THE

EIGHT

SOURCES

OF

POWER

Library of Congress Control Number: 2024932417

ISBN (paperback): 978-1-963271-13-3
(eBook): 978-1-963271-14-0

Armin Lear Press, Inc.
215 W Riverside Drive, #4362
Estes Park, CO 80517

THE
EIGHT
SOURCES
OF
POWER

A TALE OF LEADING WITH PURPOSE

DAVID C. BAUMAN

ARMINLEAR

Harvey Lee Bauman and Judith Elaine Bauman
Always in my corner.

ACKNOWLEDGMENTS

Thanks to Lila Docken Bauman for being a candid and kind reviewer as well as a patient sounding board for the many years I've been working on the book. A special thanks to Victoria K. Cliche for not only commenting on the entire manuscript, but for keeping me on track with regular video meetings during the pandemic. Thanks to Lee Siegfried who read the manuscript and helped me clarify some technical concepts. Also, thanks to Maryann Karinch for two years as my agent, editor, and lead navigator through the challenging world of publishing. Thanks also to author and executive consultant Edgar Papke for introducing me to Maryann. I also acknowledge Thawanrat Kuasakul for her feedback on specific story elements as they relate to Thai culture. I also received advice and encouragement from Richard Rokosz. I appreciate Neal Schlein's work in tracking down copyright permissions. I finally acknowledge the friends, colleagues, and family members who have encouraged me to keep writing and exploring how power works in the real world. To the many other guides, teachers, and supporters I've forgotten, "Thank you!"

CONTENTS

INTRODUCTION

"The opposite of love is not hate, it's indifference. The opposite of art is not ugliness, it's indifference. The opposite of faith is not heresy, it's indifference. And the opposite of life is not death, it's indifference."[1]
Elie Wiesel, Nobel laureate, Holocaust survivor, Author

What if everyone in your town decided to eliminate hunger among its citizens? What if everyone in your workplace decided that the least paid employees will earn an additional $5 an hour? What if everyone in your neighborhood decided that children must receive an excellent education regardless of their home situation?

On the face of it, eliminating hunger, low pay, and dropouts may seem like impossible problems to solve. But they aren't. Communities throughout human history have taken on these problems and come close to solving them. How they do it varies, but all change efforts start with individuals who gather people around a *common purpose* and then doggedly pursue it.

If you are interested in following a similar path to accomplish important purposes in your life, continue reading.

ACCOMPLISHING PURPOSES WITHOUT AUTHORITY

In my three decades working in corporations, non-profits, and academia, I've been attracted to purposes that create more freedom for myself and others. Even though I haven't always had the authority to make a change, like you I have *always* had the power to pursue a purpose. Here are three examples of how I used the power of purpose to recruit and lead others to make important changes:

- As a training coordinator in a brokerage firm, I found that inviting network engineers and technologists to design and teach courses produced several positive results. The teachers were more committed to our technology certification program, they customized their lessons to better fit our client needs, and their interactions across departments increased morale.

- As a long-term consultant for a large energy company, I found that selecting managers and engineers with the expertise and motivation to complete a project resulted in projects getting done faster and the members receiving more credit than their peers.

- As a founding faculty of a new college of business, a few of us saw an opportunity to open promotion opportunities for faculty whose journey to academia did not follow a traditional path. We questioned the existing structures, became curious about innovative models in other universities, let go of outdated ideas, and patiently found supporters for a new structure. The result is an equitable promotion system that recognizes multiple types of faculty accomplishments that go beyond terminal degrees and publications.

A common thread through these stories is that I did not have the authority or expertise to make these changes on my own.

THE TWO TYPES OF POWER

My definition of power is *any action that motivates a person to follow a leader.* Two types of power fit this definition.

The first type is the *power of authority*, which comes from holding an influential position in some institution. The position can come from birth, promotion, election, or gathering wealth. The power that comes from authority must be justified by an institution like a business or government that provides these positions of authority. People with the power of authority often lead change using rewards and punishments. The power of authority is important for:

- Organizing
- Directing
- Controlling
- Accomplishing objectives
- Solving efficiency problems

As I explain above, I have often lacked the authority or position to address big, complex problems, but I have observed and used a *second* power that anyone can access. The *power of purpose* seeks to increase freedom and flourishing for oneself and others. The power of purpose is not justified by an institution and its positions. Instead, it arises from two desires that followers have:

- the desire to move *away from* some deprivation or pain (for example, poverty, injustice, poor health), or

- the desire to *move toward* achievement and satisfaction (for example, education, wealth, security, peace of mind).

Both purposes seek to create freedom by moving away from something that costs us and towards something that benefits us.

The power of purpose is important for:

- Inclusion

- Innovation

- Ethical decision making

- Human flourishing

- Solving big unstructured problems

The power of purpose is available to those who need it, but acquiring and using it requires a different mindset and skillset. We need to let go of the assumption that change requires authority. Instead, we need to assume that anyone can influence and lead a particular change.

BALANCING THE TWO POWERS

In many cultures, the yin and yang represent two constantly balancing, universal forces. On one interpretation, opposites always exist and you cannot eliminate either one. For example, we may purify water, but the impurities still exist somewhere else. We may try to create a perfectly moral world, but the immoral will always reappear. We may try to create sustainable energy sources, but the environmental cost of making those can counter the progress made. Accepting the frame of yin and yang does not mean that we can never "win." It tells us that we have forces working together that we need to balance and manage without fully eliminating one while expanding the other.

PURPOSE   AUTHORITY

In organizations and society, the power of authority and the power of purpose also co-exist, but the power of authority often dominates our narrative of how change actually happens. Relying only on the power of authority can produce efficient solutions and faster action, but we may forfeit commitment, creativity, and including different perspectives. If we rely only on the power of purpose, we release greater creativity, commitment, and inclusion, but we may forfeit efficiency, strategy, and stability. Both types of power are needed to solve our most pressing problems.

Many books, articles, and professional speakers explain how to lead with the power of authority. It seems that each year, authors publish multiple books on how to better use the power of authority. In contrast to this singular focus, this book describes how the power of authority and the power of purpose can work together. It also describes in detail the eight sources of power that come from purpose. The eight sources of power described in the story are:

1. The Power of Invitation
2. The Power of the Open Hand
3. The Power of Praxis
4. The Power of Framing
5. The Power of Substitution
6. The Power of Solidarity
7. The Power of Building the Wheel
8. The Power of Patience

POWER, AUTHORITY AND CORRUPTION

Ordinary people have used the eight sources of power revealed in this book to produce amazing changes. Consider a teacher who organizes other teachers to learn new skills for teaching math to hard-to-reach students. Or a whistleblower who speaks out against corruption, or a person who launches a new business to meet a market need, or the lay person who starts a church foodbank, or a middle manager who leads a company turnaround from their department. These people are changing their world without waiting for the authority or permission to do it. They are using the power of purpose.

Even if the power of authority is available, people may resist stepping into these positions because power can have a negative connotation or it may lead to corruption. In 1887, Lord Acton wrote a letter to British Archbishop Creighton arguing that writing history about past leaders requires holding them to universal moral laws. Historians should not ignore a leader's terrible deeds. He famously wrote, "Power tends to corrupt, and absolute power corrupts absolutely. Great men are almost always bad men, even when they exercise influence and not authority: still more when you superadd the tendency or the certainty of corruption by authority."[2] If you believe this statement, then you may decide that avoiding power is a safe strategy. But I must caution you. Retreating from power only opens the door for someone else to lead who may lack integrity and a strong moral compass; the very leaders Lord Acton condemned.

We must realize that some type of power is essential for improving our world. Ignoring power can produce a life of compromise, like a leaf caught in a tornado. Also, if you think power only comes when you have a position in an institution – like a manager or governor or principal – then you are ignoring eight sources of power that are available to you regardless of your position or lack of position.

Yes, power may corrupt those who lack integrity, but those who have integrity and a worthy purpose must step in and use their power for the good of us all.

WHY I WROTE THIS BOOK

I believe that everyone has or can acquire the power they need to change our world. I wrote this book because ordinary people like me need to stop expecting institutions and those in positions of authority to fix what is broken. This book is *not* a call to overthrow institutions and authority because the world needs the power of authority to get things done. Think about riding on a plane. I would never board a plane unless I trusted the institutions and lines of authority that establish and govern the airlines, pilots, flight crews, mechanics, airport security, and safety regulations. But while on the plane, I may exercise the power of invitation to talk to someone about their profession, or I may use the power of framing to encourage someone who is concerned about an upcoming meeting. I have no authority to do these things, but I do have the power to do them.

WHY A HISTORICAL STORY?

I wrote this book using a historical account to show that many of the problems we face today are not unique to us. The same problems we face existed in Siam (modern day Thailand) in the late 1600s. In fact, the capital Ayutthaya at that time was larger than London with almost 1 million people. The city was a world center of trade. Like our cities today, Ayutthaya had foreign interests jockeying for influence, markets with opportunities to become wealthy, threats of war, political turmoil, military pressures, religious conflict, continual innovation, disparity between city-dwellers and country dwellers, and ordinary people trying to manage it all.

I also wrote in a historical frame to help you observe the power dynamics of authority and purpose outside of our world of smartphones, the Internet, and constant distraction. In the story you will encounter people with lives like yours, but they will have to go deeper into themselves to solve their problems. They don't have the option of constantly distracting themselves with a 30-second video or a forgettable social media post. After key lessons are covered in the story, I provide a space for personal reflection in the back of the book so that you can work on your own leadership development and plans. I also provide real-life stories of people who used each source of power to improve lives and change their world. My hope is that the stories and lessons presented help you learn to see the world anew.

WHY YOU SHOULDN'T WAIT

Few things can stop you from developing your own sources of power and leading others to a better future. You may be able to start now, and it may require more effort than you imagined. I *am not* arguing that anyone can be a leader just by reading this book. I *am* arguing that anyone who commits to acquiring the eight sources of power can and will lead others.

The time to make the changes you want in the world is now, and it starts with you *deciding* to lead with the power of purpose. Psychiatrist and concentration camp survivor Viktor Frankl observed, "When we are no longer able to change a situation . . . we are challenged to change ourselves."[3]

KING NARAI OF SIAM - 1670S[4]
(FRENCH DEPICTION)

Ayutthaya, Siam - 1684[5]

1
SAVED

Rain. Heavy rain.

A million tiny eruptions popped from the once placid water surrounding Tao's ankles. Meanwhile streams of water poured off his round straw hat. He liked feeling the stinging rain drops on his back. Through the mounting downpour he could barely hear his father shouting from the hillside. "Tao! Come in!"

Smiling, Tao continued planting his last rice plants. Thunder echoed through the mountains and vibrated in his chest. He didn't look up but increased his pace. He would be 17 in the winter. The storm didn't frighten him.

"Come on! You can finish tomorrow!" Frustrated by his son's stubbornness, his father gave up and splashed up the hillside shaking his head. Tao, a nickname that means "turtle," prided himself on outlasting everyone regardless of the test. He loved a challenge more than the comfort of a dry room.

The rain fell harder, and Tao could barely see the plants he had jammed into the mud seconds ago. Maybe he should go in. He only had 15 more rice shoots in his canvas bag. He quickly planted them in perfect rows as lightning lit up the dark sky.

Finished.

Tao turned toward home. He ran across the levies separating the rice paddies and his bare feet skidded on the slippery mud. Unable to see clearly with water pouring from his hat, he fell and landed on his back in a rice paddy. Sputtering and coughing he climbed out and continued toward the hillside and the village. Had he stayed out too long? His enjoyment of this adventure waned. The chill of wet clothes, the mud covering his face, and the stinging rain on his back exhausted him.

The last obstacle was the stream at the bottom of the hill. The villagers usually walked through the gently flowing water, but it had become an uncrossable river. Three years ago, a farmer had lost a child in a similar flash flood. Tao was older than the child, but fear started to nag him. As he approached the roaring torrent, he said out loud, "I can do this!" He ran and leapt in the air. His height was perfect, but his length was short.

Landing in the roiling water, the water dragged Tao away from the shore. He screamed. "Help! Papa!"

Within seconds he was tumbling down the stream toward the mill. The large wooden water wheel spun freely in the current. Terror filled Tao's heart. He grasped for anything to slow him down. He spun onto his stomach and tried to scream, but only inhaled water. His head hit something hard and he winced. Weak from his struggle and bruised from the punishing current, he stopped fighting the current. It was over.

But instead of feeling the crushing blows of the waterwheel, Tao felt a strong hand grab his shirt and lift him from the river. He was dragged under a tree. "Who?", he thought. He could not see who had saved him – only a shape. He tried to speak, but couldn't work his mouth. Exhausted, he blacked out.

2

AN INVITATION

Tao stirred on his bed mat. A faint taste of dirt and sand made him grimace. His body and head ached. He slowly opened his eyes to see his empty house. The morning sun speckled the wooden floor and the smell of fried eggs, garlic, and rice filled the air.

He took a minute to recall what had happened. He raised up on his elbows and looked for his mother and father.

"Tao, Tao! You're up!" His little sister Nu leapt into view. "You need to get up! Mommy was worried! She wants to see you! Tao you're all better!"

Tao carefully laid back on his mat and smiled. He loved his sister's excitement about anything he did. She would yell, "Tao caught a frog! Tao made a flute! Tao is catching a chicken!"

"Where are mom and dad?" he asked. Nu, still hopping up and down, said, "They are at the Wat (temple). Someone from Ayukya is talking to everyone."

"Ayukya? Why are they at the temple?" Tao painfully struggled to his feet. He noticed a blue bruise on his upper arm and his knees were scratched.

"I'm supposed to stay here with you. But mommy said that

when you wake up that you should come to the Wat and bring me." Nu had stopped her hopping and was now pulling on Tao's hand.

"Ok, ok! We'll go together but let me eat first."

Tao tried to figure out what was going on. He pulled on a shirt and then sat on the floor. He unwrapped the banana leaf that held his breakfast. Why were his parents at the Wat? No ceremonies were scheduled. And where is Ayukya? And who pulled him from the river? Too many questions for an early morning.

Tao and Nu climbed down the ladder from their hut. Their water buffalo stood in the shade under the hut and swung its head to watch them. Tao could tell by the sun that it was not quite noon. Nu held his hand as they half-walked, half-skipped to the Wat on the edge of the village. The huts they passed were empty.

As they approached the Wat, he heard voices. He heard a few voices over the murmur of the crowd. The loudest voice was his father's.

"You are asking me to put my family in jeopardy," his father said loudly but calmly. "How will I plant my fields? How will I harvest? I need my son to stay here!"

Tao could see that his father was addressing a stranger seated in a large wooden chair. The stranger wore a silk shirt and his round face looked as if he had spent many days in the sun. He was taller than most of the villagers and sat with a respectful and relaxed posture.

Nu escaped Tao's hand and ran to their mother. Chantara's arms were crossed, and she had a serious look on her face, but when she saw Tao she smiled and waved him over. As he stood beside her and held her hand, the stranger caught his eye and continued speaking to his father.

"Suchart, the king understands the cost to your family and he has instructed me to provide you with whatever support you and your family need. He would never put your livelihood in jeopardy. He would never put Siam in jeopardy. But the foreign powers that buy our rice, teak, and other goods are powerful. We must prepare Siamese leaders to guide our nation lest we find ourselves serving a foreign king." Then with a gesture of his hand toward Tao he said, "Your son has been chosen to be trained as one of those leaders."

What? Tao felt a warm feeling as the blood rushed to his face. The villagers turned toward him. His aunts, uncles, cousins, and friends looked at him. "Tao, please come here," the stranger said. Tao let go of his mother's hand and walked to his father's side.

"My name is Mongkut and I am from the capital Ayutthaya." Tao thought, "Ayutthaya not Ayukya." Mongkut continued, "You look much drier than when I pulled you from the creek last night. I thought I had caught the largest fish in all of Siam!" The villagers burst into laughter and Tao smiled nervously with his eyes on the ground.

"But I didn't come to your village to catch a fish. I came to catch one of the brightest young men in Siam. I sent a letter two months ago to all senior monks and village leaders to identify young people who were honorable, respectful, hardworking, courageous, and intelligent. Your priest Phra Somdej wrote to me of a young man who met these criteria. He told me of your humility in serving in the Wat, your respect for your elders, your skills in reading and writing, reciting proverbs, and managing the rice harvest accounting. I saw your courage myself as you attempted to jump over a roaring stream. Foolish courage, but still courage."

Tao was embarrassed. He saw people nodding their heads as Mongkut listed his accomplishments. Phra Somdej met Tao's eyes and nodded as well. How could this be? He was just Tao. Not some leader. He loved doing what he did. He wasn't trying to impress anyone.

"I am here to invite you to join our leadership academy. The choice is yours."

Suchart slowly turned around and looked into Tao's eyes. "Son," he said, "you are old enough to make this decision on your own. We would all miss you greatly, but the king requires the best for Siam. It would be selfish for us to keep you for ourselves."

Tao felt a wave of emotion. Fear, excitement, sadness, and joy competed for his heart. What should he do? In these types of situations, he looked to his mother.

Chantara held Nu in her arms and gently nodded "Yes." Her love for learning, her joy in serving, and her adventurous spirit shined from her eyes. She had often told him that everyone has a responsibility to use what they have to uplift others. The day had come.

"If I can serve, then I will accept the king's invitation," Tao said. The people cheered. The priest laughed. Mongkut hid a sigh of relief.

Tao's stomach felt like he had just jumped over another roaring river, but he had no idea where he would land.

3

THE KING AND THE PROPOSAL

(TWO MONTHS EARLIER)

King Narai took in the view of Ayutthaya. He was amazed at how the capital had grown since he became king. One of his counselors told him that the city boasted a population of almost one million. According to a visiting British navy commander, Ayutthaya in the current European year 1687 was more populous than London. A six-mile wall surrounded the city and miles of canals and roads ferried inhabitants, soldiers, and traders to markets, jobs, schools, and temples. The capital of Siam was alive.

From the palace balcony, the king counted the shining pagodas that filled the city horizon and seemed to prop up the orange morning sky. The golden spires of Buddhist temples also reached to heaven. The temples offered a meeting place for the community, a space to reflect on one's place in the world, and a school and home for saffron-robed monks and novices.

The king maintained the palace's location in the north-western corner of the city as a symbolic "cornerstone" that projected power and his stabilizing presence. He knew, however, that his power was always being tested by the traders representing England, France, Portugal, Spain, China, and other nations. Narai was building another palace north of Ayutthaya in case these friendly traders and their soldiers decided that conquest and colonization were more important than trade.

The palace's red brick and gray stone walls were accented with brown teak staircases and balconies. Narai especially liked walking on the third-floor balcony that wound its way along the palace and overlooked the lush gardens and pools below. He admired the tall banyan tree with its large roots spread so far from the trunk that it looked like it was walking. Next to the tree were three gardens bursting with purple, blue, and red flowers. The gardens ended at the protective 20-foot tall outer wall – a reminder of his exalted place in Siam and of the enemies who wished to take the throne from him.

Narai walked down to the second floor to meet his senior advisors. He found them waiting in a kneeling position and they bowed their heads to the floor. The king greeted each one and then requested that they walk with him for their meeting. The advisors did their best to keep up while delivering their reports on the kingdom. The king liked to walk during meetings to keep his mind sharp. The advisors wished he would slow down in the humid morning heat.

Aqu Muhammad Astarabadi, the tall, thin Minister of Treasury and Trade wiped sweat from his brow with one hand and handed the king his treasury report with the other. Aqu was of Persian descent and his family had served the kings of Siam since the early 1600s. He and his father held the title of Phrakhlang which recognized their authority over the kingdom's trade and finance. The king valued his close ties to the Persian community, and many years ago some Persians helped him take the throne from his uncle.

Narai scanned the document intent on finding the bottom line. Aqu said, "Our tax revenue could be higher, but the foreigners continue to press us for more goods, lower taxes, and more influence. We must gain control of our commerce or we will become a mere puppet to foreign interests." The king nodded as he glanced through Aqu's figures.

"Your majesty, our nation is prosperous *because* of the foreign traders," interjected Rangsiman the Minister of Foreign Relations. "We are a cosmopolitan nation. When you look over our walls, what do you see? You see the enclaves of our *partners*: the Chinese, French, British, Dutch, and Portuguese. They bring wealth and fame to our nation and to your name."

"At what cost?" Aqu retorted. "They do not respect our tariffs. They sail gunships past our walls and dismiss our complaints by saying that the boats are for their protection. But one day, will they colonize Siam? Will they enslave us?" Aqu's white handkerchief fluttered across his brow.

The king finished reading Aqu's treasury report as the group reached a room that was prepared with mats and a throne on a raised floor. He could see that his advisors were tired of walking. The king sat on his throne and the ministers found their mats and kneeled down. Two boys appeared and gently fanned the king with large palm fronds.

"I agree with both of you," the king said. "Rangsiman, Siam needs strong relations with these foreign powers. We must also treat them as a snake charmer treats a cobra. Let them buy our goods and we will tax them. But remember that they have teeth and poison. Never turn your back."

Rangsiman nodded his head, though his tight lips displayed his frustration with the king's lack of trust. He knew that the real teeth and poison aimed at the king came from within Siam.

King Narai then gestured to Aqu who was more relaxed now that he was kneeling in the shade. "Aqu's financial assessment offers a clear picture of how we are losing revenue because the traders exploit loopholes. Our people cut the teak trees and float them down the river. But then foreign buyers pay them a pittance, avoid our taxes, ship the wood to Europe, and sell it for a great sum. The same happens with the rice and coconuts we sell to China and Japan."

"With the money the traders earn," he continued, "they return with guns, horses, and armored ships. I believe the French respect our interests which is why I sent envoys to the court of Louis XIV. But Ayutthaya will *never* become an occupied city." He looked at his other two advisors and said, "What can we do?"

Somboon, the Minister of War spoke first. From his bowed position, he glanced up at the king with whom he had fought many battles. "Your majesty, on your directions I have purchased 100 more cannons from the Chinese and 1,000 muskets from the Portuguese. Our soldiers on horses as well as our elephant army are well trained and can protect us from Burmese and Khmer threats. The nobles in the provinces have 300,000 men who can take up arms, and the nobles in Ayutthaya have another 100,000."

The king took a moment to think about these numbers. To have power in Siam meant to control laborers and soldiers. While

Siam needed a strong army to repel outside attacks, a strong army within the provinces could be used to challenge his throne.

"And ships?" the king asked.

"Great king, we only have 34 ships that could be used in battle," Somboon responded. "We rarely fight on water, but our ports in Bangkok and Mergui need to be defended. I've discussed buying two more ships from the Dutch and the French, but they refuse." He looked at Aqu who nodded while Rangsiman inched forward on his mat.

"Your majesty," Rangsiman quickly interjected. "With diplomacy we do not need more weapons. These foreign guests are our friends and they represent the greatest houses of royalty. They will protect *us* from the Burmese and the Khmer."

"I appreciate your confidence in their words," King Narai responded. "I do not share your confidence in their intentions. They are here to make money, or like the Jesuits and Persians, to convert us to their religions."

"May I offer an important option that we have overlooked?"

Mongkut, the Minister of Lands, often waited until the end of the meeting to provide his advice. In the early days of King Narai's reign, the other advisors privately spoke against including a Minister of Lands as an advisor to the king. A couple of them thought Mongkut was more of a philosopher and farmer than someone who should advise on armies and trade agreements.

But the king had relied on Mongkut's counsel since ascending to the throne. Mongkut was close to the Siamese people in the city and the country. The capital was an insular place with distractions and political infighting. The king needed access to what his subjects were thinking.

"Speak." the king shifted slightly toward Mongkut without

reducing his royal prominence. The boys carefully adjusted their palm frond fans.

"Great king, I have studied the history of the nations whose representatives and companies sit at our doorstep – actually they are already in our house. Several of these nations value education and progress. We have traded with the Chinese for centuries and know their emphasis on education and art, but the Europeans rarely take 'no' for an answer either religiously or in regard to commerce."

Mongkut pulled out a scroll, bowed his head, and handed it to the king. He kept his eyes down and continued to talk.

"I recommend that we match and surpass the foreigners' knowledge of trade, building, and commerce, while protecting our own traditions. We need to train young leaders who can fulfill this mission."

The king unrolled the scroll to find a plan for establishing a leadership academy at the temple Wat Ratchaburana.

"I propose that we select the most capable young adults from Siam. With your approval, I will bring them to Ayutthaya and train them in the traditions of Siam and the practices and cultures of the foreigners. After taking courses here in language, leadership, building, and diplomacy, they will gain experience by traveling around Siam and to foreign capitals."

Rangsiman jumped on the idea. "Yes! I have heard that other nations send their brightest youth to study abroad. This is an opportunity to strengthen our relationships with our friends!"

"Wait! They will be pressured to convert to Christianity if they go to Europe," exclaimed Somboon. "We cannot allow them to lose their Buddhist heritage."

"I understand your concerns," Mongkut calmly responded, "and in this leadership academy Buddhist principles will be taught.

However, the world has changed and we cannot hide behind our walls and rivers. We must lead or be led. We must speak with a voice that the world respects or the foreigners will treat us as they have other lands – as people who must sign their treaties or be destroyed or enslaved."

The group fell silent as the king lowered the scroll and sat up straight. This was the sign that he had made some decisions. He addressed each advisor individually.

"Aqu, continue to track our taxes and tariffs. Develop a plan for impounding any ships that do not pay the taxes on the goods they are carrying. Rangsiman, keep our foreign friends happy, but be wary of their requests for more favors without paying for them. Also, while I have allowed the French Jesuits to build schools and hospitals, I do not want the French thinking that Ayutthaya belongs to them. Somboon, purchase the latest guns from the Portuguese and work with Aqu on a budget. Also, continue implementing our river defenses. We cannot rival the foreigners' ships, but we can stop them from coming up the river from Bangkok."

Finally, he turned to Mongkut. "Mongkut, you may create the Siam Leadership Academy, but only select five young people. I think ages 16 to 18 would be about right. Start small and then report your results."

He then looked at the advisors and summed up his thoughts.

"Mongkut is right. We cannot hide from the outside world. Even in our finances, Aqu is working closely with Phaulkon the Greek to improve our trade agreements. But be mindful of foreign traditions and teachers. Learn from foreigners and respect our traditions."

With these final words, the king stood and the advisors dutifully bowed their heads to the floor. "Well done," he said. "We will meet again next week."

The king walked away with Mongkut's scroll under his right arm.

4

THE JOURNEY TO THE CAPITAL

The two-day journey to Ayutthaya was almost over. Tao leaned back on his bag as the thin boat floated south on the Chao Phraya river. Mongkut slept in the bow under a canvas canopy and the two sailors kept their eyes fixed down the river.

Tao reflected on the last two days as he gazed into the swirling brown water. He already missed his family and his village. Nu's eyes were red from crying. His father forced a smile whenever he spoke to Tao and held his hand more than usual. Chantara beamed with pride – the king's representative had chosen her son to serve Siam. She had banished any fear or worry; Tao was meant to go. They embraced him and gave final parental advice about taking care of himself, watching for robbers in the city, and eating plenty of food.

The villagers slapped Tao on the shoulder, laughed, and said, "Tell the king we said hello!" Mongkut patiently waited in a small oxcart, though he kept observing the sun's transit across the sky. Finally, Tao climbed aboard with his cloth shoulder bag containing his clothes and a small bag of coins the villagers had forced on him. Looking backwards, he waved until the last person disappeared behind the green rolling hills.

Tao was still sore from rolling down the river, and the bumpy cart ride didn't help. The wooden oxcart rumbled and creaked behind the water buffalo, bouncing Tao up and down and side to side. Mongkut appeared to sit steadily, though he clutched the reins tightly. They finally reached the Lopburi river and approached a thin wooden boat waiting for them. Two sailors wearing white shirts, brown shorts, and sandals met them at the shore.

"This is Tao," announced Mongkut with a smile. "He is joining the Leadership Academy." The two men looked at each other, shrugged and bowed their heads slightly to Tao.

The long boat cut through the slow flowing dark water. Using long poles, the sailors guided the boat past sand bars and away from low-hanging trees. Eventually they left the small river and joined the large Chao Phraya river flowing south to Ayutthaya.

The air was cooler on the water and Tao felt as if he were gliding through a dream. Bright white pagodas and red temple roofs appeared around bends as the river became broader. Tao watched people washing their clothes and children fishing along the bank. Mongkut closed his eyes, deep in thought.

Before dark, the sailors pulled over to a river village and Mongkut and Tao stayed at a small inn. They awoke early and climbed back into the boat as the sun rose in a brilliant orange spectacle and lit the eastern sky.

During their breakfast of bananas and rice, Mongkut gestured to a large building project on the eastern bank of the river. Piles of stone, wood and brick sat on the banks while caravans of oxcarts kicked up dust heading out of the town. Barges full of materials lined up at the wharf and workers wove around each other. Tao had never seen such a building operation.

"What are they building?" asked Tao.

"That is an addition to King Narai's Lopburi summer palace."

"Why does he have a palace here? What's wrong with the old one?"

"Nothing is wrong with the current palace, but the environment around Ayutthaya has changed. For centuries foreigners have traded with us. Some of them, like the Chinese, understand our ways and accept Siam's authority. Our pottery has graced the best homes in China for centuries. But other foreigners do not accept Siam's authority. They seek to guide us to their ways and possibly . . ." Mongkut stopped talking and reconsidered his words.

"The king wants to keep a distance from some powerful foreigners if they turn against us. Ayutthaya will continue to be the capital and Siam's main trading center. The king will live in the Lopburi palace some of the time depending on the situation."

"How do I fit into this story?" asked Tao. "Am I here to fight the foreigners?"

"No, you are not!" Mongkut laughed. "You are here to learn about Siam. You are here to learn how to lead."

"What do you mean by 'lead'?"

Mongkut leaned forward and said, "Let me ask you something. Is it easier to float down the river or up the river?"

"Down the river," Tao said and noticed that the sailors were now paying attention to Mongkut.

"Why?"

"Because the water does all the work. The current pushes the boat and the sailors only have to steer the boat."

"Correct. The current has the power to move the boat in one

direction which makes it easy to go downstream. Sometimes leading others is like floating along with the current. You know where you are going, the people are already going that way, and your job is to 'steer' them to the destination. Most leaders use the power of their institutions – like the military or the trading companies – as the current that moves people. It isn't always easy, but everyone is moving in the same direction. Leading in an institution requires you to learn about the institution and how to use the *power of authority*."

Mongkut then pointed at a ship slowly moving up the river on the other bank. "How about that ship going against the current? What power is it using?"

Tao studied the ship carefully. It had four large white sails flapping in the wind. He then noticed three smaller boats pulling the ship up the river. The sailors in the small boats pulled on their oars and the ropes connecting them to the ship tightened with each pull.

"Wind and human power," Tao said.

"Yes. Here is a power that is different from the current or the power that comes from institutional authority. If someone wants to use a power that moves in a different direction from the current, leaders must develop the skills, creativity, and patience to harness it. The only thing really moving that ship against the current is the leader's purpose and the crew who are following. You will be learning this type of power."

"What type of power is that?"

"You are going to learn to use the *power of purpose*," Mongkut said. "This power works alongside the power of authority. It is not the power that commands people to follow you. It is the power that moves others to follow you when you *do not* have authority."

Mongkut smiled and said, "It is the power that moved you to accept my invitation."

Mongkut then turned the conversation toward Tao's life. He asked about his life in the village, his training with senior monks in the Wat, and how he managed the harvest. After lunch, Tao felt confident enough to ask Mongkut about his life, but before Mongkut could respond one of the sailors exclaimed, "The king's barges!"

The longest boats Tao had ever seen slowly appeared on the right bank. The two barges were moored to a pier and their dark red sides were inlaid with lines of gold. They both had golden dragon heads lifting up from the bow.

"I'm one of the oarsmen," the other sailor said. "We race these barges during the festivals. Have you ever been to a festival?"

"No," Tao responded. "But I can't wait until the next one!"

"And ahead is Ayutthaya!"

The sailor in back pushed hard to the left on the rudder while the other paddled on the right.

One of Tao's teachers told him how Ayutthaya was named after the city of Ayodhya in India, the birthplace of the character Rama in the Indian epic *Ramakien*. The tops of giant pagodas appeared like dark soldiers as the evening sun set behind the city. The sailors paddled the boat into a canal that circled the city walls. Tao saw canon barrels poking through notches near the top and soldiers looking down at them. As they sailed south of the city, large encampments with thousands of people lined both sides. Smoke from cooking fires wafted out of the camps and created a mystical fog hanging over the water. Tao heard strange languages coming from the camps and strange musical instruments.

Mongkut pointed here and there with his hand. "This is the

Chinese encampment. Their country is not far from here and they have traded with us for centuries. Your rice is sometimes sold to them. On the far side of those trees are the Dutch, French, and English camps. The Portuguese live south of the city. These foreigners have traveled many months to trade with Siam. You will learn their traditions and languages."

The sailors guided the boat through a gate and into Ayutthaya. Tao marveled at how many people lived outside and inside the walls. Canals branched off in different directions and roads wound their way past buildings of brick and wood. The sailors carefully maneuvered the boat past other boats filled with fresh produce or chickens in cages. As the sun gave off its final rays, the boat passed a large temple on the left and in the distance the walls of a palace came into view. Tao could not believe he was here.

Mongkut sighed deeply as they approached his home. Tao was the last of the Siam Leadership Academy students, and Mongkut could now start his experiment: to teach his students the eight sources of power.

5
CONSTANTINE PHAULKON

Constantine Phaulkon desired power and he knew how to get it.

He had traveled across the world to find an ideal opportunity to control his destiny. Siam offered him the best one and he was executing his plan perfectly. Phaulkon was one position away from becoming the Minister of Treasury and Trade and possibly receiving the royal title of Phrakhlang, but first he needed to remove Aqu.

While Tao was moving into Mongkut's home, Phaulkon was leaving a meeting with King Narai and Aqu. He had innocently created an argument between the king and Aqu and then left as if he had another meeting. As he closed the door to the king's salon, he could hear the king heatedly questioning Aqu about the faulty accounts with the British East India Company.

The time was right for Phaulkon's next move.

The meeting had gone well for Phaulkon. While Aqu's father and grandfather had once held the high position of Phrakhlang which oversaw the treasury and all trade agreements, Phaulkon knew that the king needed skills and connections that Aqu didn't have. Also, Aqu did not know about the accounting tricks used by the British East India Company to cheat Siam out of tariff fees.

Phaulkon hinted at these "accounting irregularities" during the meeting which left Aqu stunned and King Narai shouting.

Phaulkon descended a stone staircase into a vibrantly colored palace garden lit by torches. He reflected on how his life's journey would culminate in *him* replacing Aqu as Phrakhlang. He had been an excellent student in Greece but wanted to see the world. He joined the British East India Company and traveled the world. He learned business, trade, soldiering, and several languages. He never turned down an opportunity to learn a new skill or develop a friendship that may result in a promotion or more money.

When Phaulkon sailed with the British to Siam in 1678, he didn't know what to expect. He wanted to see Asia and explore opportunities for gaining real power that didn't require sitting on a ship for months. He married Maria Guyomar de Pinha who was a fascinating person and excellent chef in the palace kitchen. They had two sons, though one had died. And now he was ready to climb the ladder to the second most powerful position in Siam.

Phaulkon stopped at a water barrel under a bodhi tree and filled a hollow gourd hanging on a peg. He looked into the cup and saw his face. "What do I want?" he asked himself.

He knew the answer. He wanted to be Siam's king or at least the highest ranking official under the king. He was tired of taking orders from lesser men, especially his current boss Aqu. As he scooped another cool drink from the barrel, he realized that he didn't want to answer to anyone but himself. In his current position, he enjoyed negotiating treaties on behalf of Siam and seeing his former employers and competitors submit to him. He enjoyed telling the British corporations the rules of the game and then letting them petition him for exceptions and favors, which he regularly pocketed.

He hung the cup back on the peg and walked toward the eastern gate out of the palace. He remembered entering the same gate two years ago and deciding that he would build a power base here. He studied Siamese for months and eventually became an interpreter for Aqu and the king in their negotiations with the French and the British. Phaulkon also understood accounting and trade negotiations, so he outshined Aqu by collecting more money for the kingdom. It also helped that Phaulkon withheld important information from Aqu and then passed it to the king himself.

For the king to appoint a foreign Phrakhlang was not new to Siam. Replacing a Persian with a highly skilled Greek shouldn't cause problems in the court. Besides, Phaulkon had already discredited two other candidates in the presence of the king for their lack of expertise and shoddy oversight of foreign accounts.

Phaulkon nodded slightly to two palace guards as he emerged into the noisy streets of Ayutthaya. He followed the main lit road to a small pier, jumped into a long, narrow boat in a nearby canal and directed the driver to take him to the British compound. Phaulkon sat and contemplated his next move as the driver lit a lantern to hang on the stern and navigated out of the slip.

Next week he would make a devastating challenge to Aqu's abilities which would add to the subtle case he had been presenting to the king for months. He knew that soon the king would announce a new Phrakhlang - Constantine Phaulkon.

6

THE FIRST DAY OF SCHOOL

Tao dreamed of home.

He was harvesting rice while Nu raced back and forth on the bank, stopping only when she saw a small rock. She hummed. He looked up but couldn't see his hut. He turned and Nu was gone. His heart sank. He was the only one in the village and all the rice had to be harvested. He could not do this on his own. Where was everyone? Why did he have to do all the work?

He opened his eyes. A wooden plank ceiling stared down at him. His thatch sleeping mat and blanket were comfortable, but he felt anxious after his dream. Why was he upset? He wanted to be home, but his desire for adventure and his feeling of responsibility kept him here.

Instead of hearing familiar voices talking outside or the clucking of chickens under his hut, Tao heard loud voices from the street. He heard rolling oxcart wheels and the shouts of vendors. He smelled burning wood and ox dung.

He sat up and looked around his room. He had a mat, a basin on a chair, and a wooden door. He had never had a door before. He also had a window. He stretched and looked out of the second story bedroom window. He saw a yard with a tall brick fence surrounding it and he could hear the sounds of Ayutthaya. The smell of food came from downstairs, and he realized that he was starving.

He dressed in his extra pair of clothes, washed his face, and ran down to the main floor where a short woman with her hair tied back greeted him. "Tao! You have class soon. Come and eat, you lazy boy." He saw the twinkle in her eyes as she gently pushed him into a courtyard in the back of the house. "You are so skinny. How can you learn with no meat on your bones?"

"What is your name, ma'am? I forgot."

"I am Sunan and my husband Mongkut said that you will be our guest for a while. He has already left for the school but wanted you to sleep after your long journey. But hurry! You need to leave soon!"

Fruit, rice, and dried fish sat on the table. Tao quickly ate under the caring eye of Sunan who busied herself with cleaning away dishes. Her skin was lighter than his mother's and her movements were quick. She wore her hair in a tall bun on her head, and her purple silk dress with its small golden triangles highlighted her attentive eyes. She obviously enjoyed having someone to fuss over.

"Have some more rice. No? Here, fresh pineapple will give you strength for the day. Have more! You look like a twig!"

After breakfast Sunan gave Tao clothes to replace his farming clothes. The pants fit perfectly as well as the sash around his waist, but the shirt consumed him. "This shirt is too big," he murmured. Sunan laughed and said he looked like a prince. "Just tuck it under your sash. I'll walk you to school when you finish."

The two of them left the house and hurried past markets, sprawling temples, and roads filled with people and oxcarts. They traversed wooden bridges that spanned small waterways. Tao tried to take in all of the new sights and sounds, but it made him dizzy. He looked above the buildings on the other side of the street and saw a giant stone structure in the distance. He had heard of these huge pagodas that adorned the temples of Siam. Soon they crossed through the gates into the largest temple Tao had ever seen.

"Welcome to Wat Ratchaburana," Sunan said. "This is your new school."

The scene took Tao's breath away. Before him stood a long brick building which Sunan said was a coronation hall and a place for monks to meet. Bald monks wearing saffron colored robes milled around the front of the building. Some were Tao's age and others were much older.

They walked behind the coronation hall. Jutting up to the sky stood the stone pagoda that Tao had seen towering over the wall. Tao would later learn that the conical structure stretched 90 feet into the sky. It stood on a giant brick base with stairs on three sides that led to vaults inside the pagoda. Naga and Guaruda statues built into the base of the pagoda crouched as if holding its immense weight on their shoulders. Buddha statues chiseled out of white stone adorned the base.

Sunan gently pulled Tao's sleeve and they walked to a single-story building with a large wooden front porch. Stone lion statues stood on both sides of the porch steps. Tao was distracted by the statues and tripped on the last step. He fell forward and splayed on the wooden porch. Then he heard laughter.

Tao jumped to his feet and found himself face-to-face with two well-dressed boys his age. They were chuckling. He half-smiled, trying to join in the humor of his fall, but his first gesture of friendship failed.

"Don't you know that servants are supposed to enter through

the back door," said a tall, thin male student. "Look at how this guy dresses and how dark his skin is. He must have come from up-country." A larger and bigger boy imitated the accent of an ignorant country person and asked, "Did you bring us some rice, farmer?" The two boys laughed again and Tao fought back two impulses – to run away or to smash the big male in the face.

A female student quickly pushed between Tao and his two antagonists. She wore a red silk dress, a red wrap over her shoulders, and her black hair was wrapped in a bun. She held a book tightly to her chest. The two boys took a step back as she stared into their eyes.

"Shame on you!" she said with intensity. "This is Tao and he is joining the Academy. Ajarn (teacher) Mongkut selected him out of thousands."

The two boys mumbled, "Sorry," and walked into the main building. The girl bowed slightly to Sunan and walked in after the boys.

"First days can be difficult, but you're not alone," Sunan said apologetically.

"You definitely are not alone," came a familiar voice. Mongkut had watched the entire scene from the doorway. He stepped out into the light and said, "Come in and select a desk."

Tao's body was frozen and he wanted to go home, even if he had to swim up the Chao Phraya river.

But then he felt Sunan's hand on his arm. He turned to see her staring up into his watery eyes. She smiled and said, "I am so glad you came to Ayutthaya. You are going to do great things."

With those words she let go of his arm and walked down the

steps. "Don't be late for supper!" she yelled over her shoulder. "Yes ma'am," Mongkut yelled back.

Tao felt some of his confidence return and followed Mongkut into the classroom.

Answer the reflection questions in the Reflect and Apply section about *Opposition and Resilience*.

7
WHAT IS IN A NAME?

The classroom had wooden floors, wooden walls, and ceilings with exposed round wooden beams. Large windows with open wooden shutters allowed a gentle breeze into the room. Five reed mats were placed in two rows on the floor: three in front and two in back. They all faced a black chalkboard. A writing desk sat in front of each mat with paper, inkwell, and two quill pens on top. It reminded Tao of his lessons with Phra Somdej.

The two boys who laughed at Tao sat next to each other in the front row and continued a quiet conversation. Tao knelt behind them and pulled his mat and desk backwards to what he thought was a safe distance.

The girl knelt at the last desk on the front row and immediately organized her paper, checked the level of ink in her well, and started examining the tips of her pens. She turned her head, and noticing Tao's stare, quickly made eye contact. She did not smile but said, "You better get organized. Ajarn Mongkut talks fast."

Mongkut walked out of a small room behind the chalkboard and wrote "Welcome to the Siam Leadership Academy." He then wrote the names of the students and their nicknames.

- Olan / Muu (pig)
- Suriyothai / Faa (sky)
- Saratoon / Mot (ant)
- Somchai / Tao (turtle)
- Sorasak / Chang (elephant)

He turned to face the students who respectfully greeted their teacher with a wai (pronounced "why"), pressing their palms together at their foreheads and bowing to the ground before returning their teacher's gaze.

"I know a few of you from the palace school," he said. He looked at the girl and the thin boy sitting in front of Tao.

"I personally chose each of you to attend the Siam Leadership Academy for the next two years. We then expect you to use what you've learned to serve the people of Siam. The purpose of the academy is to prepare you to be leaders. I will tell you more about the purpose in a minute, but I want to introduce you to each other."

"Each of you has a name that means something important – something that gives hope and courage. We will use your nicknames in class, but I want you to know each other's given names and consider how you live out your name."

Tao gently dipped his pen into the inkwell and wrote his given name, "Somchai."

Mongkut pointed to the large boy in the front row.

"Olan or Muu (pig) comes to us from the south. Olan means 'great' and as you can see he is strong."

Muu jokingly raised his right arm and made a muscle.

Mongkut chuckled and continued, "Muu's family owns a teak farm and a trading business in Bangkok. I know Muu is strong because I have seen him lead an elephant from the forest pulling huge trees. He understands the land, business, and trading. Welcome to the Academy."

Mongkut gestured to the young woman. "Suriyothai or Faa (sky) is the daughter of Somdet Chaophraya Rangsiman who is the Minister of Foreign Relations and his wife Arinya who is a manager in the palace. Faa has attended the palace school for six years and speaks French and English. Suriyothai means 'rising sun' and she is a shining student, so you boys had better study hard to keep up with her."

He looked directly at the boys and became serious.

"Siam needs men and women to lead. Faa, you probably guessed, is named in honor of the great Queen Somdet Phra Sri Suriyothai who bravely fought and died alongside her husband the king many years ago. Welcome to the Academy." Faa bowed slightly to acknowledge Mongkut's introduction.

Tao was impressed and began to worry. How could he ever compete with these students? Why was he here with his ill-fitting shirt and years as an upcountry farmer? He struggled to forget the students laughing at him.

Mongkut stood in front of the tall thin boy who was sitting next to Muu.

"Saratoon or Mot (ant) is also a student from the palace. His father was a brave soldier who died in battle against the Khmer five years ago. His mother Makuta manages the palace staff with Saratoon's stepfather Rangsit. Saratoon means 'tiger' and if you have seen Mot in military exercises, then you will see that he is cunning, fast, and does not miss his target. He also speaks French. Welcome to the Academy."

Mot turned to the other students and said, "I only speak French when threatened." They all laughed.

Tao knew he was next. He needed reassurance, so he looked directly at Mongkut who looked back at him with an expression of confidence.

"Somchai or Tao (turtle) comes to us from a northern village near Chiang Mai. I had heard such excellent reports of Tao's hard work, intelligence, courage, and kindness that I traveled two days up the Chao Phraya to meet him. I was not disappointed. I first met him when I pulled him from a roaring river that he unsuccessfully tried to jump over."

Tao felt himself blushing as Mongkut continued.

"You see, this young man was working longer than any of the other farmers to plant the rice that you and your families eat every day." The other students turned and looked at Tao. Muu appeared impressed.

"Somchai means 'worthy of honor'," Mongkut continued, "and he would not be here if he did not live up to his name. Tao reads and writes the Siamese language, can read Sanskrit like a senior monk, knows how to organize the planting and harvesting of crops, has studied Buddhism with two great masters, and is a guest in my home." Tao started to feel like he belonged.

"However," Mongkut said in a serious tone, "Tao is *not* a good swimmer and should avoid jumping over canals until he learns to swim." The students laughed and Tao joined them. Mongkut said, "Welcome to the Academy."

Mongkut pointed to the empty mat and desk beside Tao.

"Our last student is away with his father. His name is Sorasak or Chang (elephant). His father is Phra Phetracha."

Tao knew this name. Phetracha was a famous military leader who led the war elephant brigades. He trained all of the battle elephants and was a close ally to King Narai. Tao's teachers told him of Phetracha's mother nursing the king when he was a boy and that Phetracha and the king were as close as brothers.

"Sorasak means . . ."

Before Mongkut could finish, a loud voice from the back of the room said, "Possessing great honor and dignity—and don't you forget it."

The students turned to see a young man in military dress. He was not tall, but he was muscular and stood with a confident look on his face. His breastplate was made of bamboo and his helmet was red with a gold insignia of an elephant on the front. His right hand rested on a sword.

Mongkut did not look surprised. "Yes, this is Sorasak. After he removes his sword and armor, I will continue his introduction."

"Must I?" Chang asked as if seeking a favor from an old friend.

"Yes. We are here to learn how to lead without force. You can defeat an army without a sword or a troop of elephants if you apply the lessons you'll learn here. In the corner will be fine."

Chang shrugged his shoulders and did as he was told. He dropped down on his mat next to Tao and gave him a curious look as if to say, "Who are you?".

"Chang's father is Phetracha," Mongkut continued. "You all must know that he leads Siam's elephant army. He loves Siam and is one of its greatest defenders. Chang is training with the military strategists and is also learning how to fight while on elephants. Welcome to the Academy."

Chang nodded to Mongkut.

Tao glanced over at Chang and noticed the handle of a knife in his linen belt. Chang caught Tao's eyes and smirked. "You can never be too careful in Ayutthaya."

8
MAKING AMENDS

The students ate lunch outside and Tao sat by himself under a tree while the other students sat on the steps of the classroom.

The sun shone down on the rotund pagodas and the monks began chanting in a pavilion on the other side of the Wat. The deep sound filled the air with an undulating, deep humming sound. Tao had never heard so many monks chanting. He leaned back on the tree trunk and finished his lunch. He looked at the branches and saw birds flitting from one to another.

Muu approached and said, "Sorry about this morning. I didn't mean to make fun of you."

"That's alright. I *am* different from you all. I'm from the country. I've never been to a city like this before. Everything is new to me." He tugged on his large white shirt and said, "And I don't have city clothes yet."

Muu sat down next to Tao.

"You're not that different. You work on rice. I work on trees. We both harvest, plant, and sell. I'm from a small village and so are you. It's just that I live in Bangkok half of the year."

"So, what do you think of Ajarn Mongkut?" Muu asked.

"I like him. I trust him. And I think he is worried." Tao said. "He just sat in silence most of the boat trip here. He believes that we can create something that the country needs. But he hasn't told me what it is. Has he told you?"

"No. But I guess we'll find out soon enough. I know that the king's counselors are concerned with the foreign countries moving into Siam. Have you noticed how many people are here from other countries?"

Tao admitted that he hadn't had time to notice, but that he had seen camps of men with light skin and roundish eyes.

"Those are probably the English and the Dutch. They export a lot of our teak to their countries. They could also be French. The French are friendly, and a couple of the Jesuit priests taught me French in Bangkok."

"Who are the Jesuits?" Tao asked.

Muu explained that the Jesuits were like Buddhist monks. They wore robes, didn't get married, and followed a prophet named Jesus who they claimed died and came back to life. The Jesuits were well educated and believed it was their mission to teach science, philosophy, commerce, and the Christian life to the world.

"My dad says they also want us to follow Jesus so that we can live forever," he continued. "But I don't know much about that."

A high-pitched bell rang twice from the classroom. Muu and Tao brushed off their pants and walked to the classroom.

9
TWO TYPES OF POWER

"I am going to explain why you are here."

Mongkut sat on a stool by the blackboard and looked at the students.

"I created the academy to prepare you to lead Siam during a time of great change. Before selecting the topics and exercises, I studied Siam's history and the history of other nations. I questioned many foreign emissaries and merchants who live in Ayutthaya. I received counsel from our wisest monks and provincial officials. Based on my research, I see two types of power for our future leaders."

"The first type is the *power of authority*, and by power, I mean *any action that motivates a person to follow a leader*. In the government and the military, we teach people to fulfill one specific role such as becoming a soldier, sailing a ship, cooking in the palace, or managing trade agreements. There are many young people like you apprenticing with Siam's leaders. They will eventually take service exams and enter jobs with more responsibility. All of them must follow the power of authority."

Mongkut stood and began to pace in front of the chalkboard.

"The power that comes from authority is necessary for maintaining our country. You see this power in our courts, in markets, on ships navigating the Chao Phraya, and in military units protecting our borders. When the kingdom needs something achieved, it creates an organization or institution to achieve it. These institutions grant their leaders authority to accomplish the task. Consider a ship leaving Ayutthaya for Bangkok with a shipment of pottery. The ship has a captain who has authority over the sailors for as long as they are fulfilling their purpose – safely reaching the pier in Bangkok. But once the ship reaches Bangkok and the sailors leave the ship, the captain's authority over them disappears."

Tao recalled Mongkut's discussion on the boat about how institutions create positions of authority, and how the institution is like the current flowing downstream.

"Why do people obey a person with authority?" Mongkut asked.

"A person in authority can punish you," said Chang.

Mongkut pointed at Chang and said, "Correct! Authority requires an institution to justify punishing *and* rewarding people. Being part of an institution is the connection between you and the leader. Have any of you gotten in trouble for disobeying a teacher?"

The students got the point. The teacher's authority comes from the school and justifies the teacher's punishment.

"Finally," Mongkut said, "the power of authority is built on a top-down structure. This allows power to be transferred from one level down to another. For example, the king has appointed me the Minister of Lands which gives me the authority to implement decisions and use resources that others cannot. My provincial secretaries receive their authority from me."

Mongkut walked to the board and wrote:

THE POWER OF AUTHORITY

1. *Requires institutions*
2. *The institution justifies rewarding and punishing*
3. *Authority can be delegated to others*

The students wrote down the definition, but Chang seemed disturbed by the definition.

"Are you saying that authority is a *bad way* to lead others because it relies on punishing and rewarding people?" Chang asked.

"Not at all," replied Mongkut. "It is essential! Any kingdom will collapse without it. You wouldn't be here if the king had not given me the *authority* to open the academy. But," Mongkut paused, "there is another type of power that does not rely on institutions."

Mongkut went to the board and drew a large tree with eight branches evenly spaced from left to right. It took him a while and the students also drew the tree in their notes. Over the tree branches he wrote in large letters, "The Power of Purpose."

"I invite you to learn about another type of power – the *power of purpose* – represented by this tree. No matter where you meet people, they will share their energy and strength with you if you help them fulfill their purposes."

Tao noticed that Chang was drawing something and was not paying attention to Mongkut.

Tao raised his hand. "What do the branches represent?"

Mongkut became excited as he traced over some of the spreading branches. "Each branch represents a unique source of power that grows from the power of purpose." Chang stopped his drawing and looked up.

"You will learn how to develop *eight sources of power* that do not require authority."

Chang smirked and returned to his drawing. Tao noticed that the drawing was of a war elephant crushing a person under its foot.

Mongkut faced the students and asked loudly, "Why should anyone follow you if you don't have any authority over them?"

The students sat in silence, so Mongkut answered his own question and began pacing again.

"I have observed that people follow those leaders who acknowledge and understand their needs and desires – who help them fulfill an important purpose in their lives. Like this tree naturally growing toward the sun, humans naturally grow toward the purposes they desire. One of the main purposes is the freedom to live a life worth living. Leaders who align their work with our desire to gain more freedom can tap into sources of power that institutions often ignore."

"People already have freedom," said Mot. "Except prisoners."

Mongkut nodded.

"Most of us have freedom to walk where we want, eat what we want, and sometimes live where we want. But not everyone has the freedom to live a life worth living. This is a life that you would wish for someone you love. Let me explain what I mean by purpose and how it motivates us."

Mongkut went to a clear space on the chalkboard and drew a horizontal line. He then wrote "purpose is to <u>move from</u> . . ." below the line and "purpose is <u>to move towards</u> . . ." above the line. At the top of the board he wrote, "Freedom."

"Purpose falls into two categories: purposes that lead *from* something and purposes that lead *toward* something. Both result in an increase in freedom. Faa, what are some things that people naturally move away from?"

Faa looked up from her detailed notes, thought for a second and said, "Hunger, war, ignorance, injustice, fear, pain."

As she spoke, Mongkut wrote the words below the horizontal line.

"Excellent. For some people, their primary purpose is to move *from* situations full of deprivation, ignorance, and pain. A leader can tap into this purpose and guide people away from a painful state to a better state. The power of purpose within these people comes from the desire to move *from* a bad situation. The result is more freedom."

Mongkut pointed to the words "purpose is <u>to move towards</u>," on the board. "And what are things that people want to move towards?"

Tao raised his hand high, and Mongkut nodded at him.

"People have lots of things they want to move towards, like money, family, wisdom, owning a business, seeing new things. A lot of things."

Mongkut wrote these words above the horizontal line. He also wrote the words, "achievement, peace, belonging, recognition."

"Tao has listed some important desires we have, and I've provided a few others. For some people, their purpose is to move *toward* situations that allow them to achieve their goals, learn new things, and change the world with others. The same leader who harnesses a desire to move *from* a bad situation can also harness a desire to move *toward* a better life. Again, the result of leading with the power of purpose is more freedom for the followers."

Mongkut wrote the following on the board:

THE POWER OF PURPOSE

1. *The leader identifies a purpose that increases freedom*
2. *Followers share their power in pursuit of the purpose*
3. *The leader uses the eight sources of power*

Mongkut put the chalk down in the wooden tray and rubbed his hands together.

"The power of purpose takes time, but it can remove the largest obstacles to freedom. This is the power you are going to learn in the Academy."

10
PUTTING POWER TO THE TEST

Chang shook his head and smirked.

"Do you disagree?" Mongkut asked.

"I do. The power of purpose is for weak people and is too slow. Why not just tell people what to do? If you're stronger than everyone else, then they must obey you."

Mot nodded in agreement. Faa glared at Chang with disapproval because of his disrespectful tone.

"In many cases," Mongkut said, "I agree that we need authority to achieve something quickly. But what if you are outside of an institution? You may believe you have no power, but that is not true. We all decide how much effort we give our leaders. People may give you a little effort if they must obey your authority, or they may give everything they own if they are pursuing a life worth living."

"I'm all for authority," Chang said and dropped his pen on his desk. Mot said, "I am as well. It works in the palace and in the military, so it must be the best way to lead."

"Let's test your love for authority," Mongkut said. "Chang and Mot, please come to the board."

The two students stood and walked to the front. Mongkut

disappeared into the back room for about five minutes. He returned carrying two ladles. Two young monks followed him dragging a ceramic cistern sloshing with water.

Chang and Mot realized that they may have fallen into a trap.

"I agree with Chang that power from authority can be effective," Mongkut explained, "especially if it is based on rewards and punishments. Maintaining this power may require constantly threatening punishment and promising rewards. Authority works only as long as the threatened pain or promised reward is enough to produce obedience."

Chang and Mot appeared uncomfortable with this new discussion of punishment.

"Which of you wants to experience the power of authority and which wants to experience the power of purpose?"

The boys looked at each other and shrugged. Chang said, "I'm the one who likes authority, so I'll take that."

Mongkut looked at Chang and said, "Your task is to deliver water to all the monks on the temple grounds. If you can do it by the time the sand drains from this hourglass, you can keep your armor in the corner."

Chang became upset. "It's hot outside and that armor belongs to me."

Mongkut stood straight and in a firm voice said, "I have the authority in this class, and you will do what I say or I will pass on your comments to your father." Chang shrank back as he realized what he had gotten himself into.

Mongkut then addressed Mot. "I *invite* you to work with Chang. The monks are thirsty, and it would bring you merit to serve them water. Also, I believe you have two cousins who are novices here and you can see them. Are you willing to help Chang?"

Mot was stunned by the invitation, and he had forgotten about his cousins.

"Sure, I'll work with Chang."

Mongkut said, "Let's go. I'm coming with you to help."

Chang looked shocked. He was the only one who was told what to do and threatened with punishment. Mongkut looked at Chang as he carefully turned an hourglass over and placed it on his stool.

Mongkut and the two students walked to the door. Chang and Mot grasped the heavy ceramic cistern between them.

"Ajarn! Can we go as well?" Faa asked.

Mongkut smiled and said, "If you would like."

For the next thirty minutes the students offered ladles of cool water to the monks and novices around the temple. It was fun for Tao who wanted to see the temple grounds and the various buildings. Chang was worried about the time, so he insisted that they hurry. Eventually they arrived back at the classroom with an empty cistern. The students returned to their mats. Chang and Mot were sweating and breathing hard.

Mongkut looked at the hourglass which still had a little sand left at the top. He then addressed Chang.

"How did you like being led by authority? You were told what to do without input. You were under the pressure of time, and you could lose something you value. Share what you experienced."

Chang was too tired to argue. He said, "The power of authority made me focus on what I would lose. I became frustrated with the others because they didn't have a time limit and wouldn't lose anything. But we did finish early and I'm happy that I won't lose my armor."

"Good," Mongkut said. "But notice that you get to keep your

armor because of the power of purpose. Mot agreed to work with you with no rewards or punishments because he wanted to move toward his cousins. The other students joined us without rewards or punishments because they wanted to move *toward* some other desire – even if it was just belonging to a team. Without them, you would have lost your armor."

A flash of realization hit Tao. He clearly saw the two types of power. He wrote down that one was effective but narrowly focused on rewards and punishments. The other was also effective, but broad, inclusive, and even fun.

Mongkut removed the hourglass and sat on his stool. He put his hands on his knees and asked, "What have we learned today about the two types of power?"

Muu raised his hand and said, "The power of authority comes from institutions, and allows people to be rewarded and punished."

"Yes. We *do* need the power of authority, but different sources of power exist. Chang, what have you learned?"

"If all you follow is the power of authority, you can feel frustrated and bound."

"I agree," Mongkut said. "There is a place for authority, but only relying on authority can sap your followers of joy and ignore their own purposes."

Tao was copying Mongkut's words as fast as he could. He heard Mongkut ask, "Tao, what did you learn about the power that comes from purpose."

"Purpose is about leading others to more freedom. You invited me to come to the Academy. You didn't threaten me or my family or promise me riches. You invited me and I freely agreed. I see more freedom if I come to the Academy than if I stay at home."

"And I am glad you came!" Mongkut said with a nod.

Turning back to the board, Mongkut wrote "The Power of Invitation" next to one of the tree branches.

He said, "The first branch is the first source of power: the *power of invitation*. So, I ask you, would you like to join me tomorrow morning to help build something at Wat Mahathat? As you know, this monastery is 300 years old and contains many treasures."

Tao raised his hand. The other students did as well.

"Thank you for accepting my invitation," Mongkut said. "I will see you at Wat Mahathat at sunrise. Tomorrow you will learn about the power of invitation."

Mongkut stood, picked up his hourglass, and walked into the room behind the blackboard. The class was over.

Tao finished writing and placed his paper and pen into his desk. Chang crumpled his elephant drawing into a ball and left it on his desk.

"See you tomorrow, Chang," Tao said.

"Maybe," Chang said. "My father is forcing me to take these classes, but I'd rather be training with the elephants."

Tao waited for Mongkut as the other students filed out to the porch. Faa waved good-bye to Tao and he returned the gesture. Then he felt a hand on his shoulder. He turned to see Mongkut behind him.

"Ready to learn French?" he asked. What could Tao say to such an invitation?

———————————————————

Answer the reflection questions in the Reflect and Apply section about *The Two Types of Power*.

11
PHAULKON MAKES HIS MOVE

King Narai appeared uncomfortable on his throne. It was not the large pillows or wooden back that caused his unease. He wasn't overly hot because servants fanned him with palm fronds at his left and right hand.

He was uncomfortable because he was about to change Siam's future. He leaned on his right arm and spoke. "Phaulkon, what do you have to show me that can't wait for our leadership meeting next week?"

Phaulkon and Aqu knelt before him in the empty meeting hall. The desk sitting before Aqu was clear because he had been summoned without any warning. He felt exposed without papers and reports sitting between him and the king.

"Yes, Phaulkon," Aqu said accusingly. "As Phrakhlang (royal title for the Minster of Treasury and Trade), I am the one who should review any requests before they come to the king. Explain yourself if it pleases the king."

King Narai nodded to Phaulkon. He had received documents earlier in the day that indicated what Phaulkon was going to say. The king, however, wanted to show respect to Aqu.

In perfect Siamese Phaulkon said, "Great king, I have worked for the honorable Phrakhlang Aqu for three years and he has exhibited great care with the trade revenues for the kingdom. But I believe that of no fault of his own that his bias toward Persian traders has clouded his analysis of their financial accounts."

Phaulkon ignored Aqu's stare and waved three documents before his face.

"Great king," Phaulkon continued, "As your servant it is my duty to ensure the integrity of all foreign accounts, and all appear to be in order, except for three. The trading accounts of Persia, Malaya, and India all have significant errors and amounts that show they are being charged less than other traders."

Phaulkon handed the papers to Aqu whose face had turned red. He reviewed the accounts, and he knew of some minor favors he had given to the Persians. Now he saw that they had taken more than they should have. Also, the Indian's and the Malaysians had done the same without him knowing it. Phaulkon had known but hidden it for months.

"Great king," Aqu started, "I was not aware of these financial problems. You know that my family has faithfully served the kingdom for three generations, and we have never allowed anything like this before. I will resolve the problems immediately."

"Aqu," the king said, "you and your family have performed excellent work for Siam. But you must admit that times have changed. Our future must include the French and not just the Persians, and these oversights can damage our larger strategy."

Aqu glanced at Phaulkon who was nodding at the king's words. He knew that the incorrect financial accounts had put him in check, and the king's desire for closer relations with the French and English put him in checkmate.

"Given these facts," the king continued, "I have decided to

name Phaulkon acting Phrakhlang starting today. I am sure he will seek your advice and counsel. Thank you for your service, Aqu. You and your family will always be a friend of mine." With these words, the king said, "Is that all?"

"One more thing, great king." Phaulkon could not stop himself. After firing a loyal servant, Narai was not in the mood for more accusations from Phaulkon.

"Speak!" Narai demanded.

"Thank you for the honor of serving Siam. I want to clarify that you said that I will be *acting* Phrakhlang. Does this mean that I now have the title of Phrakhlang as well?" He bowed his head.

"No. I will seek more counsel before handing out such an important title."

With these words the king stood, walked behind his throne and disappeared behind a curtain. The servants with palm fronds set them down and began talking.

Phaulkon and Aqu stood up together. Aqu slightly bowed to Phaulkon.

"Congratulations. You have won what you desired."

Then he put his hands on Phaulkon's shoulders and looked into his cold blue eyes. "Just remember that the higher one climbs in Siam, the smaller the rungs on the ladder. As one foreigner to another, at least I have a soft landing. Hold tight my friend because you have few friends or allies like I do. If a Greek adventurer falls in Siam, who will catch him?"

With those words Aqu let go of Phaulkon and walked out into the palace grounds. Phaulkon collected his papers and glanced up at the throne.

He whispered to himself, "I am holding to the throne, not a ladder my friend."

12
AUTHORITY IS DELEGATED

Tao was in bed early after eating three helpings of rice, beans, and papaya. He was tired from a long day of learning about trees, power, and how to say, "How are you?" and "My name is Tao" in French.

Mongkut's day as Minister of Land's had just begun. Sunan had already sorted the palace communications into two piles: "do today" and "do later." She lit an oil lamp on his desk and then sat in her rocking chair to sew.

Mongkut longed to explore a world of ideas that made sense of the world instead of navigating political battles. Sunan, however, had relationships with senior palace officials and gathered news that would help Mongkut.

As Mongkut read through the first "do-today" document he said, "Did you know that the king replaced Aqu with Phaulkon?"

"It was the biggest news of the day. You said that Phaulkon was moving quickly to discredit his boss. He finally made his move."

Mongkut finished reading the document announcing Phaulkon's new position. He chuckled.

"What's so funny," Sunan asked without looking up from altering Tao's shirt.

"The king denied Phaulkon the title of Phrakhlang. He is keeping Phaulkon in a subordinate position so that he can use him without giving him too much prestige. I'm sure Phaulkon hates doing the job without the title. But giving the title to a newly arrived foreigner would upset the cabinet and the provincial leaders."

"The king is wise," Sunan said, "but he is playing a dangerous game. The resistance to foreigners in our government is getting stronger, and Chang's father is leading it."

"Hmm," said Mongkut. He knew that Chang's father Phetracha was fiercely committed to Siam being led by the Siamese. He also knew that the king would never become a puppet of another nation, but Phetracha's intentions were not only about protecting Siam. Phetracha desired the power of authority that his boyhood friend Narai held. Mongkut also wondered if Chang attended the Academy to learn about leadership or to spy on him. Probably both.

Sunan eventually finished her sewing, rose from her chair and kissed Mongkut on the cheek. "Don't stay up too late. Remember that you're doing construction at Wat Mahathat in the morning."

She shuffled to the bedroom with one of the lamps leaving Mongkut with his documents. Mongkut laughed to himself. "I did invite the students. I guess I better be there early."

13
BUILDING UP AND
TEARING DOWN

Every time Tao walked into a monastery the massive gates, walls, buildings, and pagodas amazed him. Why was everything so big in Ayutthaya? As he and Mongkut entered the towering western gate of Wat Mahathat, he stopped and craned his neck to take in its height.

"Wait until you see the inside," Mongkut said.

The red-brick pagoda in the center of the monastery stood like a mountain jutting out of the ground. He later learned that the pagoda represented Mount Meru, the most sacred mountain in Buddhism and Hinduism. Mongkut said that the base was 360 feet around with four towers at each corner.

"It is an impressive monument isn't it," Mongkut said. "This monastery is where Siam's most important royal and religious ceremonies are held. Parts of it over 300 years old, dating back almost to the founding of Ayutthaya in Year of the Tiger 713, or 1351 in European years. The pagoda is a 'temple mountain' and it is the same style used by the Khmer people. Part of it collapsed in 1632. King Prasat Thong restored it in 1633 and increased its height from 120 feet to 150 feet."

"What's inside?" Tao asked.

"Different relics related to the Buddha and our kingdom. These buildings are symbols of who we are and who we want to be. But here is where a kingdom's true greatness lies." Mongkut gently tapped Tao's chest with his hand. He then pointed to Tao's forehead and said, "And here is also where you learn how to lead others."

They continued around to the left of the monument, passing monks and rows of Buddha statues. After a few more minutes of walking, they approached a group of workers who had gathered around a tent. Bamboo scaffolding stood along a partially constructed building. The foundation was finished and a wooden frame rose up from the foundation. Tao saw Faa and Muu standing next to a pile of bricks.

Mongkut asked Tao to wait. He walked into the tent and greeted a man who was standing at a table with papers on it. Laughter spilled out of the tent as soon as Mongkut entered.

"What do you think of Mongkut's plan to make us work all day?" Muu asked as Tao approached.

"He has a unique way of teaching. How about serving all of that water yesterday?"

"My arms are still sore," said Mot. He and Chang walked up to the brick pile.

"It serves you right," said Faa. "Arguing with Ajarn Mongkut about his lesson is disrespectful."

Chang would have none of Faa's correction.

"He doesn't mind being challenged. We aren't babies. The old man can take my opinions or leave them. Besides, what are we going to learn here anyway? And why are *you* here instead of sewing something?"

"Leave her alone," Tao said.

Faa interrupted, "Don't defend me country boy."

She stood face-to-face with Chang.

"Your insults don't frighten me. But know this Chang; I will always outwork you, out think you, and outsmart you because I am willing to learn and change. You are stuck in the past just like your father, and if you had a mother..."

Faa stopped speaking as Chang stepped toward her. His fists were clinched.

"What's going on here?" Mongkut asked. No one had noticed that he was standing behind them.

"Just giving a lesson in respect, Ajarn," Faa said with a slight bow. Chang laughed and said, "If you say so," and walked back to Mot.

"Respect, hmm?" Mongkut said. "Well, you can never lose a relationship by showing respect, and you can never gain one without respect. How much respect were you two showing?" He glanced at Faa and Chang.

"Of course, I only respect people who have earned it. Respecting idiots, thieves, murderers, name callers, and traitors makes no sense." Mongkut looked at all of the students. "I respect each of you because you have proven you are worthy of respect so far. But be careful!"

Mongkut leaned down and picked up two red bricks from the pile. He held them in front of his chest and examined them.

"When people fight for superiority over each other, they both lose respect." He looked at Faa and Chang and vigorously ground the bricks together. Red powder and small chunks of clay began to fall to the ground.

"They fight and scar and tear at each other until both of them are weak and useless." He smashed the bricks together twice which made the students jump. The bricks shattered into large chunks and red dust.

"To be a leader is to build people up and not tear them down. You should build each other up even if you disagree. If you are attacked," he looked at Faa and Chang, "do not take it personally. The attack is about the fears of the attacker. It's not about you, so why take it personally?"

Mongkut let the lesson sink in and dropped the broken and scarred pieces in the mud. "These are no good for a great building like this," he said, wiping the dust from his hands. "These will be crushed and used for a walkway – to be stepped on for generations."

His lesson delivered, Mongkut walked back to the tent. Faa took a deep breath. Chang grabbed Mot by the arm and stomped to the shade of a tree. Muu started stacking the loose bricks.

Tao felt a hand on his arm.

"I'm sorry I called you a country boy," Faa said in a soft voice. "I know you were trying to help, but when someone tells me I can't do something . . ." Her voice trailed off, but she maintained eye contact with Tao. "And yet I did the same thing to you that Chang did to me."

"My mother taught me to find the good in everyone," Tao said. "It's difficult. It hurts when rich people like you look down on me because my clothes don't fit or my accent is strange. But why should I carry someone else's hatred in my heart? Like Mongkut said, 'that's their problem.'"

He looked at Faa and said, "I accept your apology. And thanks for sticking up for me yesterday. I *did* need help."

Faa said, "You're welcome."

Answer the reflection questions in the Reflect and Apply section on *Tearing Down and Building Up.*

14
THE POWER OF INVITATION

Mongkut returned to the students walking with a woman wearing a round wicker sunhat that was firmly tied under her chin with a red piece of cloth. She wore a dark blue long-sleeved shirt and was shorter than most of the students. Her nose was flat, and she had a wide smile that lit up her suntanned face. Her hair was short under the hat.

"Welcome to Wat Mahathat." She said in a joyful voice. The students respectfully wai'd (pronounced "wide") her and she returned their greeting.

"I am Siriporn and my father Thongsit has put me in charge of building this school for monks. Just as my father invited me to build with him, you can have a part in building something that will honor our king and our people. Maybe your children and grandchildren will come here and see your work." She paused and glanced at Mongkut.

"For those who wish to build with us today, I *invite* you to review the architectural plans and then to help us build the south wall. If you do not wish to work, you can sit over by that tree for the day."

Mongkut and Siriporn turned and walked toward the tent. Tao, Muu, and Faa joined them. Tao glanced back at Chang and Mot who were considering their options. The shade tree was appealing, but sitting all day would be boring. Eventually, they caught up with the group and entered the tent.

A wooden table sat in the middle of the tent and large sheets of brown paper with building diagrams covered the top. Mongkut gathered the students around the table.

Siriporn took a scroll from a wooden rack and rolled it out on the table over the other documents. The paper revealed four views of the building outside of the tent – one view of each of the sides. The architect had sketched the long wooden posts rising to the ceiling and the beams to support the ceiling and connect the walls to each other. Siriporn explained the vision of the building and how the location was selected to encourage contemplation. She noted that several trees were left in place to provide shade and that large openings on the walls would allow breezes to cross through the building.

Siriporn took a blank piece of paper and began to write for all the students to see. Tao leaned past Muu's large frame to see what she was writing. She wrote:

THE POWER OF INVITATION

1. *Ask someone to join you on a journey.*
2. *Together, determine*
   - *where you are going*
   - *where you are*
   - *how to get there*

"Imagine that you have an idea to go on a journey or build a school or start a business," she said. "You can do it alone, or you can invite others to join you. If you have others with you, the work can go much faster and you all will learn from each other. When you invite someone to join you, a good way to start is to agree on *where you are going*. Any idea or vision starts with describing your destination. For example, this building is designed to serve people and not to serve the architect. The architect sat around the Wat for days and invited senior monks and novices to tell him what they most desired in a classroom building. He asked them to define what is beautiful and what inspires them. Before he drew one line on this paper, he understood who would use the building and what was important to them. Then he knew *where* they wanted to go."

"An important second step of inviting someone to join you is to describe *where you are*. While these diagrams give us a clear picture of what we want to see in the world, they don't tell us where we are now. We need to know what resources we have, how much they will cost, and who else we need to invite on our journey. I invited Mongkut and he invited you!"

Siriporn looked at the students and Mongkut as if satisfied with the students, and then continued.

"Finally, you need to agree on how to get from where you are to where you are going. Working together, the leader and those who are invited create a detailed plan that everyone can understand and follow. This explains *how to get there.*"

Mongkut said, "You can invite new people for each of these discussions and some people may leave after they share their ideas. What doesn't change is that the leader is the one who knows the destination, the reality of what is, and the plan for reaching the destination. The power of invitation is a way to lead others to accomplish a purpose without using authority."

Siriporn moved the paper she was writing on and began pointing to items on the building diagram.

"Note the exact measurements for the footers. Note the instructions on what type of wood to use. See the angles for setting each corner post? This is a vision that we as builders can understand and can follow."

Mongkut said, "An invitation is a source of power. It creates a channel for people to join together to talk and create something new. The plan then becomes an agreement for moving forward together. Just look around."

Tao looked outside of the tent. He saw workers hammering boards into place, mixing cement for the bricks, and constructing a pulley system to lift ceiling beams into place.

Mongkut continued, "They are following the plan and they have freedom to decide how to do their part."

"Correct" said Siriporn. "These workers are invited to fulfill what needs to be done. The plan provides a goal, a channel, and a boundary. The goal is the final picture, and ideally it is a vision that inspires people to join. The channel is how you do the work using your own skills and knowledge. The boundary lets you know where you are straying from the plan and need to get back into your channel."

All the students were interested now. Muu was skeptical and asked Mongkut if the workers volunteered or were paid. "If they are paid, then they were not invited."

Siriporn shook her head. "Just because you pay someone to join you doesn't mean that they were not invited. I know many workers I did not invite to work on this particular building. Don't confuse the power of invitation and volunteering."

"Siriporn, please tell the students how you came to be in charge of this project," Mongkut said.

Siriporn adjusted her hat proudly and told of how the Supreme Patriarch of Wat Mahathat had requested a meeting with her father and an architect. He explained that he needed a school building for the new novices coming to the monastery. The Patriarch had the funds, but now he needed a plan and a builder.

"By inviting us to discuss the project, he started a chain of actions which has led to the building you see taking shape," she said. "To give an invitation is to open a space for things to move – to initiate action – and that is a power that produces results. Invitations also sort out those who are not interested from those who are interested and motivated. We were the third builder that the Supreme Patriarch invited to build the school."

"Why were you the third, ma'am?" Faa asked.

Siriporn laughed, "Because the Supreme Patriarch wanted a team who would build what he wanted, and not what the builders wanted. My father and I listened while the others wouldn't stop talking!"

The students nodded as if they understood.

Siriporn looked out at the building and became pensive. She said, "We *wanted* to build something great. Something that serves the people of Siam. Something that we would be proud to send my grandchildren to see. So, we received the invitation and accepted it."

Chang had been closely examining the drawing of the building. He looked up from the brown paper and asked Mongkut, "What if someone doesn't want to come? Regardless of the plan, some people will not follow."

"You are right. Leading without authority means that people are free to reject your invitation. Then you must adjust the vision, find other people, or reconsider the timing of your ideas. But don't take it personally. The power of purpose is based on freedom, not coercion."

Mot said what most were thinking. "But what if after all the invitations, you do the work alone?"

"Then you can try one of the other sources of power," Mongkut said. "But sometimes you will work alone if your vision is important. Siriporn's father started this company alone."

Siriporn nodded and took a drink of water from a wooden cup. "My father started a construction company many years ago and my brothers and I had built all kinds of buildings, houses and walls growing up. My husband was a fisherman and drowned in a storm, and I was left with two older children. I began to feel sorry for myself, so I asked my dad if I could work with him. He said yes, and here we are." She took another sip of water.

"My dad set me up repairing floors for people without much money. Then we did some walls and roofs. Eventually we bid on a stable for the palace and Mongkut hired us. We 'invited' three workers to help. I say invited because I couldn't pay much, but they also wanted to work on a palace building. We completed the stable and ever since then our company has grown."

Mongkut said, "Students, do you see the power of invitation! Prove that your vision is worthwhile, create a space for other people to join you, and those who are interested in your vision will accept your invitation."

A worker came into the tent and bowed slightly to Mongkut and Siriporn. "We are ready for the students."

"Enough talk about invitations and plans," said Siriporn. "Who wants to build a school?"

The students rushed from the tent following the worker. Mongkut walked slowly with Siriporn.

"Thank you for teaching my class. You're a natural." he said.

Siriporn gave Mongkut a friendly shove. "Thank you for inviting me. I'll keep building the schools if you keep teaching the students."

Answer the reflection questions in the Reflect and Apply section about how you can apply the *Power of Invitation.*

15
PHETRACHA COMPLAINS
TO THE KING

Phetracha did not like waiting.

He paced on the broad porch outside of the throne room. The decorated warrior in charge of the kingdom's war elephants had many things on his mind. He scheduled his meeting with King Narai two weeks ago, but recent events made the meeting more urgent.

The distant sound of elephant trumpeting could be heard from the porch. Phetracha housed about 20 elephants in the palace stables for parades, special ceremonies, but primarily for battle training. Most of the elephants were strategically placed outside of the city. Unlike other senior leaders of Siam, Phetracha was always on a war footing. He loved Siam and had risked his life several times defending the kingdom from Khmer invaders. He remembered the stories of being under Khmer rule decades ago, and he would never allow it to happen again.

But Phetracha saw a more sinister enemy: foreign interference in the kingdom. Phetracha protected the kingdom's external borders and the king was supposed to protect the internal borders from invasion.

The presence of a court messenger woke Phetracha from his thoughts and his rising frustration.

"The king will see you now." The messenger gestured to Phetracha to follow him. Phetracha went along with the messenger, as if he did not know every inch of the palace. He and Narai played in every room of the palace as children. His mother nursed, disciplined, and loved them both. But eventually a prince becomes king and the nurse-maid's child becomes a servant.

Phetracha walked into the throne room and knelt down on a mat before his friend. King Narai laughed, walked down the steps from his golden throne, and asked Phetracha to stand. "My friend!" he said. "I have missed you!"

"I've missed seeing your face as well, your majesty," Phetracha said. He felt his frustration dissolve in the presence of the king.

"Let's go for a ride!" the king said. "Do you have my elephant ready?"

Phetracha was taken aback by the king's enthusiasm. "Well, don't you want to talk first?"

"We'll talk and ride. I need to get out of the palace for a while. Let's go. I'll see you in an hour."

Phetracha nodded and knelt down with his head touching the floor until the king left.

Within an hour Phetracha and the king were riding two elephants around a corral in the elephant paddock. The king's elephant was clad with a gold inlaid saddle and harness. The head of the elephant was partially covered with a red and purple silk triangle with green emeralds and garnet rubies that glinted in the sun. Phetracha's elephant had a battle saddle and a green silk triangle with the seal of Siam prominently displayed. The elephants lumbered along as the two riders talked of past battles, how to best calm the elephants under gunfire, and the new palace in Lopburi.

The king knew that Phetracha wanted to talk to him about Siam's government because that is what he always wanted to discuss. He appreciated his friend's advice, but Phetracha had a narrow view of the world in King Narai's opinion. He didn't see the interconnecting treaties and trade agreements that made Siam resemble other wealthy nations. Foreign emissaries and trade agreements affirmed that King Narai was a king like Louis XIV in France. Kings knew best, and he intended to guide Siam into this bigger world.

The king finally asked, "What specifically do you want to talk about?"

"Your majesty, I know that you only make decisions that benefit the people of Siam. I was surprised, however, that you replaced Aqu with Phaulkon. While Aqu is not Siamese, his family has lived here for generations and served past kings well. Phaulkon is an unknown foreigner who now manages the lifeblood of our kingdom. I realize that I do not have all the facts, but why appoint this wandering Greek to this office? Don't you have anyone from Siam to hold this position?"

King Narai looked ahead as the elephants curved around the corral. "My friend, I do not have anyone like Phaulkon who can speak multiple languages, understands trade across the seas, and keeps a close eye on our trading partners. I know that I am taking a risk appointing him to lead this department, but I am watching him. Also, I have not given him the position of Phrakhlang."

King Narai smiled and turned to Phetracha. "You know how to keep a new soldier motivated? Let them see the medal, but don't give it easily. I want to keep Phaulkon focused on earning the position, which means working in the interests of Siam."

"But what of the Chinese? Certainly, Phaulkon will bias our nation toward England, France, and the Dutch?"

"He may," the king admitted, "but that is to our advantage. I communicate with the kings of these lands, and they have much to offer us in terms of science, medicine, and building techniques. The Jesuits let me look through a telescope not long ago to see the surface of the moon!"

Phetracha grunted, "I am concerned that Siam will lose her heritage. Our Buddhist traditions. Our ability to survive against our enemies! The provincial governors are also concerned that..."

"They worry too much," King Narai interrupted, switching to an authoritative tone. "You and the governors need to trust me. Keep your eyes on our borders and I will keep my eyes on the traders."

King Narai wanted to change the subject from Phetracha's worries. "How is Chang doing in Mongkut's leadership academy? Mongkut said he is preparing leaders for Siam so that we won't need to rely on foreigners in the future."

Phetracha got the message that the king was finished discussing his concerns. At least he had assured him that Phaulkon was under control and that his western ideas would be held in check.

"Chang is a soldier at heart, so he's not interested in lessons about persuading others to follow. But Mongkut has made him think of alternative ways besides commanding obedience. The class is building a wall at Wat Mahathat today to learn something about leading."

"Good!" King Narai exclaimed. "Let them build and learn. There is nothing like doing something with your hands to teach your mind discipline. Like how you taught me to race an elephant many years ago."

With that both men looked at each other. Phetracha quickly prodded his elephant with a bamboo rod. The king laughed and did the same. The elephants started running and the king yelled in delight. Phetracha put on his best smile and goaded his elephant forward. For the sake of Siam, he would watch the borders, but he and his spies would also keep a close eye on the king's minister of finance.

16
MANAGING WORLD VIEWS

The students worked on the school at Wat Mahathat for three days. Each day they learned about structural engineering, the strength of different materials, and how to join bricks with mortar. Each night they went home tired but inspired by their contributions. Siriporn organized the work so that the students would complete a full section of wall by the third day. They could always point to that wall as their wall. Each student scratched their name onto the cornerstone.

That weekend Mongkut and Sunan gave Tao a tour of Ayutthaya. They left the house as the sun was rising. The reddish-orange sky lit the rising fog from the canals and created a mystical scene. Figures walked out of the fog and nodded as they passed by. Carts pulled by water buffalo creaked past them and disappeared on their journey to a market, a port, or the countryside.

After stopping at a food vendor for rice and fish soup, they walked north-west toward the palace complex.

At the palace Tao asked about a large building sitting in front of the palace. Sunan explained that the future kings would live in this palace as a symbol of the future stability of Siam.

"Does King Narai have a son?"

"Yes," said Sunan. "He is very young and private tutors teach him languages and military tactics. Maybe you can meet him someday."

Further north, they approached the walls of the main palace. The sun sat above the horizon now and the palace behind the walls shined, though Tao could only see the roof.

They approached the main gate which was guarded by several soldiers. Mongkut greeted the guards with a humorous comment about not letting even an ant into the palace. He knew each of their names. They laughed and spoke of their terrible breakfast and how they were looking forward to a cool day.

"Can we go in?" Tao asked.

"Not today," said Mongkut. "I have another place for you to see."

The three continued walking west to a canal where Mongkut rented a long, thin boat with an old driver who had no teeth. The driver pulled out his pole while Sunan and Tao sat in the bow. Eventually they passed through a large gate and were outside the city.

"Where are we going," Tao asked.

"We are going to see the French Jesuits." Mongkut said. "I am inviting Father Guy Tachard to teach a lesson in our academy."

As they traveled down the river, Tao saw men on both banks who did not look Siamese. Some had dark beards and stood six feet tall. Others looked like Siamese people but wore dark blue shirts and pants. Sunan explained that these were the compounds where the foreign traders lived. She pointed out the Portuguese camp on the left where five ships gently rocked next to wooden docks. Eventually their boat joined the Chao Phraya river and they sailed past the Chinese, English, and Dutch compounds. Buildings stretched from the piers into the country.

The driver guided the boat next to an open dock at the French compound. Mongkut asked the driver to stay, and he nodded his head and began preparing a pipe to pass the time.

The French camp had several permanent buildings. Mongkut pointed to a Catholic chapel (Tao noticed that it was not elaborate or covered in gold like the Wats), a school building, and a large building for managing French trade with Siam. Siamese worked around the camp stoking fires, doing laundry, and preparing meals. They stared at Mongkut and Sunan who acknowledged them with a smile and a nod.

"The French have been in Siam for almost one hundred years," Sunan explained. "They brought their own religion – Catholicism – and want everyone to worship their god Jesus. These French Jesuits were sent by King Louis XIV and have been here since 1662. They study the stars, teach languages, and opened a few hospitals."

"And battle the Portuguese missionaries for converts," Mongkut added.

Sunan countered, "But they have done many good things for Siam. They opened the General College near the palace and also Monsignor Lambert founded the hospital in Ayutthaya."

"Unfortunately, western religion has become tied to trade, and trade is tied to kings, armies, and money," Mongkut said seriously, but then took on a lighter tone and said, "King Narai is open to the French Jesuits teaching here and benefiting the nation. We are friends with the Jesuits because we can learn much from them."

They walked up to a two-story house with a balcony and open windows. Mongkut knocked on the door frame. To his and Sunan's surprise, Phaulkon stepped out of the doorway and greeted them.

"Hello Mongkut and Sunan. What a surprise to see you!"

Phaulkon bowed slightly. Tao had never been so close to someone with such white skin. He looked into Phaulkon's eyes and saw that they were blue! He also noted a flash of panic in his eyes, but then it was gone.

"What brings you to the French compound?" Phaulkon asked as he quickly stepped out into the street.

Mongkut, who was also surprised, said, "I'm here to ask Father Tachard to speak to the Siam Leadership Academy. The students need to learn about different religions and the leaders of the countries that trade with us."

"Great idea," Phaulkon exclaimed. "Maybe some of them will become Catholic. I've become a Catholic."

Sunan looked down and asked Phaulkon, "Will your decision be accepted in the king's court?"

Phaulkon laughed confidently. "Of course! King Narai loves the Jesuits and the French. Maybe someday he will become Catholic as well. But I must be going now."

With a quick bow of his head, Phaulkon marched off toward the river.

Before Mongkut could say anything, a tall European man in a black robe walked out of the doorway and embraced Mongkut. This must be Father Tachard.

In French the man said, "Mongkut and Sunan! So good to see you. Please come in."

Tao entered the house and looked around the main room. It was filled with books on shelves and papers stacked on a thick wooden table. A painting of Jesus' face with a halo around his head hung on the back wall in a wooden frame. Next to the painting hung a wooden cross. But what caught Tao's eye was a five-foot long, shiny brass tube sitting on a wooden tripod.

Father Tachard walked over to Tao who was carefully examining the tube. In Siamese with a strong French accent, he said, "This is a telescope. King Narai used this same one to view an eclipse of the moon."

Tao nodded his head and put his hands behind his back.

Father Tachard asked, "What is your name?"

"My name is Tao. I'm a student at the Siam Leadership Academy. I've heard of telescopes but never seen one."

"Well now you have, and you can use it." He moved the telescope next to a window. "At night we go on the roof and study the moon's surface and look for objects which are like our own planet. Of course, at this time of day you can only look across the street!"

While Tao carefully examined the telescope, Father Tachard sat down with Mongkut and Sunan. As they talked in French and Siamese, Tao used it to look out of the window at different shops and the tops of trees. He eventually put the telescope aside and picked up a book on astronomy that was sitting on the table. He glanced through the book, but he didn't know enough French to understand what it was about.

Tao heard Father Tachard say, "I'll see you in the coming weeks, and I'll stay within the boundaries you outlined."

Tao carefully set the book down and walked up to Father Tachard.

"Thank you for sharing your telescope," he said. "By the way, who is Galileo?"

"So, you can read some French!" Father Tachard exclaimed. "Galileo wrote the book you were looking at. It is called the *Dialogue Concerning the Two Chief World Systems*. He was a brilliant astronomer who argued that the earth travels around the sun, which agrees with the theory of Copernicus. We Jesuits are still discussing his conclusions and observing the stars to prove for ourselves if he is correct as opposed to those who say the sun travels around the earth."

"Which do you believe?" Tao asked.

Father Tachard thought for a second and said, "I believe Galileo. He proved that Venus – you know the brightest light in the winter sky – has phases like the moon, which means that it travels around the sun. I've seen and measured these phases. Galileo, however, was arrogant about his discoveries and insulted the leader of my church in this book. He makes him look like an idiot, and the leader didn't like that at all."

Father Tachard guided them out of the door and said to Mongkut, "With students like this, I can't wait to talk to your class."

As they walked toward the river a concerned look grew on Sunan's face. She put her arm in Mongkut's arm and whispered.

"Are you sure you should have a priest talk to your students? You know how some in the palace feel about the Christians and Muslims trying to convert Siamese."

"It is a risk, but I am actually *reducing* the risk of us losing our traditions. Ignorance of their beliefs leaves us two options: let them overtake us or violently oppose them. But understanding and being in a dialogue with their ideas gives us a common ground for discussion. We can present our own beliefs in contrast to their beliefs. We can protect ourselves from being colonized."

"What stops the French or Dutch from colonizing us?" asked Tao.

Mongkut was surprised that Tao was listening.

"I believe it is because we have so many foreigners here trading that none of them is strong enough to overcome us and each other. If the French try to take over, the English and Dutch will fight them as well as the Siamese. The king balances these relationships through trade, taxes, and favors. As long as these competing forces are held in balance, the foreigners seek our favor instead of dominance. Their kings are busy enough trying to manage other colonies around the world."

"What if one of your students converts to Christianity," Sunan asked, "like Phaulkon and his wife? Consider what Phetracha would do!"

Mongkut knew that Sunan had reason to be concerned, but he also knew that most converts to Christianity in Siam were among the Dutch, English and Japanese. Very few Siamese became Christians.

He held Sunan's hand. "The students are old enough to choose which religious path they take. My mission is to create a space for them to test and evaluate a variety of beliefs. They can choose whichever one will lead them to a freer and more powerful life of service."

Answer the reflection questions in the Reflect and Apply section about *Managing Power Relationships*.

17
THE POWER OF THE OPEN HAND

On Monday morning the students loudly entered the classroom. They became silent when they saw a Buddhist monk sitting on a raised platform at the front of the room. The monk was older than Mongkut. He had a round face, a bald head, thin arms, big feet, and his eyes were closed. His dark saffron robe cast an orange hue on his tan face which gave an impression of peaceful meditation.

The students quietly knelt on their mats and took paper out of their desks. Mongkut appeared next to the monk who opened his eyes and smiled at Mongkut with white teeth.

Mongkut said, "Good morning. As you can see, we have a distinguished guest visiting us today. We have Phra Udom Vimutti who is an elder teacher at Wat Mahathat. Many great teachers including Phra Luang Pu Thuat taught him.

The students greeted the guest with a deep wai, and Phra Vimutti gave a friendly nod.

Mongkut continued. "I have asked him to talk to you about Buddha and a source of power that his teachings reveal to us."

Mongkut gestured to Phra Vimutti and then walked to the back of the room. The monk remained seated with his legs crossed.

In a soft voice he asked, "How many of you have heard the story of Siddhartha Gautama who became the Buddha?"

All five students raised their hands.

"Good! But how many of you know one of his greatest teachings on leading others?"

No hands raised and Phra Vimutti clapped his hands together.

"Excellent. This means you will learn something today. Let's start with his life journey. Who was Siddhartha and his parents?"

"He was a prince born in India near the great mountains." said Faa. "His father was King Suddhodana and his mother was queen Mahamaya. Astrologers told the king that his son would either be a great king or turn his back on wealth and power and become a spiritual leader."

"Correct!" said Phra Vimutti. Tao noticed the contrast between the monk's peaceful sitting position and his excitement.

"What did the king do to protect his son from becoming a spiritual leader?"

Mot raised his hand. "The king didn't allow the prince to see people who were suffering. He kept him in the palace all the time and surrounded him with gold, delicious food and beautiful things."

"And then the prince wanted to go out into the city," Phra Vimutti continued. "His father removed all of the sick, old, and dead people from the streets so that Siddhartha would not see suffering. But from his chariot the prince saw an old man lying on the ground. He was shocked to see that people grow old and suffer. On future trips around the city he saw a sick person and a dead man. What did he realize?"

"The truth of life," said Faa. "Humans are born, they get sick, they grow old, and they die. Change is constant."

Phra Vimutti took a deep breath and slowly stood up. He straightened his robes, walked to Faa's desk and looked at her. "Yes. Siddhartha saw that all physical things are constantly changing. We cannot hold onto anything permanently, and we suffer when we try to cling to things. He then formed his one question, 'What is the nature of suffering and how can we escape it?' He was 29 years old."

Tao had heard the story many times, so he was drawing a telescope on his paper. He glanced up from his drawing and saw Phra Vimutti looking directly at him. His heart jumped and Chang chuckled.

"Young man, how did he try to answer his question?"

Tao said, "Siddhartha left the palace on his horse and became a beggar in another city, but living as a homeless beggar didn't answer his question. He then joined people who renounced all pleasure."

Phra Vimutti said, "Yes. He lived with a group of ascetics for six years. He starved himself and punished his body. These ascetics believed that a state of pain and weakness would reveal the answer to the question of suffering. By focusing on the body, they thought the mind would be free. Siddhartha also practiced different types of meditation to gain a higher consciousness. So, did he get his answer?"

Muu joined in the discussion. "I don't think he did. Didn't he get his answer under a Bodhi tree?"

Faa jumped in. "After many years he sat under a Bodhi tree and remembered being a boy at a planting festival. He watched the farmers dig up the field and he felt sad when ants and their homes were destroyed."

Phra Vimutti became more animated as if she had reached the main point of his lecture. He looked at the students and spread his arms wide.

"Siddhartha felt sad because he had compassion – even for ants. In his compassion he felt joy. Compassion and joy are the fabric of all life. At that moment, a peasant girl named Sujada was walking by the tree and saw that Siddhartha was starving. She had compassion on him and offered him kheer (rice porridge). He ate it and suddenly realized that his obsession with punishing his body did not answer his question."

Phra Vimutti had their attention and continued the story.

"Siddhartha sits under the Bodhi tree and says, 'I will not leave this spot until I have attained wisdom.' Mara the god of death, rebirth, and desire appears and threatens to destroy him and tries to seduce him. None of his attacks work. Siddhartha then touches the ground with one hand and the earth shakes. The earth was his witness that he would be enlightened, and Mara fled. That night Siddhartha meditates under the tree and becomes awakened and enlightened to the answer to his question. He identifies the middle path. You? What is that path?" He pointed at Chang.

Chang said, "Is it the middle way between seeking pleasure and torturing yourself?"

"Yes, it is! Now Siddhartha becomes the Gautama Buddha, the awakened one. He understands the truth about suffering and he can experience freedom from the cycle of birth, death, and rebirth. What is the truth that he discovers?"

Tao answered. "My teacher told me that Buddha said, 'I teach suffering, its origin, cessation and path. That's all I teach.'"

Phra Vimutti nodded at Tao and then walked to the chalkboard and picked up a piece of chalk. The priest's robes shook as he vigorously wrote on the board. The sound of the chalk attacking the board was loud. The chalk broke twice but he continued writing with the nub that was left.

When he finished, he stepped back, rubbed chalk dust from his hands, and reviewed what he had written. The students wrote down the following.

1. Suffering comes from misplaced desires and the three poisons.

2. A person can extinguish the three poisons.

3. When the poisons are extinguished, the person can use the power of the open hand.

"Buddha teaches that suffering and dissatisfaction have many sources. While some suffer because of the evil actions of others, or being born into a poor family, or sickness, all of us suffer from our frustrated desires. As a leader of others, you must acknowledge that suffering exists in many forms, and that it is a temporary reality. A leader who ignores the suffering of others cannot inspire them to follow. A leader who acknowledges and relieves the suffering of others builds a strong relationship with them."

Muu raised his hand. "What are the three poisons?"

Phra Vimutti exclaimed, "You are hungry to learn! The three poisons are the three causes of being unsatisfied: greed, anger, and ignorance. *Greed* drives us to constantly look for what we desire, and yet acquiring it never satisfies our deepest needs. *Anger* and hatred come from focusing on what we don't like or don't want until our spirits burn. Finally, *ignorance* is believing that all things are permanent."

Phra Vimutti wrote the three poisons below his list and left blanks next to each.: Greed or _____ ; Anger or _____; Ignorance or _____.

"When you exercise the power of the open hand, you are practicing the three opposites of the poisons. Each opposite first frees you and then frees others to follow. Instead of practicing greed, we practice *compassion* every day. Remember, compassion is why the Buddha left the comfort of his tree to teach others. He had to share his joy and freedom!" He wrote "Compassion" in the first blank next to "Greed."

"We practice *generosity* toward others and this frees us from anger and hatred. Buddha taught us that all material things are an illusion and impermanent, so giving is easy since you cannot own anything." He wrote "Generosity" in the blank after "Anger or."

Phra Vimutti scanned the students' faces. "We know that suffering exists because of misplaced desires and that the path of compassion and generosity leads us away from these desires. What is left?"

Mot asked, "How can we be free of ignorance?"

Phra Vimutti paused, closed his eyes and said. "Excellent question for a student in Mongkut's class."

When he opened his eyes, he looked deeply into the student's eyes as if he were going to reveal an important secret.

"Extinguishing ignorance requires curiosity." He wrote "Curiosity" in the last open space in his list.

"We are ignorant because we believe that things are permanent. We may even believe that *beliefs* are permanent. Ignorance is committed to the illusion that we can grasp ideas and material objects while still being free. Curiosity, however, is committed to the universal constant that nothing is permanent. Reflecting on impermanence makes you *curious* about what you don't know, and this completes the power of the open hand."

"But before I describe this power anymore, let me show you something." Phra Vimutti reached into his robe and took out a gold coin. He held it in his palm for the students to see.

"Consider this little piece of metal. Just by bringing it into your view, have I created a fire in your spirit?"

Tao did feel excited for some reason. He realized that he wanted to hold it. He wanted to spend it. He thought of buying a telescope. He leaned back and wondered where these feelings came from.

"For some of you," Phra Vimutti said, "I have ignited a burning suffering in your heart by showing you this gold coin. What if I said that the best student can keep the gold coin? Then some of you will feel *more* suffering. Greed, anger, and dissatisfaction start rising in each of us. If gold is not to your liking, I could show you a silk robe from the south, a position of authority, a shining sword, a book, or a delicious meal. You will want to acquire these things because you think that they will satisfy your desires; that they will make you happy."

The students looked at each other and were embarrassed. The gold piece and the other items the monk listed had triggered something deep inside them. Each of them felt dissatisfied.

"It depends on the sword," Chang said.

Phra Vimutti laughed. "Yes! We all desire some ideal in our hearts and this drives our ignorance in thinking that we can acquire it and hold it forever. But that is ignorance and a cause of suffering."

He put the coin away and wrote on the board:

THE POWER OF THE OPEN HAND

1. *Compassion frees us from greed.*
2. *Generosity frees us from anger.*
3. *Curiosity frees us from ignorance.*

"People will follow a leader who practices the power of the open hand. First, these leaders show compassion by being *gentle* to themselves and others. If you are angry at yourself or others, check your own desires and impatience. Remember, you are choosing a path of purpose, not authority. Be gentle by asking rather than telling."

"These leaders also show generosity by *sharing* what is needed with themselves and others. Are you generous with your time, your food, your skills, and your knowledge? We all are attracted to generous people who are not stingy. Their hands are open so that physical items are never grasped tightly but shared."

"Finally, they practice *curiosity* by keeping their hearts and minds open to new ideas. It is ignorant to believe that you are smarter or dumber than everyone else. Avoid clinging to ideas that make you feel superior or inferior to others . . . The tighter you cling to the certainty of your superiority or inferiority, the smaller your freedom and that of your followers."

Phra Vimutti seemed satisfied with his explanation. He returned to his mat, crossed his legs, and placed his robes around his boney knees. He lifted his right hand and his index finger pointed to the ceiling. "I am teaching you the power of the open hand. Practice compassion, generosity and curiosity. All that the leader has is held in an open hand. You are not losing anything! You are gaining everything! Now, ask me questions about how this power influences others."

Faa had written down Phra Vimutti's every word. She raised

her hand while looking down at her notes. "If I want to lead people to start a school in a village, how does the power of the open hand help me?"

Phra Vimutti rubbed his chin and said, "First, consider an ignorant person starting the school. She believes that things are permanent and grasps them tightly. She does not adapt to the needs of the families and the students, but instead forces her ideas onto them. She is not generous with praise and is harsh with punishments. She tries to control rather than guide; telling rather than asking. She holds ideas so tightly and greedily, that she is trapped in a box that can receive no new knowledge. Does she have any power to influence others if it were not for her authority?"

The class was silent. Muu furrowed his brow. "I had a teacher like that. He threatened us all the time. He demanded that we repeat his ideas, but we knew from our other teachers that he was incorrect."

Phra Vimutti nodded. "Leaders who live by the three poisons are a heavy burden on followers. Their lives are spent seeking pleasures that will never satisfy. The leader who is truly suffering causes others to suffer as well."

Phra Vimutti shifted his body side to side and said, "Let's consider a person who uses the power of the open hand – compassion, generosity, and curiosity. What kind of school will she create?"

Faa said, "She believes that things are impermanent and is curious how they will change. She learns about the students before starting to teach. She lets go of the ideas that do not work and is curious about what ideas are most effective. She is at peace because she is generous and does not envy others. She sees the flow of change and gently guides it. She frees others to change and allows them to grow."

"Well said!" Phra Vimutti exclaimed. "People are inspired by her open hand. She is free from grasping and her students are freer as well."

Mongkut started walking toward the front of the classroom and said, "Thank you for the lesson."

Phra Vimutti raised his hand and said, "May I tell one story about the power of the open hand in conclusion?"

Mongkut nodded and stepped back.

"There once was a novice who came from a wealthy family. He was afraid of giving up his life of good food and buying whatever he wanted, but his family insisted that he become a monk. He secretly kept a bag of five gold coins under his pillow and during the day he hid the coins under a board in the corner of his small room. The longer he hid the coins the more he worried about them. He was impatient with the other monks and was often disciplined for arguing. No one liked eating with him or talking to him. He thought he knew more than his teachers because he believed that his family and his gold made him superior to others."

Phra Vimutti chuckled to himself and then laughed out loud. "One day the monk went into his room to count his gold, but it was gone!"

The students stared at the monk who was joyfully laughing, and tears came to his eyes, "It was the happiest day of my life! I was free of my worry! I wasn't constantly thinking about the bag and checking it three times a day! I now opened my hands and my mind to a life free from a bag of metal."

He continued, "I started listening to my teachers and med- itating. I discovered that I became curious about new ideas and perspectives instead of defending my own. My teachers moved me to different temples, and I found peaceful satisfaction wherever I lived. My compassion and generosity inspired my students and the people in the villages, and they became more compassionate and generous toward each other. I have been living my life by the power of the open hand and now I am honored to share this power with you."

With those words he stood, and Mongkut walked to the front of the room. The students were quiet.

Phra Vimutti pulled out the coin he had shown earlier and gave it to Mongkut. "I found this on the street this morning. I'm sure you can buy more chalk since I've broken many pieces banging on your board."

Mongkut and the students bowed their heads to their hands as Phra Vimutti walked out of the classroom.

Mongkut left the room and the students erupted with exclamations about what they had just seen. Chang said he would not have given up the coin. Muu said it would be impossible for him to give up his family's house. Faa expressed her struggle of holding ideas with an open hand.

Tao listened quietly and organized his note pages into a neat pile and put them in his desk. He thought of the contradiction of acquiring power by giving away power. And yet deep in his heart he felt the freedom of not owning anything because he *didn't* own anything. He was also curious about what he didn't know. But would he be gentle and generous when he actually owned something?

Answer the reflection questions in the Reflect and Apply section about how you can apply the *Power of the Open Hand*.

18
THE TRIP TO LOPBURI

Over the next two days, Mongkut and the students discussed how the power of the open hand can open one's mind to see changes and trends that others might not see. They spent a day working with a master potter who explained how molding a pot requires strength to shape the large clumps, but gentle pressure to finish the spinning pot.

The students also went out before sunrise with some monks as they collected their daily food. Mongkut asked the students to consider how compassion for others can fill basic needs and how clinging to what one owns can limit freedom and the resources available to others. He also hinted at a trip they were going to take and that they needed to pack a bag and bring it to class on Thursday.

Thursday morning came and the students met Mongkut at a dock along the Chao Phraya river. Three long wooden boats bobbed up and down next to the dock as the dark water flowed by.

"Where are we going?" Mot asked. His tall and slender frame stood above the other students.

"We're going to a place where you can use the power of the

open hand," Mongkut said. "In particular, sharing what we have and being curious."

Mot smiled but expected more of an answer. Mongkut finally understood that Mot wanted a location. He said, "We are going to a village north of Lopburi to learn about two more sources of power. Carefully climb into the boat or you'll feel the power of the river carrying you to Bangkok!"

The students sat down and stored their bags in the middle of the boats. Tao was happy that Sunan had joined them. She wore a large straw sun hat and sat next to Faa. They talked, pointed at things, and laughed.

A short, muscular man Tao had never seen before walked up to his boat and dropped a heavy blue sack into the boat with a crash.

He looked at Mongkut and in a rough, low voice said, "Trying to leave without me, Mongkut? Without me, you won't have any fun!"

Mongkut laughed. "I think you overestimate your ability to create fun. The last time I saw you, no one was laughing."

"That's because they weren't following my instructions. Besides, no one died. That makes for a good day."

The man climbed into the boat and sat next to Tao. He took off his hat and wiped sweat from his brow with a brown rag.

"Hello young man. My name is Chatchai and I am a bridge builder. Who are you?"

"I'm Tao and I'm a student. I'm curious. What did you mean when you said that 'no one died'?"

"Ha! I meant that a bridge I designed in the north required the workers to dig deep holes for the main supports. But they dug shallow holes because they were lazy. After a heavy rain half of the supports were swept away along with two workers. They were injured but survived. They ignored my instructions and it almost cost them their lives."

Tao remembered his near-death experience in the river near his house and shuddered.

"Are you going to build a bridge on this trip?" Tao asked.

Chatchai put his big arm around Tao's shoulders, leaned in close and whispered, "*You* are going to build a bridge, but don't tell anyone."

With those words Chatchai stood up and went to talk to Mongkut who was supervising the loading of the third boat. The experienced boat drivers lashed down burlap sacks that contained iron nails and spools of rope.

The three boats finally left the shore and progressed north. The trip reminded Tao of the trip down from his village. Each boat had two drivers – one in the middle with a long pole and one in the rear who used a rudder that also pushed water. They stayed close to the shore as they poled their way up the river. The students talked, napped, and ate snacks during the four-hour journey. Mongkut read a letter that Chatchai had given him, folded it, and then stared out at the river.

In the afternoon, Tao saw a familiar site from his trip to Ayutthaya; the pier for the Lopburi palace. The drivers and a couple students took up oars to row the boats across a gentle part of the river and up to a pier. Other boats were moored to the pier and oxen pulled creaking carts of wooden crates, bricks and stones up a dusty road that disappeared among wooden shops, houses, and government offices. Tao assumed that the materials were for the palace.

Tao also saw carts full of teak wood parked at another pier.

Workers unloaded the contents onto flat wooden barges with French names on the sides.

Mongkut instructed the students and drivers to empty their boats into two nearby oxcarts. He then called the students together around the carts as the oxen stood dutifully still, swatting flies with their thick tails.

"Welcome to Lopburi. I'm sure you want to know why we are here. The village of Dusit has used the *power of invitation* and asked us to build a bridge across a river. As Minister of Lands, I volunteered you to help with this project."

Chang groaned and shook his head. He whispered to Tao, "More free labor when we could be learning something in the classroom."

Mongkut continued. "The village also used the *power of the open hand* to ask why they didn't have a bridge and they are also generous with their labor and materials. But they are lacking a power that is necessary to make their invitation a reality. Do you know what it is?"

"Ajarn, they need workers," Muu said.

"Good Muu, but they have men and women ready to help. But most of them are farmers and merchants. What else do they need?"

"They need a bridge builder," Mot yelled.

"Correct. They lack the third type of power – *the power of praxis.*"

Mongkut saw the confused looks on the faces of his students. Chatchai looked down and chuckled. He found Mongkut's bookish ways both humorous and fascinating.

"You may not know what this word means. It is a Latin word that the Romans adapted from the Greeks. It means to put your knowledge into action. The villagers need someone who can take the knowledge of building bridges and put it into practice. They need someone with the power of praxis in the area of bridge building."

Mongkut put his hand on Chatchai's shoulder and said, "When someone needs a bridge, Chatchai has the power of praxis. He has extensive experience and knowledge of how to build bridges, and he puts it into practice across Siam."

Chatchai took a step up and winked at the students.

In his rough voice, Chatchai said, "Mongkut is rather philosophical about what I do, and I'm not sure if I have the power of praxis or not. But he is correct that I have built different types of bridges for 17 years. Bridge building is an exciting job because a bridge creates connections and joins worlds. Building a bridge can also be dangerous because you are suspending people over water or ravines."

He let that thought sink in. "Also, sometimes the people on one side of the river may not want to connect to those on the other side. I leave that part up to people like Mongkut."

Mongkut said, "We'll talk more about the power of praxis later, and now we need to travel six miles to the village of Dusit."

The carts shuddered as the barefoot drivers urged the oxen on with long switches. Eventually the large cart wheels turned and rumbled through deep ruts in the road. Mongkut pointed to the right and said, "Those large walls and buildings are the king's new palace. We'll visit on our way back to Ayutthaya."

Tao remembered what Mongkut had said about the palace being a safe refuge in case foreigners decided to take over Ayutthaya, but he kept his thoughts to himself.

After a couple miles, Tao, Muu, and Faa walked together and talked about praxis and what part they would play. They agreed that they didn't know anything about building bridges, but they did know other things.

"What good is knowing French and English out in the country?" Faa asked.

Muu had found a long stick beside the road and used it as a walking stick. "Probably not worth much, but you won't know until you arrive."

"Muu's right," Tao said. "A bridge builder like Chatchai doesn't have much power in a trade negotiation with the British East India Company, but a person who speaks English does have some power in that situation."

Muu smacked a low hanging branch with his stick. "As long as the person is willing to use what they know and not hide it."

Faa said, "So the power of praxis is only useful in specific situations."

"Yeah," Tao said. "If anyone needs to plant rice or irrigate crops, I'm the one with the knowledge."

"If anyone needs to eat rice, Muu has the knowledge and the motivation to act – praxis." said Faa in a serious tone.

Muu and Tao burst out laughing.

Tao looked ahead and saw that Mongkut was watching them. He smiled back at Tao, but Tao noticed that Mongkut's eyes and shoulders seemed heavy with worry.

19
TAKING ADVANTAGE
OF REBELLION

Phetracha's house was close to the elephant drilling grounds so a fine film of dust always covered his wooden floors. His house-keepers constantly cleaned the furniture and the floors to meet Phetracha's high standards of cleanliness and order.

The knock on the door was expected and Phetracha opened the large wooden door. Two of his most trusted friends: Somboon the Minister of War and Chatchawee Commander of the Infantry. The men removed their shoes and entered. The three joyfully exchanged pleasantries and loudly made their way to the dining room in the back of the house. Servants appeared and placed several steaming plates of fish stew, spicy pork, and rice on the table. The men sat down and Phetracha excused his servants who closed the doors behind them. The mood became serious as the conversation moved from gossip about the kingdom and army to the reason Phetracha had called this group together.

"What news do you have of the foreigners and their armies?" Phetracha asked Somboon.

Somboon put down his utensils and wiped his mouth.

"The English and the French have increased their presence in the country. The king has given significant tax concessions to the French so that they have the same deal as the Dutch. To protect their goods, the king has allowed French troops to station themselves in Songkhla. The French claim that the value of their shipments requires more protection from Indian, English, and Chinese pirates. This may be true, but it still concerns me. I told King Narai, but Phaulkon ..." Somboon's voice trailed off as the two generals stared at him.

"Phaulkon!" exclaimed Chatchawee. "How did this Greek adventurer ever become head of Siam's financial affairs?"

Somboon continued in a calm tone. "The king made the decision and has carefully monitored Phaulkon's decisions. However, it is my opinion that Phaulkon wants to increase his power and convert the king to Catholicism. His greed for power and wealth is greater than his commitment to Siam."

Chatchawee wiped the sweat from his bald head with a napkin and breathed out hard. The spicy pork was obviously taking effect. He shoveled another spoonful into his mouth and said, "I'm not sure about Phaulkon's intentions, but if he wants to protect himself, he must also protect the capital. My troops can defeat the English and the French in the open field because we outnumber them three to one."

Somboon nodded and picked at the remaining rice on his plate. Phetracha listened.

Somboon said, "I agree with Chatchawee that we can defeat the English and French. I've explained this to the king. But the problem is that Phaulkon is close to the English. He is negotiating contracts with the British East India Company and I heard a rumor that he has a side business with two British friends. The king has ordered more guns and powder to prepare our troops, but he may not understand the dangers Siam faces."

Phetracha sat quietly and looked at Somboon.

"What has the King told you?" Somboon asked Phetracha. "You are like a brother to him."

Phetracha sat back in his chair, took a long drink of water, and said, "The king has assured me that Phaulkon is tightly controlled, and that he is doing more good than bad to the kingdom. He is willing to take the good with the bad. But we must be vigilant." He put his cup down with an authoritative thud.

"Today," he continued, "we must leave Phaulkon where he is. His contacts and communications with the foreign companies are invaluable to us. According to him, we have a pressing problem outside Ayutthaya."

"Phaulkon has informed Somboon and me that the traders from the city of Makassar are upset about the special concessions that the king gave the Dutch. Twenty years ago, the Dutch pushed the Portuguese out of Makassar and took over. Because we've given concessions to the Dutch, the Makassarese community in Ayutthaya plans to retaliate against King Narai."

The men knew of the Makassar princes who lived in a large compound south of Ayutthaya, next to the Malay camp.

Chatchawee shook his head, "You mean the Makassar princes may turn on the same king who supports and protects them? This is how we are repaid?"

Somboon nodded and in a hushed tone said. "Phaulkon learned from an intercepted letter that the Makassarese, their princes, and some Malays may launch an attack on Ayutthaya. The king and Phaulkon are already in the Lopburi palace making plans."

Phetracha pointed to Chatchawee and said, "We must act as

well. You are to quietly reinforce our city and the palace defenses and wait for orders. Use 3,000 soldiers and tell them that we are preparing for a possible attack."

Chatchawee realized that Phetracha had given him an order. He took a long drink of water, wiped his forehead once more, stood, bowed and walked out, closing the door behind him.

Phetracha turned to Somboon with a mock look of surprise. "You withheld information my friend. You did not tell him that the princes asked one of King Narai's younger brothers to rule in Narai's place if he converts to Islam."

"We know that the princes asked him, but he didn't accept their request," Somboon said as he reached f121or more rice. "It's not important for defending the city."

"True, but it may be important if Phaulkon tries to take over with the support of Narai's brothers."

"The king will not let that happen."

Phetracha poured himself more water.

"Yes, he will not allow it to happen. But, the king—may he live forever—is human and if he were to become ill or die in battle, we must have a plan to protect the kingdom."

Somboon stopped eating. "Do you have a plan?"

"I am thinking of one."

Somboon grunted and continued eating.

Phetracha looked out of the window. He needed to diminish the king's younger brother's power after the Makassarese uprising was defeated. He needed to clear the way for his own move to power in the future. King Narai's younger brother was a sacrifice that must be made for the sake of Siam.

20
THE POWER OF PRAXIS

The weary travelers arrived in the village as the sun dropped lower in the west. The evening sun lit up the village and made it look like it had been painted red. People walked out of their homes and businesses to greet the work party.

The students ate a meal at the Wat and then Sunan assigned each student to a family for the night. An elderly man and woman stepped forward and took Tao by the hand when their names were called. They asked Tao about his family, Ayutthaya, and if he knew the king. They talked until late, but eventually the man saw that Tao was about to fall asleep. He and his wife showed Tao to a mat that was laid behind a hand-woven blanket hung from a string that stretched across the hut.

As Tao laid on his mat, he listened to the chirp of crickets and frogs. He thought of home. He missed home and his family. As he lay in the dark, he wondered if Mongkut's training would make any difference for Siam. He was learning about different types of power and how to speak French. But couldn't he do more for his family and village if he stayed and planted rice? He had rehearsed thanking Mongkut and Sunan for their hospitality, and then admitting that he was not some special "leader." He was just a country boy and would not waste any more of their time.

But Phra Vimutti's lesson had changed his mind. "The Buddha wanted to stay under the tree and enjoy the peace he had found. But his compassion for others moved him to go and teach the truth to others."

Tao didn't understand this level of compassion, but when he thought of the invitation to learn with Mongkut, he did feel a commitment to Mongkut and his vision. He also understood that the invitation to study in the academy was a gift his family could never afford. He wanted to honor the gift.

As he fell asleep, he imagined his mom kneeling next to him, her hands in her lap, and her soft voice humming a familiar song.

Tao's hosts woke him while it was still dark. They fed him breakfast and as he ate, they told him about how some of the citizens still did not support building a bridge. His hosts didn't go into the details, but they personally supported building a bridge to make transporting rice to other villages easier. After breakfast, Tao joined the other students, Mongkut, Sunan, and Chatchai at the village's Wat.

Mongkut was dressed in blue work clothes. He asked the students to kneel on mats which the monks had positioned like in their classroom in Ayutthaya, just without desks. A small blackboard hung from the wall and Mongkut reached into his right pocket and produced a piece of chalk.

"So much for taking a break from class," Mot whispered to Chang.

"Before we start working," Mongkut said, "we need to talk about the *power of praxis* that I introduced yesterday. Have any of you thought about the power that comes from having a deep knowledge of something and then putting it into action?"

Faa looked at Muu who then raised his hand. "We talked about how knowledge is specific to some area like business, or ship building, or talking with foreigners or teaching. It seems to us that the power of praxis only works when you know something that fits a particular situation."

Mongkut nodded his head and wrote on the board,

THE POWER OF PRAXIS
1. Match your knowledge and expertise with the need

"What this means is that even though you may want to lead people, you will not have the knowledge to change everything you want. At least, not enough knowledge to inspire people to follow. For example, Chatchai has the knowledge to build bridges and organize workers. But he does not have the knowledge to teach Sanskrit or negotiate contracts with the Chinese."

The students heard Chatchai say "Ha!" in the back of the room. "And I don't wish to have either of those!" he exclaimed.

Mongkut continued. "Don't be fooled into thinking that you can meet every need you see. People who follow you will quickly discover where you lack expertise. You may have the motivation, but not the knowledge. When using the power of praxis, be honest about your limitations or your followers will distrust you."

Chatchai again sounded off from behind the students. "Talking about bridge building is easy. Building a safe, solid bridge that will stand for 100 years requires experience and learning from your mistakes."

Mongkut wrote another point on the board.

2. Practice in real situations.

"The second aspect of the power of praxis is that it creates a trap for some leaders and freedom for others. The trap is that some leaders feel that they never know enough about something to act on it. They learn more and more, but don't share what they know. Or they never act on what they know to solve real problems. Knowledge is *not* power unless it is put into practice, so practice what you know in real situations."

"How does praxis create freedom?" Tao asked.

"If you focus time and effort on learning something well and you start to apply it, like bridge building or running a store or leading an army, then you create a space for others to meet their needs. For example, the villagers must now walk two miles to cross the river. They have needs that cannot be met. But Chatchai's knowledge and practice now opens a space for them to do things that were impossible yesterday. The power of praxis – gaining knowledge and putting it into action – creates a space for more freedom of movement."

"What about the army," Chang asked. "How does a general use the power of praxis? Doesn't he just tell soldiers what to do?"

Mongkut nodded his head and pointed at Chang with his chalk. "Excellent question! Students, consider a general who has the knowledge required to fight a battle against an invading army, and has practiced fighting this same foe. How does this general create freedom?"

The students sat silently as they thought. Chang finally raised his hand.

"The general's knowledge and experience inspire confidence

in the soldiers so that they'll follow him. They will be less fearful and freer to act quickly and bravely."

"Good!" Mongkut said. "Anything else?"

Mot jumped in, "The general is also more likely to win, which frees the people from being under the rule of a foreign king."

Mongkut nodded and gestured broadly with his arms. "You see how the power of praxis creates freedom. Note as well that a general who only *studied* strategy and battles but never fought in one may not be able to create the freedom you describe."

Mongkut walked to the board and wrote the final point.

3. Multiply the power of praxis through others.

"Faa, what do you think this point means?" Mongkut asked.

Faa thought about the question for a moment.

Mongkut prodded her by saying, "Think about what we are doing here?"

"Do you mean that putting knowledge into action creates even more power?"

"Yes. How does the power of praxis create more power?"

Faa looked up at the board and said, "Knowledge is something that can be learned by others, so knowledge can multiply. People can also learn by practice, so experience can multiply as well. The power of praxis can be multiplied as more people learn and practice?"

"I couldn't have said it better myself," Mongkut said. "You can and should pass on the power of praxis. Can you imagine a village full of people who know what to do and practice their knowledge each day? An army? A government office? That group can accomplish great things and create more freedom!"

"Why don't we see more of this power?" Muu asked.

"Another trap of the power of praxis is when someone identifies so closely with their knowledge and experience that they refuse to share it. They deny others freedom for the sake of keeping the power for themselves. They need to practice the power of the open hand."

"Over the next three days we are going to apply the power of praxis. First, Chatchai has the knowledge that meets the need of this village. Second, he has learned and practiced the art of engineering and bridge building which will create more freedom for this part of the country. Finally, Chatchai is sharing his knowledge with those of us who will help him. In fact, he is training two apprentices who have worked with him on two other bridges."

A man and a woman had been quietly standing next to Chatchai behind the students. When Mongkut mentioned them, the students turned, and the couple nodded.

"One final point," Mongkut said. "While you are working on the bridge, I want you to take time and consider what area of knowledge you will commit to learn in the coming years? What will be the area in which you can earn the power of praxis?"

Mongkut dismissed the students and they walked outside of the Wat. The sun was starting to get hot, and several villagers were waiting on Mongkut to finish. It was time for Chatchai to take charge.

Chatchai stood on the steps of the Wat and the students and villagers gathered close to hear him. He introduced his two apprentices as a married couple who had worked with him for two years on bridges from Bangkok to Lopburi. He thanked the villagers for acquiring the bridge materials and digging the footers in the riverbank as he had directed last month. He outlined a work schedule for the next three days and divided the villagers into three work groups. Chatchai and his two apprentices would lead each group. The students found themselves in Chatchai's group with Mongkut and Sunan.

Chatchai then walked up to each work group and took on a serious tone. He asked each group a question. "Are you willing to do exactly what your leader says on the bridge site? If not, then please stay here. If you are willing, then I invite you to join us." The members of the groups each said "yes" and realized that they were making a personal commitment to follow their leader.

After Tao said "Yes," he realized that something had happened to him. He was now following someone based primarily on the power of praxis and the power of invitation.

Answer the reflection questions in the Reflect and Apply section about how you can apply the *Power of Praxis*.

21
FOLLOWING THE EXPERT

The clear water of the Bang Kham river flowed slowly past the clearing that had become a building work site. Tao estimated that the bridge would stretch about 100-feet across the river. At this point the river did not curve. Pairs of large wooden pylons made from tree trunks stood at attention at the river's edge and continued in 10-foot intervals to the other bank. Water gently swirled around the pylons creating small, lazy whirlpools that wound and unwound in the current.

One of the work teams climbed into three flat-bottomed boats and started paddling to the other side of the river.

"The river is low," Muu said.

"We rerouted part of the river upstream to make our work easier," Chatchai said. "We're also building in the dry season, but we always watch for flash floods."

One of the apprentices took the second work team to a huge pile of wooden planks and beams, while Chatchai took the students and his team to another pile of wood. He and Mongkut dropped two heavy bags of tools next to the pile.

"All of you listen," Chatchai said in a serious tone. "You can be injured and even killed while building this bridge." He had everyone's attention.

"You will do what I say while you are on my team because I am responsible for your health and the bridge. If you are carrying wood, watch out for who is around you. If you are carrying tools, put them into a bag and tie them to your belt. We don't want any of them lost in the water. If you are not working, then you need to sit in the shade over there." He pointed to a place on the bank under two large trees. "Standing around in the work area slows the work and creates a distraction."

Chatchai then explained that this team was going to frame the bridge over the next three days. He winked at Mongkut who acknowledged the hidden message. Tao thought that maybe the next lesson on power would involve framing, foundations, building, teamwork, or bridges.

Chatchai assigned two or three helpers to each of the experienced workers. The helpers would bring them planks, rope, long iron nails, and water when they were thirsty. The helpers would also hold planks in place. Tao and Chang were helpers for a jovial man who called himself Hua Na – the boss.

During the morning and into the afternoon the teams carried heavy pre-cut beams into the water. The beams connected two of the pylons along the width of the bridge. The experienced workers sat on narrow boards nailed between the pylons and used ropes to lift the cross beams. There they secured the beams between the pylons using rope and then large iron nails. Hua Na worked quickly and precisely. When the cross beams were secured, more thick pieces of wood were fastened along the left and right sides of the pylons so that soon the pylons were connected width-wise and also along the length of the bridge.

Tao and Chang made a good team and kept Hua Na well supplied. Tao worked hard, and took time to kneel in the cool water to escape the rising heat.

During lunch he and Chang sat on the riverbank eating. Tao asked Chang about his training as a soldier. "Have you ever been in a battle?" Tao asked.

"Not yet, but my father has had me train with our best archers and gunners for the last three years. If an enemy comes, I'm ready to fight."

"I hope that won't happen any time soon." Tao said. "Isn't that one reason why we are in this academy? To negotiate with foreigners so that we avoid war?"

Chang shrugged his shoulders. "I don't know if you can negotiate without the threat of force to back it up. I see what Mongkut is trying to do, but his kind of power doesn't command much respect."

Tao said, "Don't you think the power of purpose can be used regardless of one's strength? He talked about how a general can use the power of praxis."

"I guess so," Chang said, "but my father doesn't know any power except for the power of authority. At least that's what I've learned."

The two became quiet at the mention of Chang's father, and Chang picked up a rock and threw it into the river. Tao broke the silence by pulling a river rock out of his pocket and handing it to Chang.

"Take a look at this rock." The smooth brown rock fit perfectly in Chang's palm, but didn't seem special. He flipped it over and noticed that Tao had scratched the word "Power" into the rock with a nail.

"It's okay," said Chang and started to hand it back.

"Look at the color under my scratches," Tao insisted.

Chang re-inspected the rock and then saw the deep green color emerge from the scratches. He began to laugh and said, "If that is real emerald, you'll be rich."

"It would be the first time. My dad taught me to look for emeralds near rivers, but we never found any. Maybe this is real."

"If it is, keep it hidden like Phra Vimutti's gold."

Hua Na was up and walking out into the river. He whistled to the boys and they slowly stood up.

Chang handed the rock back to Tao and said, "Thanks for sharing it with me."

By the evening, the workers had transformed the free-standing pylons into a frame that would hold the bridge floor. When they entered the village, Chang pointed to two soldiers who were talking to an old man and a monk. The old man motioned Mongkut and Chatchai over. Tao's team stood away from the discussion, but he could tell that something had happened. Mongkut listened and nodded his head. After about five minutes Mongkut led the two soldiers to the team.

"Before I left Ayutthaya, I heard that a group of Makassarese following their princes may attack Ayutthaya. The soldiers told me that their attack did not succeed because most of their Malay supporters deserted at the first sign of conflict."

He looked at Chang. "Your father has requested that you and Mot return to Ayutthaya to support the palace guard." At first Chang appeared surprised, and then said "When do we leave? I'm ready to leave now!" Mot didn't say anything, but instead looked at the ground.

One of the soldiers said, "We leave at dawn. Eat and get a good night's sleep."

The group made their way to the Wat where a large meal was set out for the workers. The talk was about the possible attack on Ayutthaya, the possibility of them coming to the Lopburi palace, and who these people were anyway. Several local young men volunteered to go with the two soldiers, but they said that the opposing force was small, and their help was not needed.

Tao sat next to Faa who had not touched her food. He said, "I'm sure your family is safe."

Faa gave a weak smile. "My mother and father live in the palace grounds. I wish I were with them."

"Why don't you write a letter and send it with the soldiers. Let them know you are thinking of them."

Faa's face brightened a little. "I'll do that."

She became quiet again, then asked, "How do you manage living far from your family? It must be difficult."

Now Tao looked down at his food and thought for a moment. "I miss my mom and dad and little sister. But they want me to use this opportunity to go to school. This is a path they could never give me, so I feel obligated to follow it."

He looked up at Faa and admitted that he thought about leaving Mongkut's academy every day and returning to the comfort of his village.

"Why do you stay?" she asked.

"Because I believe Mongkut sees something that most people don't see."

"What does he see?"

"He sees a Siam that needs leaders like us."

He continued, "I miss home, but Mongkut has given me a

chance to learn how to lead. I want to honor the gift he's given me and my family."

Faa was comforted by his words. She finished her dinner and then asked Sunan for paper to write a letter.

22
CHOOSING AN EXPERTISE

Early the next morning Mot and Chang started walking down the road to Lopburi with the two soldiers. Tao ran after them and touched Chang on the shoulder. Chang turned and Tao handed him his rock.

"This is for good luck. It will give you something to polish when you're standing guard."

Chang looked at the rock and then at Tao. As he turned the rock over in his hands, he didn't know what to say. Eventually he said, "Thanks. I'll give it back when you return."

Tao said, "You and Mot be careful."

The soldiers and Mot had continued walking. Chang put the rock in his shoulder bag and ran after them.

Tao went to breakfast in the Wat and noticed a group of people talking to Mongkut. They were intent on checking items off of a piece of paper that Mongkut held. A woman who was the age of Tao's mother appeared to be the group's leader. She stood erect with her arms crossed while Mongkut checked items off of the paper. She would nod approval or shake her head with a smile.

When the group was satisfied with the document, Mongkut

turned and said something to the woman. She took the paper, rolled it up into a scroll, and then bowed slightly to Mongkut. The group followed her on the path to the bridge.

Tao had focused so intently on the meeting that he had not eaten his fish soup. Mongkut signaled for the remaining three students to follow him into the room with the chalkboard. With a mouth full of soup and a handful of small bananas, Tao followed after Faa and Muu, eating as fast as he could.

Mongkut pointed to five mats on the floor. The chalkboard still had the three points describing the power of praxis.

Muu turned to Tao and said, "I sort of miss Chang and Mot. I hope they're safe."

Mongkut erased the board and then turned to the students with his hands on his hips.

"I want to start by saying that the village leaders are impressed with your work ethic and respect towards the people of this town."

"Second," Mongkut said, "I want to return to the question I asked you. The power of praxis requires you to know some topic very well. Have you decided what you would like to become an expert on?"

Muu said, "It's hard for me to say because I like many things like building, working in my family business, and meeting new people. But I think I want to become an expert on trading. I like bringing people together to exchange things and negotiating a good deal. It isn't that I don't like cutting trees and planting new ones, but I like delivering them to the dock and watching my father negotiate the best deal with the Dutch and English."

"Good. I'll make arrangements for you to spend more time with our Ministry of Finance. Faa, what have you decided."

Faa was still distracted by the possible attack on Ayutthaya, but she sat up straight and said, "Ajarn, I'm not sure what to focus on because . . ." She paused and said, "Women are not allowed to hold important offices."

Mongkut rubbed his chin and said, "What you said is true in Ayutthaya, but I want you to consider what you want to study regardless of position. Remember, we are talking about how to gain power without an institution granting you its authority."

Mongkut looked at the three students and said, "If you are waiting for a high position to lead others, you are limiting your opportunities. Only about eight positions report to the king which means out of all of Siam, only eight people can have these positions at a time. I happen to have one of these positions, but after I am gone only one person will take my place."

He pointed outside at the village. "Do you think these people know who runs Siam? They don't, but they do know that Chatchai can help them build a bridge if they follow him."

Mongkut continued and his voice expressed a passion and intensity Tao had not heard before. "You must look beyond positions because they change with each new leader. Instead, consider who needs you to use your power to fulfill a purpose. And if you happen to be in a position with the power of authority, use that power to do the same thing – increase people's freedom."

"I want to focus on medicine or helping people," Faa said quickly. "I seem to be drawn to those who are weak or hurt. I helped my host family build a stone wall behind their cooking fire so that they won't continually breathe smoke. Their two children have a hard time breathing, and I believe this will help them."

Mongkut nodded. "Excellent choice Faa. I will connect you with Father Tachard and you can start learning about treating patients in the Jesuit hospital."

While Mongkut had been talking, Tao was juggling different topics in his mind while finishing his last banana. He wasn't sure what to select. He was the son of rice farmers, and he knew Sanskrit and writing. He loved learning but was not fantastic at French.

"Tao?" Mongkut prodded. Faa and Muu turned to look at him.

"I don't know," he confessed. "I've only had one option most of my life and that is farming. I'm not used to having options."

Muu said, "Can I make a suggestion?"

Tao nodded.

"You have courage to try new things. You are always asking good questions about people and how things work. If I had all those questions in my head, it would burst."

Tao laughed.

Muu looked at Mongkut. "Ajarn, what should a curious person focus on?"

Mongkut addressed Tao, "Which of these jobs would you like to do if they were offered to you: farmer, builder, teacher, monk, soldier, trader, government administrator."

Tao thought about each of the positions. "Could I be a teacher who starts schools? I love learning and sharing what I've learned with others. But if I'm only in one classroom, I'm limiting the students I can reach. I sort of like your job!"

"Well, you can't have my job... yet," Mongkut chuckled.

Then he said strongly, "Never underestimate the impact of one teacher in one classroom, one negotiator in one contract, or one doctor to one patient. Think of how a small spark can light a candle that others can use to light their homes. If educating others is what you want to do, you can work with Phra Vimutti and one of the Jesuits. They are excellent educators and know how to establish schools."

Mongkut stood back and admired his students. "You have just taken an important step into leading others by focusing your thoughts and actions. Avoid distractions if you truly want to attain the power of praxis."

Mongkut erased the board and said, "Now let's learn about the fourth source of power."

Answer the reflection questions in the Reflect and Apply section about *Identifying and Growing Your Expertise*.

23
THE POWER OF FRAMING

"Look at your hands and reflect on what you see," Mongkut said.

Tao looked at the calluses on his palms and a small gouge in his right thumb where a splinter cut into his skin. Faa was still wearing a cloth on her left hand. She untied it and revealed a bruised palm. Muu rubbed his hands together and said, "I'm used to working with wood, but my hands are sore from holding the bucket of nails."

"Your hands are reminders of how you framed the bridge. When we arrived, we saw pylons sticking out of the river, but then we built a frame that supports all who will cross the bridge. It takes time and effort to frame a bridge, especially when the water is pushing against your legs and the beams are heavy."

The students nodded.

"Like the frame on a bridge that supports people on their journey, we can describe or 'frame' the past, the present, and the future in a way that moves or stops people. We do this through stories, arguments, and our imaginations. I want to explain how you can use the *power of framing* to influence and inspire others."

Mongkut pulled a chair toward the students and sat down. He

groaned and rubbed his right leg as he sat down and said, "I have my own reminders of framing the bridge."

"Let me tell you how we got here – to this moment when the bridge is almost finished. Two years ago, I visited this village with four people in my ministry and a few people from the Ministry of War. We were traveling across Siam and asking people about farming, trade, and safety. The king asked us to learn of their concerns. Some villagers complained that they could not easily trade with the villages across the Bang Kham river. Each day they either loaded their goods into boats and crossed the river or journeyed two miles south to a safe river crossing. The trips can be slow and dangerous in the rainy season. Three villagers drowned in the river the year before we came."

Tao recalled his own close call with drowning.

Mongkut continued, "Here in town, some argued that a bridge was an expensive luxury. People crossing the river needed to be more careful. Three former soldiers voiced their concerns that a bridge opens the door to enemies and criminals. Crime would increase and invaders would have an easy path to attack the village."

"All of us talked about the benefits and costs of building a bridge and it seemed that the loudest voices against the bridge were winning. Their main concern was the cost of the bridge and the fear of crime and attack. But then Supawadee stood up."

Mongkut gestured to someone behind the students. The woman Mongkut talked with during breakfast walked to the front of the room. She stood up straight and had a confident expression on her tan face. Some of her black hair curved over her left eye, but she didn't push it back.

"Supawadee, these are my students. Please tell your story."

Supawadee had a strong, low voice and she crossed her arms tightly as she spoke.

"My husband and I have four children and we operate a silk business. We raise silkworms and also do some weaving."

Mongkut interrupted and said, "Supawadee's silk is highly valued in Ayutthaya. Also, her family is respected in the village because of their generosity to those in need."

Supawadee nodded to Mongkut and continued.

"Some of my friends were afraid of crime, being invaded, and the cost of building the bridge. Fear took over our discussion. I, however, believed the bridge was important for the future of our village."

"I kindly and strongly challenged the picture of fear and disaster that people had in their minds. I gently addressed each concern. First, I said, the village could put a gate on the bridge at night to protect the village from criminals and enemies. I also explained that most crime in the last two years came from a gang of thieves from Lopburi. I asked my friends, 'Should we dig up the road leading to Lopburi to ensure our safety?'

Supawadee shook her head. "Of course, no one agreed to that idea."

"Next, I acknowledged their fear that an attack is always possible, but this happens with or without a bridge. I explained that the village has always learned of movements by the Khmer days before they made their way this far west. Then one of the soldiers said that defending a narrow bridge is easier than defending an entire riverfront. It is a single path that gives us a high point to see oncoming troops."

Mongkut asked, "How did you address the fear of the cost?"

"My family has been in business for three generations, and I know that the villagers could pay for half of the bridge if we all set aside some of our earnings for a year. The other half would come from bridge tolls on goods – but not on travelers. The merchants can afford the toll while individuals may not be able to pay it. The merchants will pass the additional cost on to the traders."

Faa asked, "Did this convince the people who didn't want the bridge?"

Supawadee shook her head. "Not immediately, but it did eventually." She then looked over at Mongkut and signaled that he should take over.

Mongkut went to the board and wrote:

THE POWER OF FRAMING

1. *Address fears about the change*
2. *Describe how the change will create more opportunities*
3. *Reinforce the frame by asking others to describe their vision*

"Let's go step-by-step through how Supawadee used the power of framing. First, she addressed their fears by explaining that the bridge would not increase crime, the threat of attack, or create a financial burden. Second, she described how the bridge would create more opportunities. No one would drown crossing the river, the villagers could avoid river taxis that demanded higher prices, and they could control who crossed the bridge. Also, the village's prosperity would grow because they could trade more easily with villages on the other side. Those villages would benefit as well."

"While Supawadee spoke, those of us from Ayutthaya watched as the villagers moved from fearing the bridge to seeing it as an opportunity for growth and more freedom."

"What do you mean by more freedom?" Muu asked.

"Freedom in this case is moving toward new journeys and opening opportunities for a better future. The power of framing must describe a realistic future with more freedom, health, safety, and growth."

Tao said, "This sounds like the power of the open hand."

Mongkut thought for a moment and said, "The *power of the open hand* releases you from thinking that reality cannot be changed. The *power of framing* describes a new reality."

"Finally," Mongkut concluded, "she connected these opportunities with the lives of the villagers. She asked them to consider their new future."

Supawadee said, "I asked the villagers to think of the benefits for themselves and their families. One of the people who was against the bridge at first said that he counted 33 children in the village. He said that the bridge would be a legacy for our children. They would no longer be tied to one place, but could travel and learn of Siam. They could develop friends from other villages. Teachers could come from the east without traveling through Lopburi. They would have a better future."

Mongkut pointed to the third point on the board. "See how she allowed others to reinforce the frame with their own ideas, and she continues to help others reinforce the vision today. We all know that a bridge needs reinforcing because the flowing water presses on it daily. Without starting the project and reinforcing it daily, the idea will wash away and the fears will return."

Supawadee joined in again.

"What Mongkut calls the frame is actually a story of the future. We wrote it on some paper and started building with words, drawings, and invitations. The bridge team negotiated with Mongkut to buy wood from the king's holdings at a discount. He also sent Chatchai to talk to us and the village. After about a year, we had set half of the pylons and paid for the ropes and nails. All of these actions reinforced the frame of the future until it became a real bridge and not just a description. Like magic, we've turned words into something that stands over water."

Faa raised her hand. "Ms. Supawadee, what if no one joined you? What if the fears were too strong?"

"If you believe in a change that must happen – a change that will serve others – sometimes you have to start it by yourself. At the same time, test your own facts and make sure your vision is possible. Ask people for their perspectives. Consider if the timing is right or if some other need or problem is more important. We knew, for example, that if we lived on a part of the river that was too broad, the bridge would not work where we put it."

Supawadee paused for a moment and said, "And, if the timing is right, then commit yourself to starting. My family donated 20 percent of the bridge funds in the first three months, and that action made the bridge 20 percent more real to everyone else."

"Remember that the power of framing leads people *without* authority," Mongkut interjected. "Supawadee and her team listened to fears and aspirations instead of ordering people to follow."

Mongkut thanked Supawadee and the students wai'd as she walked out.

Mongkut erased the board and said, "That's enough for today. We need to work during the morning and leave for Lopburi after lunch. I believe the king will meet us after dinner."

Tao looked at Muu in amazement, and they both looked at Faa who didn't appear surprised.

Tao asked Faa, "What should we do? I've never been in a palace before."

"Follow Mongkut's instructions and do what he and Sunan do. The people in the palace will be watching us closely."

"Why?" Muu asked.

"We *are* Mongkut's frame of a new future. Some people are invested in a frame of grabbing power from the king. Others frame the future of one where Siam becomes a colony of foreign governments. We must show them that we represent a new story for Siam."

Answer the reflection questions in the Reflect and Apply section about how you can apply the *Power of Framing.*

24
VISITING LOPBURI PALACE

The road back to Lopburi was shaded and the tall trees protected the travelers from the sun's heat. Eventually, the clouds darkened, and rain began to fall. Tao kept his head down and watched drips from his round straw hat jiggle then fall.

As he walked he thought of his last view of the bridge stretching across the river with workers crawling on the structure. The sound of hammers rang across the water until it was time to say good-bye. Many of the villagers gathered together on the rocky riverbank and gave flower necklaces to Mongkut, Sunan, and the students. Supawadee walked out from the group and wai'd Mongkut and Sunan. She then took three green silk shirts from her husband and gave one to each of the students. "Thank you for helping us," she said as each student bowed their heads and accepted her gift.

Chatchai pushed forward and joked with the students and said that he would invite them to the next bridge building if they wanted to have some more fun. Hua Na patted Tao on the back with his rough hands and said, "Keep learning. We need people like you watching out for us in Ayutthaya. Don't forget us." Tao said that he wouldn't forget them.

As they entered Lopburi the rain stopped, and the sun lit the grounds of an ancient temple. Three large pagodas cast shadows across the wet grass and monkeys scampered across the road and into the trees on the other side. Monks walked among the towers on the wet, glistening grass and entered the temple buildings.

After removing their bags from an oxcart, Mongkut led the group to the grey stone walls of Lopburi palace. Tao noticed soldiers posted around the walls. Some held long lances and others carried swords or muskets. Tao didn't see Chang or Mot.

The students followed Mongkut and Sunan through the palace gate. A man in a golden robe greeted Mongkut. "What is the situation in Ayutthaya?" Mongkut asked.

The man said, "We received news this morning that the Makassarese rebellion dissolved without an attack on the palace. Phaulkon was negotiating with the prince who initiated the rebellion. He'll fill us in this evening. And Faa," the man said, "your parents are safe and your mother is here waiting for you."

Faa said thank you. The man directed the rain-soaked group across a large courtyard and into a brick building.

Once inside, the palace staff ushered them into rooms to dry off and change their clothes. Tao and Muu shared a room. Tao was given pants, a shirt, and a red silk robe that was too long for him, but it felt good to be free of his heavy wet clothes. Muu's blue robe fit perfectly, and he said, "I hope I get to keep this."

A servant knocked loudly on the door and asked them to follow him. Tao and Muu walked to a large dining hall where many people were eating and talking. They saw Faa wearing the green silk top and standing with a woman. She gestured that they come over.

"This is my mother, Arinya." Arinya looked at the young men standing before her and nodded.

"Faa said that you two are excellent students and good friends. She said that you are like brothers."

Tao said, "Faa is the smartest in our class. I've learned a lot from her."

Faa looked embarrassed while her mother thanked Tao. Arinya pointed the students to the main food table. Tao's eyes opened wide at the steaming bowls of chicken, vegetables, fish stew, pork, rice, and a variety of fruits and desserts. Arinya told them to eat now and that the meeting with the king would be later in the evening.

Sunan joined the students for dinner. She said that Mongkut was in meetings with the other ministers about a Siamese counterattack on the Makassarese camp last night. Phaulkon was returning from the battle which he led with French and English military commanders.

After two hours of eating and talking, Tao and Muu sat resting against a wall when a royal messenger asked Sunan and the students to follow him to the Royal Audience Hall. They walked outside toward a tall stone building along a path lit by flaming torches. When Tao entered he noticed about ten soldiers in a side room. Some of them were dirty and appeared to have blood on their breastplates and legs. A few soldiers had bandaged arms and heads. They were laughing and in high spirits.

As they entered the main hall, Tao looked up at its tall ceiling inlaid with gold and examined the tapestries that hung on the walls. About 15 people stood talking to each other and the sound of their voices echoed off the stone walls. Square Persian carpets were placed in rows on the stone floor with a narrow aisle passing down the middle.

Faa pointed to a raised balcony at the far end of the hall with a staircase on each side. The balcony was about 10 feet high and a wooden throne inlaid with gold stood in the middle. A long tapestry depicting two soldiers riding elephants hung from the front of the balcony. "That is where the king will sit when he comes. Remember that your head must *always* be lower than his. My mother said the king built this balcony to make it easier for visitors to talk with him."

As she finished talking Mongkut appeared in royal robes and asked Sunan to have the students move to the back of the hall. She directed them to the next to last row of carpets and they knelt down. Other people in the room wandered to their places and Mongkut and the other ministers gathered in the front. A tall European entered the room and all watched him as he confidently walked to the front and knelt next to Mongkut. Tao recognized him as Phaulkon from the Jesuit's house.

"Did you miss us?" a voice said. Chang and Mot knelt down on mats behind Muu and Faa. They were wearing uniforms, but they were not covered in mud like the other soldiers.

"We missed you when we were lifting heavy wooden beams." Muu said with a smile. "What have you been doing? Were you in any battles?"

Chang shook his head. "No. We've been stationed here with about 1,000 other soldiers. My father is charged with securing Lopburi." Chang seemed frustrated that they had missed the battle, but Mot appeared happy to be away from danger.

"Did anything happen in Ayutthaya?" Muu asked.

"Yes!" Chang muttered. "While we were here protecting the palace from no one, Phaulkon led an attack on the Makassarese camp. He ruined their surprise attack and it turned into an all-out war. We lost a couple French and English commanders and about 20 soldiers. My father said it was incompetent of Phaulkon . . ." Chang caught himself as he looked back over his shoulder.

Tao followed Chang's gaze. He saw a distinguished man in a general's uniform glaring at Chang. He stood as straight as a beam and his eyes were dark. He slowly nodded his head at Tao and then stared straight ahead.

Tao looked back at Chang who quietly turned toward the front of the room.

"Who is that?" Tao whispered to Muu.

"That is Chang's father Phetracha. He must have missed the battle."

Chang quietly said, "The king ignored my father's advice and the foreigners created a disaster. The sooner they leave, the better."

A royal herald appeared at the front of the room and banged a large staff on the floor three times. Immediately those milling around found their carpets and knelt down with their faces to the floor. Tao glanced up and saw Phetracha walking to the front and kneeling next to Phaulkon. All of the ministers placed cone-shaped hats on their heads.

Seeing that everyone was in place, the herald pounded his staff on the floor three more times and said in a loud voice, "His majesty, the great King Narai."

Tao wanted to look up to the balcony, but instead kept his head down and his eyes on Faa. He heard a person being seated and some whispers by the balcony. A deep strong voice from the balcony said, "Welcome to the Lopburi palace."

Faa looked up slightly but remained in a kneeling position. Muu and Tao also looked up at the king. The king leaned back on his throne with his hands on the arm rests. He spoke to a nearby servant. Tao was in awe of what he saw. The king wore a golden long coat that was open in the front, golden pants that stopped above his ankles, and golden shoes on his feet. He wore a cone-shaped hat that had three rounded sections that progressively got smaller at the top of the hat like a temple pagoda. A jewel encrusted handle of a knife protruded from his belt, the scabbard covered in small red and green stones. The king's face was round with high cheekbones that seemed to lift him even higher on the balcony. His eyes were dark brown and as he looked upon the kneeling crowd he spoke with an authoritative voice.

"We will now discuss the Makassarese rebellion. Phaulkon led the attempted capture of the Makassarese prince."

Phaulkon spoke loudly so that the entire hall could hear him. Even though he spoke with a slight accent, Phaulkon spoke Siamese like a native.

"Great King Narai," he said. "After the prince ignored and refused your generous offers of a pardon, we carried out your orders to insist that the prince apologize for the rebellion. Myself, Captain Henry Udall, negotiator Ok-phra Chula and 5,000 soldiers surrounded the island south of Ayutthaya. Before dawn we moved our ships and barges into position. When the first group of soldiers landed, they were attacked by the Makassarese. We fought through the morning at different points of the island and pushed them north. Captain Udall was stabbed and shot in his attempt to push back the Makassarese. I continued to fight with our soldiers but was eventually pushed back to the barge."

At this point the king leaned toward Phaulkon's direction and said, "Why were you fighting? We have trained soldiers for war, but only one Minister of Finance." Phaulkon dropped his head without appearing to take the discipline seriously.

"Continue," the king said.

"Eventually we secured the island at the cost of 22 Siamese soldiers who bravely fought the rampaging Makassarese. As for their prince, a French soldier shot him before he was able to stab an English soldier. He died."

Phaulkon paused to let the death of the prince affect the audience.

He then said, "Only four Makassarese soldiers remained, and they bravely faced their execution by being attacked by a tiger. We did take two of the prince's sons into custody and Father Tachard has agreed to take them as students. My apologies, great king for the trouble this attack has caused."

The king shifted on his throne and appeared to be pleased. "Well done Phaulkon, and I thank the commanders of the English, French, and Siamese troops. We honor those who lost their lives and Captain Udall who died on behalf of Siam."

The room sat in silence for a moment.

The king then sat up straight and asked, "Is there any other business for tonight?"

Tao glanced around the room and no one moved, but then from the front, he heard someone clear his throat and speak. It was Phetracha.

"Great King, if it pleases you, I would like to take a battalion of troops to secure the Makassarese camp. I'm sure you have heard of the ship that docked in Bangkok which contained more Makassarese?"

The king said, "I understand that commander Chevalier de Forbin has secured the ship at the cost of several French soldiers and Phaulkon has ordered that the commander pull the chain across the Bangkok harbor to stop any reinforcements from reaching Ayutthaya. You can stand the troops down in Lopburi and take 500 troops from the Ayutthaya palace to the Makassarese camp."

"And what of your younger brother and his relationship with the Makassarese prince?" Phetracha asked.

The boldness of his question shocked the room. Tao saw Mongkut quickly glance at Phetracha who maintained his straight posture and looked directly at the king.

The king tightened his mouth and leaned forward.

"Thank you for your concern, but my brother played no part in this rebellion. If you do your job protecting our nation, then I will do my job managing the royal family."

"Yes, your majesty," Phetracha said. He bowed his head but not his body to the floor. He had planted the seed of doubt about one of his rivals, and now he would let the gossip and political machinations of the palace do the rest.

Mongkut then spoke. "Great King, I have good news though it is not as exciting as battles fought and won. The Siam Leadership Academy students have helped build a bridge across the Bang Kham river in the north. Soon the bridge will be open to travelers and commerce. Thank you for supporting this bridge and our academy."

The king looked down at Mongkut and relaxed. "Where are these students?" the king asked.

"They are in the back. Students, please acknowledge your presence and say your name," Mongkut said.

One by one the students looked up to the balcony, stated their name as loudly as they could, and returned to their bowed position. The king nodded at each student.

"Well done," he said. "You are welcome in Lopburi." The king paused for a moment and then addressed the entire hall.

"What Mongkut is doing is important for the future of Siam. While we must have a strong military, we must also have strong partnerships with France and England. How many French and English soldiers died on our soil during the last 24 hours?"

"The kingdom is built on strong foundations, and we will always have a strong military to protect us." He looked directly at Phetracha, but then looked again out at the audience.

"But the foundations of our kingdom's future are not built on the gun or the sword or the battle elephant. Instead, they are built on laws, Buddhist principles, and friendship. I expect that Mongkut's students will strengthen our country while maintaining our sovereignty and our heritage."

With those words the people in the hall shouted, "Yes! Yes! Yes!"

The king nodded to the herald who thumped the floor three times. Once again everyone bowed their faces to the floor and Tao heard the king leave. After about 30 seconds, the room burst into talking. People walked up to the students and congratulated them on their work.

Tao saw Phetracha's straight and stoic form walk toward the students, and he eventually strode into the middle of the group.

"The king is right!" he said, addressing the group in a loud voice as if talking to a band of soldiers.

"We need strong relationships and trade. He is also right to say that we need a strong military. What I would add is that without a military to keep our foreign friends in check, we are in danger of inviting a tiger into our house. I'm sure your 'relationships' will keep the tiger happy. But when he becomes hungry for more..." he paused for effect and rested his hand on the hilt of his sword, "then I will be there to protect Siam."

"Khun Phetracha, I agree with your assessment." Tao saw that Sunan was standing next to him and addressing the General. "But isn't the best path to keep the tiger out of the house in the first place?"

Phetracha half smiled and said, "Yes, Kru Sunan it is. We'll see how long talking at a tiger can keep it out." He quickly nodded to the students and walked toward the door. He turned his head and barked, "Chang, you are with me."

Chang turned and followed his father.

25
POLISHING THE EMERALD

Tao and Sunan spent three days in Lopburi touring the city and the palace before returning to Ayutthaya. They ate lunch with Chang before they left. The day was clear and the restaurant by the river served especially spicy fish. Sunan ate it without a word, while the young men drank more and more water to try to put out the fire on their tongues.

After lunch Chang handed Tao his emerald.

"Here's your stone. I polished it while I was on guard duty."

While the stone was still brown on the outside with the word "Power" scratched into its surface, Tao noticed that about a quarter of the stone now revealed a dark green color.

"Thanks! How did you polish it?"

Chang handed Tao another, rougher and larger stone.

"You rub one stone against the other. It also helps to apply some water where you are rubbing."

"May I see it?" Sunan asked.

Tao handed her the emerald. She studied it carefully and gave it back to Tao.

"Polishing this emerald reminds me of what Mongkut is

doing in your classes. He is rubbing and grinding away at your rough edges, the ideas and habits that don't quite fit what the world is becoming. He knows there is something precious and valuable underneath. You may not like it, but you both have to be polished."

Chang politely smiled as he stood from the table.

"He can polish all he wants," Chang said, "But I know that power comes from the throne and the sword."

"True, but happiness and fulfillment do not." Sunan said sharply. "The throne is just a chair. The person who sits on it can be the most fearful and the most unfree person in the kingdom unless he applies the lessons Mongkut is teaching."

Chang was unconvinced, but politely said good-bye. Before he could walk away, Sunan grabbed Chang's hand, stood, and gave him a hug. She looked into his face and said, "You be careful. Be a smart soldier and we'll see you in Ayutthaya."

Chang's shoulders dropped, he smiled at Sunan and promised that he would be careful.

Within the hour Tao and Sunan were sailing on a large boat down to Ayutthaya with twenty other people. Sunan rested and Tao worked on polishing his emerald with the rough stone and river water.

Tao missed his village and his own home, but Sunan's and Mongkut's house was just as inviting. When they walked into the house he bounded up the wooden stairs to his room. He unpacked his bag and wrote down all he had learned. He would place these notes on the power of praxis and the power of framing with his other class notes.

In the capital, the people talked about the Makassarese rebellion. Mongkut had cancelled classes for a week because the king wanted him and the other ministers to discuss how they would manage the foreign camps on Ayutthaya's doorstep. Mongkut's absence, however, was not a break for Tao; his French lessons continued every day.

Tao now knew his way around Ayutthaya, so Sunan let him walk to his French teacher's house on his own. He could tell that she loved having a "borrowed son" as she said, and he appreciated her being his "borrowed mother." He often took fruit to his French teacher Jean Pierre. Jean Pierre was a former cook for the French navy, but now tutored the children of wealthy Siamese. He also baked and sent Tao home with fresh bread – something that Tao had not tasted before.

Mongkut returned on a Sunday afternoon and looked tired. He didn't talk about the meetings in Lopburi except to say that he was happy to be away from the palace.

26
THE POWER OF SUBSTITUTION

On Monday, the students arrived early and took their places. Muu brought a bag of mangosteen from a tree at his uncle's house. Faa appeared rejuvenated after spending time with her family and laughed easily at Muu's silly jokes. Chang sat silently and drew pictures on a piece of paper.

Mongkut entered the classroom and Father Tachard followed behind. They were both laughing and enjoying each other's company. Tao actually understood some of what they were saying in French. Father Tachard said that his dark Jesuit robes were not made for the humidity of Siam and that he wished he could wear a more open robe like the Buddhist monks.

Father Tachard sat near a window where sunlight streamed in and it gave his face an orange glow. Mongkut walked to the chalkboard and wrote down the aspects of the two types of power covered in the first class.

THE POWER FROM AUTHORITY

1. *Requires institutions*
2. *The institution justifies rewarding and punishing*
3. *Authority can be delegated to others*

THE POWER FROM PURPOSE

1. *The leader identifies a shared purpose that increases freedom*
2. *Followers share their power in pursuit of the purpose*
3. *The leader uses the eight sources of power*

"Class," he said, "we have experienced these types of power in the last months. Like the yin and yang sign that represents a natural balance, we see that both authority and purpose are necessary for balancing a life and a nation."

"In the last two weeks we saw the king use the power of authority to command the Siamese generals, the French, and the British to protect Ayutthaya, and we've learned four sources that come from purpose. You built a school using the power of invitation. In the village, you practiced compassion and generosity using the power of the open hand. You also started the journey of becoming an expert in a specific field using the power of praxis, and we saw how Supawadee used the power of framing to banish fear and create a shared vision for her village."

"These four sources of power arise from having a purpose and not from having a position of authority. They don't rely on institutions, but rather on our willingness to pursue greater freedom for ourselves and others. You *can* use these sources of power if you have authority, but I want you to lead whether you have a position or not."

Mongkut continued, "I've invited Father Tachard to talk to us about the fifth source of power. He is a leader in our community. He and the Jesuits built the city hospital and also the school near the palace wall. He is a scientist who studies the stars, a follower of the holy man Jesus, and he is also a Frenchman. Father Tachard chose to leave his country to serve the king and people of Siam. He is also a good friend."

Mongkut stepped back and gestured for Father Tachard to address the students. He embraced Mongkut and walked to the front of the room while Mongkut sat in a chair near the front.

Father Tachard spoke in Siamese. "I want to begin with a story from my tradition that is also shared with Muslims and Jews. We believe that all things that you see came into existence from one all-powerful God. By His power He spoke everything into existence – the sun, the stars, and the earth. By speaking, He substituted nonexistence with existence. We are also told that everything was dark. Think of deep darkness, like when you are outside of the city and there is no moon. But then when you light a fire, the darkness is pushed back and you can see. God did the same thing. He substituted darkness with light when He commanded, 'Let there be light!'"

"God also created humans in his likeness. We believe that all of us are made in the image of God. He placed beings on earth who are like Him. They can think, learn, experiment, love, laugh, and sing."

Father Tachard walked to the board and drew a tree. "Let me tell you about another substitution. Just as the Buddhist tradition starts with a tree, my tradition starts with a tree. The tree is located in a beautiful garden that God created for the first man Adam and his wife Eve. God told them that they could eat fruit from all of the trees in the garden, except for the tree which he called the Tree of the Knowledge of Good and Evil. If they ate fruit from that tree, they would eventually die."

Though Father Tachard was speaking Siamese, he wrote "Knowledge of Good and Evil" in French under the tree.

"The story tells us that a clever snake told Eve that she *should* eat the fruit of this particular tree because it would make her wise like God and that she would never die. He called God a liar and deceived Eve into eating the fruit. She ate the fruit and gave some to Adam who also believed the lie and he ate it too. My tradition says that at that moment, 'Their eyes were opened.'"

Father Tachard began pacing slowly in front of the board.

"Immediately, they saw that they were naked, and they felt shame! Their joy and peace were replaced with fear and shame. They couldn't hold on to peace and at the same time be filled with fear. Adam and Eve covered themselves with leaves and hid from God. So, I ask myself, 'What happened? What happened inside them when they chose the knowledge of good and evil? Why were they ashamed and afraid?'"

The class was silent as this was a strange story and they were not sure where it was going.

Finally, Mot raised his hand. "Were they ashamed because they disobeyed God?"

"Yes, they were ashamed of their disobedience. But they were also ashamed of their bodies. Shame replaced acceptance. When God asked them what they had done, they blamed each other and the snake. When we blame others for *our* mistakes, we are trying to make someone else evil so that we appear good. We want to substitute our rejection with acceptance."

Father Tachard looked at each of the students. "I believe that all humans are accepted and not rejected. Some will judge you as evil and seek to substitute your joy with shame. You may judge yourself and reject yourself. But I know that you are accepted by the One who created the earth, sun, moon and stars."

Mongkut had his arms crossed and softly cleared his throat. Earlier he had reminded Father Tachard that the king did not want any preaching of the Christian message to the students. Father Tachard glanced at Mongkut and nodded his head. "I just wanted to tell you that according to my tradition you are loved and accepted without exception, which leads me into the main topic of my talk."

He erased the tree on the board and wrote *The Power of Substitution*.

"Note how life is filled with substitutions. In the stories I've told you, see how existence replaced non-existence, darkness replaced light, and shame replaced joy? When something is substituted for something else, sometimes things change for better or worse. When you use the power of substitution, you can make the lives of others better or worse."

Father Tachard then wrote the word "Trust" on the board.

"If you have authority, people may trust you or distrust you because of the institution you represent. If you do *not* have authority, people will trust or distrust you for other reasons. We are going to discuss three ways you can use the power of substitution to increase trust."

On the board he wrote:

THE POWER OF SUBSTITUTION

1. *Substitute ignorance with knowledge*
2. *Substitute uncertainty with confidence*
3. *Substitute fear with love*

He looked at Tao and said, "Please come up and help me with an experiment."

Father Tachard took Tao into the back room and they reappeared, each carrying a medium-sized wicker basket with a lid. They carefully placed them on the floor in front of the class and Father Tachard asked Tao to stand behind them.

Father Tachard said, "Without looking inside, tell me what is in these baskets."

Tao looked at the outside of the baskets and said, "I don't know. Mine wasn't very heavy."

Father Tachard said, "Humans are often ignorant about what makes things happen, what something is, or why we are here. Knowledge can replace ignorance and create trust. For example, I know how to measure the temperature of water and when it boils. I share this knowledge with others and help them make a better cup of tea. Their ignorance is substituted with my knowledge, and this creates trust."

"Tao, what if I told you that one of these baskets contained a cobra and the other contained delicious French bread. Would you be willing to put your hand in the baskets to find out?"

The students laughed as Tao crossed his arms and shook his head "No."

"What if I told you that the basket on your left has the bread, and Chang paid me to tell you that? Would you put your hand in the basket?"

The students again laughed. Chang yelled out. "The bread *is* in the left one!"

Tao still stood with his arms crossed and said "No!"

"Why won't you put your hand in the left basket?"

"Because I don't trust you since someone paid you to give me a message. If I'm wrong, a snake may bite me."

Father Tachard stepped toward the class and said, "The risk is high because you don't know if you can trust me or Chang. Also, you are ignorant about what is in the baskets. You lack knowledge. Remember that Phra Vimutti told you that, 'Curiosity frees us from ignorance?' Be curious! How can you find out what's in the baskets to substitute knowledge for ignorance?"

"I could ask Mongkut because I trust him," Tao said.

"How else could you find out?"

"I could look in each basket and see for myself, or I could ask Muu to look in the baskets."

Muu yelled "No way!"

"I could start to put my hand in one of the baskets and see if you will stop me. Since you built a hospital and are a teacher, I trust that you would not allow me to hurt myself."

The room became quiet and Father Tachard put his hand on Tao's shoulder.

"Excellent. You described three ways to substitute your ignorance with knowledge. You can ask questions, experiment, and rely on those you trust. Notice also that as you gain knowledge, we all become freer to make a good decision. The more knowledge increases, the more power we have to make a correct decision. This is the power of substitution."

Father Tachard stepped back and said clearly, "Tao, I promise you that the bread is in the right basket."

Tao hesitated and the students' held their breath. Then Tao confidently stepped to the basket on the right, untied a leather thong attached to the lid, reached his hand in and pulled out bread rolls. The students applauded as Tao handed out the rolls and then sat down.

Father Tachard continued, "How many of you trust me more than at the beginning of the class because I told the truth?" The students nodded.

"These seeds of truth and knowledge can be planted all the time and trust will grow, but avoid lying because one lie can destroy trust."

He looked at Chang and asked, "Will a general with knowledge of an enemy's strengths and weaknesses be able to defend against them better than an ignorant general?"

He looked at Faa and said, "Will a doctor with knowledge of why a person is sick be able to relieve suffering?"

The students nodded and Muu raised his hand, "How can we get the knowledge we need?"

Father Tachard placed his hand on the edge of the chalkboard and gently leaned against it. "First, learn as much as you can as Mongkut taught you with the power of praxis. But on another level consider what the Greek philosopher Socrates said. He argued that the most capable leaders are always seeking what is true and real. He tells a mythical story of people who grow up in a cave and stare at a wall. In the cave, people only see shadows of objects projected on the wall and they think that these shadows are reality. Then Socrates says that if a person escapes from the cave and sees the real world, he is closer to knowing what is true and what is an illusion. A leader must journey out of the cave and seek knowledge of what is real."

"Then, like the Buddha who desired to stay under the tree but left it to teach others, the leaders with knowledge should return to the cave and share what they've learned. Of course, some knowledge is not accepted and those in the cave may reject and despise the person."

Father Tachard said, "Let's consider the substitution of uncertainty with confidence. Which leader would you believe? Which leader would you believe? A leader who is afraid of learning new things or one who was confident about what they know?"

"The confident one," Mot said.

"I agree. A confident leader can substitute the uncertainty of the followers with confidence. Mongkut told me of your experience building the bridge. What if Chatchai said, 'I'm not sure about how to build bridges, but I can try?' Would you have followed him into the river?"

"I may have followed him because of his experience, but I would have worried about my safety," Tao said.

"Exactly. Chatchai is confident about what he can and cannot do, and you substitute his confidence for your uncertainty. I am confident about running my school and the hospital, and that replaces the uncertainty among my followers. But consider . . . my confidence is based on my knowledge and experience. This combination drives out uncertainty and creates trust."

"But what about someone who is only *acting* confident, but is actually lying?" Faa asked. "Uncertainty is substituted with confidence . . . in a lie."

"Great observation. My only answer is to return to the first point. If you lead using the power of substitution, you must continually seek to substitute ignorance with knowledge. If someone is trying to deceive you, don't let their confidence move you. Find the facts for yourself and look at the past record of the leader before you let go of your uncertainty."

Mongkut leaned forward and said, "Also, the power of the

open hand tells us to hold knowledge lightly and stay curious. Ignorance is a poison when we think someone's ideas must be unquestioned, especially our own ideas!"

Father Tachard nodded and then drew a circle around his third point on the board. "The last aspect of this power is to substitute fear with love."

"The power of substitution becomes active when you have knowledge and are confident – you create trust. But consider these warnings about knowledge and confidence:

- Knowledge without concern for others can be cold and offend people.

- Confidence without knowledge can lead to pride and deception.

- Knowledge without confidence can create fear in your followers."

"The hidden dangers of knowledge and confidence can be resolved by the last point. You must substitute *fear with love*. Notice that fear repels, but love attracts. As Mongkut taught you in Dusit, a frame of fear can be difficult to replace because fear masks and distorts reality. It can freeze us so that we can't move or make us run away from a battle or lie to a friend. Love, which is valuing the lives of others, can replace your fears just as light replaces darkness. Think of someone you would die to protect . . . and you have found the power of love over fear."

Father Tachard became excited and started walking among the students. "You know what I'm saying, that love casts out your fears. And when people know that the leader values them, cares for them, and sacrifices for them, then they begin to trust the leader. They are willing to listen and substitute their ignorance for the leader's knowledge. They are willing to substitute their uncertainty for the leaders' confidence."

Father Tachard returned to the front of the classroom and laid his hand on the unopened basket. He said, "There is a cobra in this basket. That is the truth. And I would not let it harm you, so I've secured the lid." He slowly turned the basket to show that the lid was tightly closed with a leather thong.

"Is your fear gone?" he asked. "My concern for you led me to tell the truth about the lid. I am also confident that this leather tie can hold the basket shut. Who would like to carry the basket back to the room."

All of the student's slowly raised their hands and Father Tachard selected Faa. But as she approached the basket, Muu said, "I don't believe there is a cobra in the basket."

Father Tachard smiled, "Good! Not everyone will trust you when you share your knowledge with them and share it confidently. Some need to see for themselves. Come up and look into the basket."

Muu stood and walked to the basket. He carefully untied the thong and pulled back the lip of the lid about half an inch. His eyes grew big and he carefully let the lid down.

"There is a cobra in the basket" he said and sat down. Everyone took a breath and didn't move, except for Faa. She re-tied the thong, picked up the basket and carried it into the back room.

Father Tachard laughed, "See! The power of substitution: ignorance is substituted by knowledge, uncertainty is substituted by confidence, and I hope your fear was substituted by my love for you. Faa now has the freedom to carry the basket with a deadly snake in it. Trust is built and freedom is increased."

Mongkut stood and said, "Father Tachard, we are ready for

lunch. Do you have anything else to share that doesn't involve a poisonous snake?"

"No. Not today. But we do have a field trip in a few days, so I'll see you then."

Without further explanation, Father Tachard gave a small bow to the class and retreated to a chair on the side of the room.

Mongkut said, "Thank you for the invitation. Class is dismissed."

Answer the reflection questions in the Reflect and Apply section about how you can apply the *Power of Substitution*.

27
MAKING A SPECIAL DEAL

Phaulkon's arms and legs were sore from the battle. He carefully sat down at his desk in Ayutthaya. He had fought pirates as a sailor, but he was not a trained soldier. Sitting in meetings and writing contracts hadn't prepared him for storming a beach.

He shook his head as he sat down and asked himself, "What was I thinking? Joining a military operation?"

But then he answered himself, "Now the king trusts me more than any other advisor and Phetracha is not popular in the palace."

Phaulkon groaned and called his assistant to bring him some tea and the latest draft of the British East India Company trade contract.

As he sipped his tea, he edited the contract by making slight tax increases for teak, palm oil, and coconuts. He was also concerned that the company was losing money. Negotiators from other European countries knew that the British East India Company was extremely inefficient and that some of the commanders and sailors were undisciplined. They took too much time in port, let the sailors drink too much, and didn't properly store the cargo. Some of the goods they purchased would be damaged before they reached

England. The company would then blame Siam for high prices, bad quality, and taxes.

After an hour of editing, someone knocked on his door. Phaulkon's assistant stuck his head into the office. "Sir, two British officers are here to see you."

A familiar voice with a British accent yelled, "Phaulkon? Are you home?"

Phaulkon laughed and said, "You can let them in."

Two British sailors walked in, took off their hats, and bowed to Phaulkon. "Is this the proper way to salute a minister?" one of them said jokingly.

"Only if you want to lose your head," Phaulkon said. He walked around his desk and vigorously shook the men's hands.

In a perfect British accent, he said, "I say . . . what brings Richard Burnaby and Samuel White to the humble Kingdom of Siam?"

Richard said, "We heard you may need help escaping the Makassarese since I've never known a Greek who could use a sword or a gun." They all laughed.

Richard was tall and thin with a tan face and a big smile. Samuel was shorter than Richard, muscular, and with bright red sunburned cheeks. Both wore British navy officer uniforms and carried swords attached to broad leather belts.

Phaulkon gestured for the men to sit down and returned to his seat behind the desk.

"We are here to complete our deal before you finish negotiating with the Company," Richard said. "We want to make sure that we are in the clear for this operation. Is it going to be like the one we did for you two years ago?"

Phaulkon nodded and checked to make sure the door was shut.

"Let me show you."

He took a brass key from his vest pocket and opened a wooden cabinet behind him. He reached up on the top shelf and pulled out a large scroll.

He unrolled the scroll across his desk and the men stood and leaned on the corners. The scroll was a map of Siam with each port on the east and west coast. The port city of Mergui on the west coast facing India was circled. Burnaby and White had been stationed there many times.

"We are still on for the operation," Phaulkon said. He described the area the two commanders were to patrol. He said, "You will receive arms to protect Siam against the Makassarese and also any ships from the Kingdom of Golconda in south India. They often make trouble for us."

Samuel tapped the dot on the map that indicated Bangkok and leaned toward Phaulkon. "You know we are not here to float around and look threatening. We've done enough of that in the Bay of Bengal for the government. What's in it for us?"

"The ships that are not flying a flag of one of Siam's trading partners are not legally trading with Siam. You may stop them and take whatever cargo they have by the authority of Siam."

Samuel was not convinced. "Where is the approval that says we can stop these ships?"

Phaulkon stood, reached into his cabinet, and produced a leather pouch containing signed documents stating that the two men were acting under the authority of Siam.

The men inspected the documents. Phaulkon rolled up the map and watched them.

"What percent do you want?" Samuel asked.

"After you take what you think is fair for yourselves," he said, "send me eighty gold pieces per ship."

Phaulkon then switched to a more authoritative tone.

"I've chosen you to be privateers and NOT pirates. I trust you because you are smart enough to know which ships to attack and which ones to leave alone."

He paused for effect and then said, "However, you must recognize that we are foreigners and we stand out. Everything you do will be watched, so be discreet. Don't spend all your money on whiskey and women, and don't stop ships working for the British East India Company."

Richard smirked and said, "Don't worry your little Greek head. We'll be discreet. As for the Company, we know which ships to board and which ones to avoid. Leave that to us."

"You don't understand," Phaulkon said. "I am surrounded by enemies who seek to remove me, and I don't want them to have any reason to doubt my allegiance to the king. I watched a tiger tear apart four Makassarese soldiers. It took hours before they died. The tiger became bored in between attacks and just sat and watched the soldiers tied to stakes."

The two men looked at each other, but they did not seem to care about Phaulkon's delicate position.

Richard and Samuel stood to leave. Phaulkon told them to wait.

"One more thing. I've made arrangements with the local authorities to provide you with everything you need in the city of Mergui. Richard, the king has agreed to appoint you as governor of the city next month and Samuel will be the top customs official.

My Siamese representative Wemanmek will see that you have everything you need."

Richard was surprised. "This is a lot of responsibility for a foreigner. Will the locals support me as governor?"

Phaulkon handed him the map and said. "Wemanmek commands 200 troops to support you. Also, the French know that a British friend of the king will be governor. Do your best and keep me informed of any problems."

The three nodded toward each other and Phaulkon ushered them out of the door.

As the door closed, Phaulkon took a deep breath. He trusted Samuel to do his duty, but he knew that Richard may get greedy. He didn't have time to deal with another uprising.

Phaulkon returned to his desk and yelled to his assistant, "Sawat! Bring me the list of the British East India Company's tariff charges...and a basin of hot water for my feet!"

28
SERVING OTHERS

The students followed Mongkut and Father Tachard along a street next to the palace walls. The two teachers drew attention as they passed people on the street. Mongkut was shorter than Father Tachard and he wore a dark red silk shirt and white pants. Father Tachard wore a black robe and a black cloth hat in the shape of a box. He also had a necklace with a small teak cross on it that sat surprisingly still as he walked and gestured. They spoke French to each other and would often laugh.

"I can't believe we are visiting the Jesuit hospital," Faa said excitedly. "My parents didn't want me to go, but Mongkut explained that he would be with us."

"Why are they afraid?" Tao asked.

"They don't want me to become a Jesus follower," she said. "My father is a strict Buddhist and believes that the Catholic church is a French tool for invading our country."

"Do you think this is true?"

"I don't think Father Tachard wants to take over Siam, but more French priests and traders are coming each day. My father says we must watch the foreigners because they want to make the king a Jesus follower. That's what Phetracha says."

Chang was walking behind them listening. He said, "All the foreigners need to be controlled or we'll become a colony like Makassarese. The Dutch took over their country. Why do you think the prince is here in exile?"

"That's why we are in the academy," Tao responded. "We're supposed to learn how to manage these relationships without cutting Siam off from the rest of the world."

The group turned right into the hospital grounds. Inside a brick fence, a white two-story building stood surrounded by flowers and trees. The building had a center entrance with a wing build to the right and left of the main door. Windows were open across the front of the building and a balcony jutted out above the door.

Mongkut gathered the students together by the front door.

"This afternoon we are going to practice three of the sources of power: invitation, the open hand, and substitution. Father Tachard has invited us to serve the patients' lunch."

Chang groaned and said, "More work for free," under his breath.

Mongkut ignored him and continued.

"First, why build a place to help sick people unless you are using the power of the open hand? The Jesuits built this hospital out of their compassion for the people of Siam, and they are making an important change in our country. The king allowed it because he is not stuck in ancient beliefs about medicine. Second, they invite interested people to join them in learning how to heal the sick. Third, the nurses here substitute the fear of death with a love for life. Today, while you interact with the patients and staff, think of the invitation, the open hand, and substitution. Be curious and ask them what they need. Ask them who they are and listen. Any questions?"

No one spoke. Father Tachard directed the students into the main hallway which separated the two wings. Another priest and three Siamese women wearing white clothes met the students. They explained that the students were going to serve lunch and talk with the patients.

The nurses took the students to the left wing of the hospital where six men were lying on cots. A few looked up at the students while others appeared to be asleep. Faa went upstairs to the women's ward.

"Please ask the awake patients their names and if they are ready for lunch," the first nurse said.

The students spread out among the beds. Tao went to the bedside of a muscular man who was laying on his side. The man's right arm was wrapped in bandages. A red blood stain ran down the bandage on the side of his arm.

"Hello, I'm Tao. Are you ready for lunch?"

The man shook his head no and with a raspy voice said, "Water."

Tao looked around and found a water jug. He poured water into a cup and then helped the man sit up and drink.

"My name is Suchart," the man said as he adjusted himself into a sitting position. He carefully moved his injured arm and winced in pain as he sat up.

"Would you like to eat?" Tao asked again, feeling a little anxious.

"No thank you," he said. "Sit down Tao and let's talk."

Tao sat down on Suchart's cot and said, "My father's name is Suchart."

"What does your father do?"

"He is a rice farmer in the north. I'm from a small village, but I'm here to learn about leadership from Mongkut."

Suchart gestured for Tao to give him more water, and Tao filled the cup again and Suchart quickly drained it.

"I am a leader in the Siamese army. I was injured during the attack on the Makassarese camp. Someone slashed me with a blade. Thankfully there was no poison on the blade...they poison their blades you know? Anyway, I led my troops until I collapsed from a loss of blood. Now I'm stuck here until the cut heals, or I escape." He chuckled and gave Tao a sly smile.

Now that he was sitting up, he looked around the room. He stopped scanning when he saw Chang delivering a bowl of soup to a patient who was burrowed into his covers and shivering.

"You know that man there?" Suchart asked.

"Yes. That is Chang, the son of—

Suchart interrupted. "I know who Chang is and I know his father Phetracha. They are brave soldiers, but . . ." His voice trailed off and he handed Tao his empty cup.

Tao leaned forward but didn't say anything.

Suchart ran his left hand over his face and head and whispered, "Be watchful of Chang and his father. They have plans for Siam that don't involve Jesuits, the French, or anyone except for themselves and their friends."

Tao sat still. "What do you mean?"

"I'm just saying, keep your eyes and ears open. Learn all you can from Mongkut. You never know when you'll be called on to help the kingdom."

Suchart took a deep breath and looked at his bandaged arm. "This is my sword arm. I hope I'll be able to fight again. You know

Tao, use your life to do good for others, because once you're dead you can't do anything. Now how about some soup – and make it spicy!"

Tao realized that talking had given Suchart energy. Had Tao somehow substituted fear with love?

He went to the kitchen and told a nurse that Suchart was ready for his soup. The nurse looked surprised. "He hasn't eaten in two days. You must be a healer!"

"I'm just being curious," Tao said.

Tao took the soup to Suchart and held the bowl of steaming broth with chicken while Suchart ate with his left hand. He finished the bowl and then indicated that he wanted to lie down again.

Tao helped him lay on his back. Suchart also asked for a pillow to elevate his injured arm.

Mongkut came over and said hello to Suchart as if he knew him. He thanked him for his courage.

"Thanks for teaching these students," Suchart said. "As you know Mongkut, the sword is a costly way to lead. It only works as long as you are strong. Once you become weak, those you've conquered are quick to put you under their sword."

Mongkut nodded and gently rubbed his own arm as if he and Suchart were sharing a secret. "We have to go my friend," he said and gestured that Tao needed to go. As Tao walked away he heard Suchart say, "Thanks for the soup."

"You're welcome," Tao said. "I'll visit you later in the week if you'd like?"

"Only if you want to."

Tao nodded and joined the other students in front of the building. Each of them had a story to tell of the patients they met.

Seeing that all of the students were there, Mongkut said, "You have now learned five sources of power. I want you to reflect for a moment on this: the power of purpose is not only for you, but for the freedom and wellbeing of others. Whether you are building a bridge, a school, or serving a sick person lunch, we use whatever power we have to help others achieve their purposes."

The students reflected on Mongkut's question, but he could see that Mot and Chang were still skeptical.

"You need to trust that power without authority delivers freedom and success," he said. "Sometimes, gaining followers comes after planning and years of work like this Academy, and sometimes gaining followers comes from serving a sick person a bowl of soup."

29
DOWN TIME

The next day Mongkut became ill and cancelled classes. Sunan and Tao were worried about him. His fever was high, and his loud cough echoed through the house. Mongkut tried to work but became exhausted quickly.

Father Tachard and another Jesuit with medical training visited him a few times and recommended that he rest and drink liquids. Mongkut agreed but found it difficult to avoid glancing through the paper pile that grew on his desk.

"You know," said Tao, "I invite you to rest because it will allow you to do more work sooner and open the Academy again. I am also confident that you need to drink water and lie down."

Mongkut looked out from his blankets and smiled at Tao.

"Are you using your power to influence me?"

"Yes," said Tao. "And Sunan and I love you and want you to get better."

Mongkut seemed stunned by Tao's compassion. He rolled on his back, looked at the ceiling, and sighed.

"I accept your invitation to rest. Would you please bring me more water, and I promise I'll stay away from my desk for two days."

Tao left the room and told Sunan that Mongkut had committed to resting. She shook her head and said, "That will be a first."

But Mongkut did sleep for two days. Eventually he coughed less and walked around the house. Sunan secretly sent word to the king that Mongkut needed time to heal. No documents arrived from the palace for a week.

Mongkut also asked Sunan to write letters for him. Tao could hear him dictating in the bedroom. Mongkut would stop when his coughing became too bad and Sunan would read back to him what she had written.

"You would be a better minister than me," he said. Sunan hushed him and said, "You just get better."

Tao spent his time reading, going to French lessons, and visiting Suchart at the hospital. He learned that Suchart was a senior leader of Siam's ground troops. He told Tao of strategies for cutting off enemy supplies and fooling them into thinking you had more soldiers than you did.

"Once we set a lot of campfires at night and had men walk around them. At night it looked like we had a big army. This kept our enemy at a distance." He also invited Tao to tour the soldier training school when he was released.

Faa invited Tao and Muu to lunch and they toured the palace and talked about the bridge they built. They also visited the school they helped build. The brick walls looked like any other walls, but Faa pointed out the bricks that she placed.

After two weeks, Mongkut began going to the palace for meetings. The next week he reopened the Academy for the next lesson.

30

THE POWER OF SOLIDARITY

On Monday morning, rain fell in great sheets and thunder echoed across the city. People rushed along the streets hunched over as if they could avoid the water pouring from the sky and the shop awnings. Some leapt over puddles that were turning into small ponds. Others huddled in their doorways talking and laughing.

The students noisily entered the classroom. Most of them took off round wicker hats that provided some protection from the rain. Mot's legs were covered in mud and he sat on the floor to wipe them off with a rag.

Muu and Tao were so busy talking, laughing, and shaking water off of their clothes that they didn't notice the guest standing in the front of the room.

Eventually Tao looked up and saw a man at the front of the class watching the students with amusement. He had brown skin and wore a dark blue shirt with a red cloth belt secured tightly around his waist. He had black hair with some grey on the sides and his dark brown eyes surveyed the students. He crossed his arms and waited for the students to notice that he was there.

Mongkut appeared from the room behind the chalkboard,

which was covered by a white sheet. He set a bundle of sticks on a small table, and then asked the students to hurry to their mats because the guest speaker had another appointment later in the day.

The students quickly sat down and pulled fresh paper from their desks. The rain clattered loudly on the roof.

"Today," Mongkut began, "we have the good fortune to learn about the sixth source of power which is closely related to the power of substitution. Our guest teacher is Aqu Muhammad Astarabadi or Aqu. He is the grandson of the Persian Sheik Ahmad. His family arrived in Siam almost 100 years ago. Over these many years a member of his family has always served in Siam's finance and trade offices. Aqu served as Phrakhlang – our top finance minister – for several years and now works as a trade advisor to the king, especially in the areas of trade with Persia, the Malay peninsula, Sumatra, and other Islamic countries. I thank him for his time and I encourage you to listen closely as he explains a unique source of power."

With those words, Mongkut walked to a chair near the wall and left Aqu standing before the students with his arms still crossed. The students wai'd him and he nodded in response.

"Students," he said in a loud, low voice, "you must be thankful every day for Mongkut and what he is doing. You five are the most blessed students in the Ayutthaya kingdom. What you are learning will change you forever and will change Siam. You may not believe me, but treasure this time and what you learn because a time will come when you will need to choose to lead or to hide. If you hide, you open the space for the kingdom to be governed by those who care more about wealth and position than serving the Siamese people."

Aqu's confidence had captured the students' attention.

"I am here to talk about the *power of solidarity*. It is the power that creates change by binding your present and future with the lives of others."

He uncrossed his arms and started pacing in front of the board.

"I am an example of this power. When my grandfather traveled from Persia to Siam, he saw an opportunity to serve. Siam became my family's kingdom. He helped the previous kings build trade relationships with many nations and trained my father and I to do the same. My family follows the teaching of Buddha since that is the custom of this land and we gladly work alongside the Siamese so that it will grow for a thousand years. I have bound my present and future to the people of Siam even though I am of Persian descent."

"In an earlier class, I understand Phra Vimutti talked about the power of the open hand. He explained how compassion reveals itself as gentleness to yourself and others so that you can see what is emerging. In the last lesson, Father Tachard talked of how the power of substitution helps others by substituting something that limits freedom with something that increases freedom; like replacing fear with love. Both of these sources of power create trust which is required for leading others when you do not have authority. The *power of solidarity* takes these and the other sources of power directly into the lives of others. No more hiding from people."

Aqu resumed his stiff stance as he pulled a sheet off of the chalkboard. Under the sheet he had written the following in elegant, tight script:

THE POWER OF SOLIDARITY

1. *Listen to the stories of others*
2. *Invest in the dreams of others*
3. *Bind your future to the future of others*

The students wrote down the list as Aqu continued talking.

"These three actions provide a unique power to lead others. I'll start with the first action which is to *listen to the stories of others*. The Persian poet Mowlana Jalaloddin Balkhi Rumi, or as he is known by many as just Rumi, wrote stories and beautiful poems four hundred years ago about love, friendship, the soul and travelers. In one book he wrote a story about the people of Zarwan who had great fruit orchards. These people didn't want to share their fruit with the poor and planned to keep it all for themselves. Rumi explains that instead of withholding help from the poor, they needed to recognize the stress and struggles they endured. One way to help them is to listen to their stories."

Aqu stared above the student's heads, as if trying to recall something deep in his mind.

He then said,

Unblock your ears of heedlessness and heed
The separation felt by hearts that bleed!
When you hear tales from such a person, you
Are giving alms to that lovelorn one too. [6]

"Rumi compares the stress people feel to a house that's filled with smoke. Many people are full of bitter smoke produced by trials and difficulties. These stories are trapped in their body of clay. When you ask someone about their name and their story, you are opening a window so that they can breathe again. You are letting them pour out the smoke so that they can see and hear and think clearly again."

Faa raised her hand and Aqu nodded to her.

"I believe we did this at the hospital, so I don't see how this is different from the power of substitution."

Aqu said, "Substitution is about replacing something that limits people with something that creates more freedom and energy. You substitute a fear of loneliness with a love that cares for others. The power of solidarity requires you to commit to someone or some group. The first step of solidarity is asking someone to share their story with you. You are not judging their story. You are listening without seeking to change the other person. Sometimes to lead others you use the power of substitution to address a specific need. Other times, you use the power of solidarity to secure more freedom for a person over a long period of time."

Aqu moved from his position in front of the class and stepped to the side of the chalkboard.

"Let's consider the second step which takes you deeper in solidarity with the other person. This is when you *invest in the dreams of others*. Visiting someone for a meal can build trust. But sometimes you need to invite others for a meal and do it often. You are investing your time hearing their stories and their dreams. You may decide to provide resources for someone out of your own pocket or connect them with others who can support them. Has anyone ever been in solidarity with you in this way? Has anyone ever invested in your dreams?"

Aqu stood silently to allow the students to consider his question. Finally, Tao raised his hand.

"Phra Luang Suk in my village used the power of solidarity.

Ever since I was a young boy he took an interest in me. He taught me to write and read Sanskrit. Once I was very sick and he came by every evening to check on me and quiz me on my reading. He let me know that I had a future beyond my illness. He invested in me even though he didn't know that I would be in this class today."

Aqu nodded in agreement and called on Chang whose hand was up now.

"General Rana has invested in my dreams of becoming a soldier. He taught me to ride elephants and how to use a bow and arrow. He is like an uncle to me and I can always go and see him. He never turns me away."

All hands were in the air now and each student talked of a teacher, family member, or friend who invested in their dreams. Mot described how his older sister helped him recover after he was hit by an oxcart. If she had not fed him and forced him to practice walking, he would still be lying in his bed. Tao was surprised that everyone had experienced the power of solidarity, and that the experience had changed their lives.

After all the students had shared, Aqu told the story of how his father invested in his dreams as he learned how to negotiate trade agreements. He learned how to protect Siam's resources and tax revenue while maintaining peace with foreign governments and powerful trading companies.

"My father always said, 'If you ever have a question about a decision being right or wrong, ask yourself if you would tell the king of your decision. If you would *not* tell the king of your decision, then it is the wrong decision.' Our family name is built on solidarity and I seek to honor his investment in me."

Aqu had loosened his rigid stance a little and seemed more comfortable after telling his personal story. He smiled and said,

"Stop and think about how you feel towards each other now that you have told your story."

The students sat in silence.

"What is one word that describes what you are now feeling towards each other?"

The students called out, "Trust," "Friendship," "Respect."

"You have now experienced the power of solidarity. Sharing your personal stories has bound you together in a short time. You are in solidarity with each other when you listen to the stories of others and those who invested in their dreams."

Aqu returned to the chalkboard and pointed at the third step. "The final step is for those who recognize that leading others will require more than listening to their stories and investing in their dreams. The power of solidarity may require you to bind your future to their future. Your purpose to their purpose. This is the highest level of commitment which results in the most power to lead."

Aqu walked over to the wall, pulled on a leather coat, put on a hat, and picked up a leather shoulder bag. He slowly walked past the students, glancing at each of them, and stood by the door. The rain was still pouring down outside and distant thunder rumbled across the grey sky. He looked out of the door into the drenching rain, and then turned to the students.

"Solidarity leads you to bind your future to those of others. I have bound my future to someone. I invite you to come and visit him."

With those words he walked out of the door and into the rain. The students looked at each other in surprise. They turned to Mongkut who looked back at the students, shrugged and said, "It's your choice if you want to take his invitation."

Tao found himself jogging toward the door. He grabbed his

hat and started walking after Aqu who was already at the gate. Tao
ran down the stairs and the rain quickly drenched his clothes. He
caught up with Aqu who did not look at him, but kept walking.
Tao looked around and saw the wet shapes of Faa and Muu not far
behind. Chang and Mot stood in the doorway.

Aqu led the three down the main street in front of the school
and then zigzagged through back alleys. Large puddles seemed
to boil with the pounding rain. Muu looked at Tao and they both
smiled. This was exciting.

Aqu finally stopped next to a feedlot where five cows stood
looking at the wet visitors. They didn't seem to care about the
downpour. They chewed their cud and blinked water from their
eyes. The students followed Aqu through a wooden doorway and
into a dark single room shack. Aqu said, "I'm sorry I'm late."

In the darkness Tao saw someone move who had been laying
on a mat. The shape of a man and two children appeared in the
grey light of a window.

"Muu, please light a fire," Aqu said. He directed Muu to get
some wood from the corner.

"First we need something to start the fire," Aqu said and
looked at Tao. Tao looked around and couldn't find anything. Then
he realized that the cows must eat hay. He went outside and found
some dry hay in a stable and handed it to Muu.

Aqu handed Faa a flintstone and she crouched down and lit
the straw by gently blowing on a spark that jumped from the stone.
Muu followed with some wood. Within five minutes an orange
light filled the room. The faces of the inhabitants appeared from
the dark and everyone gathered around the fireplace to capture
whatever warmth they could.

Aqu introduced the man as Ahmed Muhammed. He tended

the cows for the British. Aqu explained that Ahmed's wife had died of an illness last year, leaving him with two children. Ahmed's wife was one of his family servants. Tao noticed that Ahmed was missing his left hand.

The boy and the girl silently crouched down by the fire. Their eyes sparkled as they assessed their visitors.

"Thank you for the fire," Ahmed said. "I was up early milking the cows and taking the milk to the British compound. I fell asleep when I returned."

Aqu nodded and then pulled rice and dried fish wrapped in banana leaves from his shoulder bag and set it on the table. Ahmed produced a candle, lit it from the fire, and placed it on the table. After a short prayer, they stood and ate. Ahmed made sure his children ate first.

Soon the children were giggling and Ahmed was telling stories of British sailors, cows, and how he had started a business selling milk.

Tao listened intently. The sticky rice was delicious and the fire in the corner grate felt wonderful. Aqu told some funny stories about how the British didn't understand the Siamese and often mistake spicy food for mild food. Ahmed laughed and his white teeth shown in the candlelight. Time went by quickly. Tao glanced around and realized that the sun had started shining in the door. He hadn't noticed that the rain had stopped.

Aqu said that they must go, but that he would be back in two days. He also told Ahmed to go to the Mosque and offer to sell milk to the Persian traders. He could bring his children to Aqu's house while he was working.

The students said goodbye and walked out into the sunshine.

Aqu followed with his empty bag over his shoulder. As he

walked he said, "Solidarity does not let you sit in your dry classroom for long. Binding your future with others requires movement on your part. I have bound myself to Ahmed's future and will see him through to his dream of owning a dairy business. In fact, two of those milk cows are his. I loaned him the money and he already paid me back."

The group reached the classroom where Chang and Mot were talking with Mongkut. They looked at the wet and muddy group and wondered why they looked so happy.

"Where did you go?" Chang asked. "Why didn't you wait for the rain to stop?"

Aqu walked to the front and said, "We went to be in solidarity with someone who needed a fire and some food. His need and the needs of his children cannot wait on the weather. They exist whether it's raining or dry. By acting in solidarity, we substituted warmth for cold, food for hunger, and friendship for loneliness. Do you see the power you have?"

Mongkut directed the students back to their desks. Three thin sticks, about one foot in length, were sitting next to each mat. Tao noticed that one was bamboo and the other two were from a bodhi tree.

Aqu resumed his place beside the chalkboard after taking off his coat, hat, and leather bag.

"The power of solidarity," he said, "requires you to listen to people's stories, invest in their futures, and when necessary, bind your future to theirs. This is a power that requires your time and action. Many obstacles will tempt you away from the power of solidarity, but you can overcome them."

"Now I want to conclude with a lesson about the power of solidarity. In addition to Rumi's instruction for us to listen, he also talked of how we need to be *with* others if we are going to succeed on our journey. Sometimes we need others and they need us. Rumi wrote,

> *This road demands courage and stamina, yet it is full of footprints!*
>
> *Who are all these companions? They are the rungs of your ladder! Use them!*
>
> *With company you quicken your ascent.*
>
> *You may be happy enough going alone, but with others you will get farther, and faster.*[7]

"The lesson is that some journeys offer companionship, and you may want to join in solidarity with your fellow travelers."

Aqu then reached over to Mongkut who handed him a thin stick of bamboo.

Aqu said, "Pick up the bamboo stick next to you and I want you to bend it without breaking it."

The students did as they were told, but the snapping of the sticks was heard. Muu and Chang smiled as they held their broken sticks. Faa's stick also broke.

Aqu glanced at Mongkut and said, "You have some strong students!"

Turning to the students he said, "With enough stress, all of you can break your sticks. Please, go ahead and break the bamboo . . . if you haven't already." Tao and Nat easily broke their sticks with a loud crunch and a laugh.

"Now," Aqu said, "take your remaining sticks and join them together with those of your classmates. You'll need to stand up to do this."

The students gathered the remaining sticks and Muu put them into a bundle. Aqu handed Faa two leather thongs and directed her to tie the sticks together. When she finished, Muu held the bundle of ten sticks.

"Break the bundle!" Aqu yelled.

Muu was the strongest, and he couldn't break it, even over his knee. Chang shoved Tao aside and tried himself, and then he and Muu tried to break it over a desk. Bark fell from the bundle, some of the outer sticks cracked, but the bundle could not be broken.

Aqu asked the students to stop and hand him the bundle. They returned to their mats.

"What did you learn about solidarity from the individual sticks that you broke, and the bundle you could not break?"

Tao raised his hand. "Being in solidarity strengthens everyone, but standing alone is risky. It is easier for others to break you."

Aqu nodded and said, "Yes, and solidarity with even one person can protect you, not only from others who may break you, but powerful people, poverty, bad weather, and illness. But what is the key to the power of solidarity?"

Tao responded, "I must decide to join with others, and they must agree to join with me."

"Correct again Tao. I encourage all of you to substitute some of your solitary life with a life of solidarity. You may feel safest alone or surrounded by a close group of friends. But endless debating within yourself or with others about how to help others will wear down your resolve. Take courage! Walk through the door of solidarity. When you bind yourself to others – to suffer with them, to encourage them, and to celebrate with them – people will follow you. It just happens."

Answer the reflection questions in the Reflect and Apply section about how you can apply the *Power of Solidarity*.

31
FOLLOWING FAA

The next day Mongkut gave the students the entire day to work on a project of their choosing. They were required to walk around the city and take time to observe and reflect on what they saw.

Mongkut instructed the students while standing on the front steps of the school building. "Observe people. Observe their patterns of behavior. Observe how and why they do things the way they do. Think about this: you would not follow someone who demands that you change who you are or what you are used to doing. In the same way, those who follow you do not want to be told to change who they are. Instead, see what is important to them and how they solve their problems. If you can, observe someone leading others and ask yourself what the leader is doing."

Chang asked a question that the students had discussed in private.

"Ajarn, what is the point of *us* leading people? People are happy doing what they're doing, so why change anything? And who is to say what we are recommending is any better than the way things are right now? I'm just an 18-year old soldier. Who am

I to invite others to follow me, or substitute their fears, or frame a new view of their world?"

The students appreciated Chang's boldness in asking questions that they wouldn't ask, though his condescending tone made them uncomfortable.

Mongkut thought for a few seconds and said, "Good question. Sometimes I can get so close to the battle that I forget to describe what victory looks like."

"Let me first explain the changes that are happening around us and why Siam needs leaders to guide us through these changes. First, the power of the open hand reveals that all things are changing – trees, animals, humans, markets, knowledge, and governments. It is the nature of the material universe and humans to grow, and these changes can restrict freedom or increase freedom. For example, about 80 years ago advisors to the king refused to change from fighting with martial arts, swords and spears. They saw no need to use guns until the Khmer purchased guns from the Portuguese. The world changes and we must manage the most important changes or they will overwhelm us."

Mongkut invited the students to sit on the steps in the shade.

"I don't want you to lead others to change things that do not make them freer and more able to live a good life. Instead, observe how you can strengthen people and help them grow. That is the horizon that you need to look to. This academy is about multiplying freedom, whether by removing obstacles or showing a new direction. Think about how many lives are freer from obstacles because of the school building at Wat Mahathat, the bridge at Dusit, and the hospital."

Tao was beginning to understand Mongkut's vision. Mongkut could not give instructions for every person, situation, and change they would encounter. But he could supply the tools and wisdom needed to apply what they had learned.

Mongkut continued. "Now why should *you* lead others and why should they follow *you?*" He pointed at Chang, and then addressed all of the students.

"The answer to this question is up to you. People should only follow you when you have a shared purpose. When the purpose is clear, then you use the sources of power. People will follow when you address their fears, invite them to do something better, stand in solidarity with them, and act on your expertise. People will follow you because they trust your knowledge, confidence and love. Does that answer your question?"

Chang nodded his head, but still seemed uncomfortable with such abstract examples.

Mongkut dismissed the students. Mot and Chang walked together toward the military barracks while Muu, Faa and Tao walked slowly around the largest pagoda in the Wat.

"Where do you want to go?" Muu said. "I'd like to go to the market by the river."

Faa smirked and Muu said, "Not to eat! To observe the traders from different countries."

Tao had no idea what to do, so he said, "Faa, why don't you choose a place for us to observe. You've lived here the longest."

Faa immediately said, "I want to observe the palace kitchen."

She started walking toward the palace and Tao and Muu followed. "Maybe we'll get to eat anyway," Tao said.

The streets of Ayutthaya were full of people, carts and animals on their morning errands. Tao was always surprised by the variety of people from many nations and different walks of life who lived in Ayutthaya.

The guards at the palace gate knew Faa and her parents. She explained that her two friends would be her guests. The guards looked at Tao and Muu closely, their hands tightly holding their pikes which pointed to the sky. They stepped out of the way and allowed them to enter the palace grounds.

The palace complex was like a city within the city of Ayutthaya. Buildings with sharp, steep red roofs lined the walls and the golden horns on each corner pointed up to the blue sky. Three massive pagodas jutted into the sky. Faa explained that they were in the Wat within the palace grounds. She said that the Sanphet Maha Prasat wooden palace once stood next to this Wat, but it burned down over two hundred years ago.

They walked past some barracks and finally the palace came into view. The palace was more impressive than the one in Lopburi. It was four stories high with brick foundations and wooden walls. The roof was covered in red tiles and its many tiers rose ever higher over each other as if it was a stairway to heaven. Windows were evenly spaced across the first and second floors and balconies extended out from doors on the third and fourth floors.

Faa walked slowly so that Tao and Muu could take in the view. She then led them to a back entrance.

As they approached they could smell meat cooking and see smoke rising from grills and clay ovens. They heard goats and chickens in the distance. A large wet barrel said "fish" on the side. Men and women hurriedly carried trays, baskets, dishes, and linens out of the palace.

Faa led them into a huge kitchen that was filled with the sounds of clanging pans, shouts for spices, and people bent over tables creating food that looked like art.

"Breakfast has just finished and they're starting to prepare lunch," Faa said. Then she gestured toward a woman who was rushing from a food staging area to a cook filling a pot with chopped vegetables. "She is who I want to observe."

"Her name is Maria Guyomar de Pinha and she is second in charge of the royal kitchen and a master chef. Her Siamese name is Thao Thong Kip Ma."

Faa caught Maria's eye and waved. Maria smiled and nodded her head at the three students and then went back to advising the cook.

"Who is she?" Muu asked. "I've never heard of her."

"She was born here in Ayutthaya. Her mother's family is Japanese and they came here to avoid persecution for being Christians. Her father is from the Portuguese colony of Goa in India. He is Portuguese and Japanese. Maria is also Phaulkon's wife. She has one child and in addition to operating this kitchen, she must spend time meeting foreign dignitaries and other aristocrats."

They turned when they heard Maria exclaiming to the cook, "This is exactly the taste I want. Good work!"

Faa watched her admiringly and said, "She also invents new dishes for the palace."

Maria left the cook and walked over to the students. She had a white face, a small mouth, and dark eyes that took in everything around her. Maria was taller than most Siamese by about six inches and she stood up straight which made her thin frame seem even taller. A white handprint of rice flour made an interesting design on her red apron.

"Faa, it is good to see you. And are these your friends from the Academy?"

Faa introduced Tao and Muu who respectfully wai'd Maria.

"What can I do for you?" Maria asked while glancing quickly

at an assistant who was placing thin cuts of chicken on wooden skewers.

"Today our assignment is to observe people," Faa said. "May we observe you and your team this morning? We'll stay out of the way."

"Why observe when you can join us?" Maria said. "I'm sure you can cut fruit while observing our team. We have a big lunch to prepare because the British East India Company delegation is eating with the king's cabinet before meeting with him. We are also preparing lunch for the king and his family."

Within minutes the three students were learning how to determine the ripeness of pineapples and oranges by touch and smell. The person in charge of fruit platters taught them how to cut melons into bowls and then fill them with fruit pieces.

Tao worked carefully but slowly because he wanted to see how Maria worked with others. Faa and Muu were also glancing around as Maria orchestrated every aspect of the meal.

After an hour of cutting fruit and arranging it on platters, eight servers arrived. Maria indicated which dishes to take first and she inspected each platter before it left the kitchen.

She called the students over to a table that contained plates of something that looked like piles of golden string.

"This is a creation that I learned from my father and have adapted it for the Siamese court. I call it Foi Thong (golden threads) but in Portugal they call it *fios de ovos*, or egg threads. It is made from egg yolks that are strung thin and cooked in sugar syrup. Try it!"

The dessert was sweet and tasted like sugary and salty noodles.

While the students enjoyed their Foi Thong, Maria continued

to release each of the dishes at the right time. Finally plates of Foi Thong were carefully placed on silver plates and carried out of the kitchen. Maria asked the students to help clean the kitchen because the dinner chef and crew would arrive soon.

After 1:00 and a big lunch of the best chicken Muu had ever tasted, the students went outside and sat under a tree. Maria joined them for a few minutes.

"So, what do you think of our operation? Would Mongkut approve?" she asked.

"I saw you use many of the sources of power that our teacher has taught us," said Faa. "First, you invited us to join you in making lunch for the king and you had a plan about what needed to be completed. Then you assigned us to work with someone who is an expert in making beautiful fruit creations and she led us to make something new. You are always substituting ignorance with knowledge and fear with love. You also encouraged your cooks to do better without telling them what they are doing wrong. You said, 'add more pepper' where other chefs may say, 'you didn't put in enough pepper.' Our teacher would say that you are being curious and compassionate."

Maria listened to Faa's observations and nodded. "I want the people I work with to be able to do my job in the future. I want them to learn enough so that they are confident to try new things."

Tao said, "That matches what we call the power of solidarity. You are investing in their futures."

Muu had been quiet but then blurted out, "You are a great cook! The golden dessert was delicious."

"Thank you Muu. Is there a 'power' that covers introducing new things to the world?"

Faa said, "Yes! We call it the power of framing. You framed the idea of dessert from something that uses beans, rice, and fruit to one that uses eggs and sugar in a creative presentation."

"This is a Portuguese dish, but it took me a month to convince the head chef to introduce it to the king. He was afraid that the king wouldn't like it, but I described it as a dish that would impress foreign visitors. The king tried it, loved it, and now everyone in the palace wants to eat Foi Thong."

Maria looked up and saw two servant girls approaching quickly. "I must go and dress for dinner. My husband Phaulkon and I will dine with the British. This time I get to sit and eat!" This time I get to sit and eat!"

She smiled at the students and said in a thoughtful voice, "What you are learning about power is important. I see a lot in the palace, and I know that one person can bring a kingdom crashing down and one person can lift it up. Study hard. You never know when you'll be asked to step up and lead."

Maria rushed off to her house on the other side of the palace with her servants trying to keep up.

The students began walking back to the Academy.

Tao said, "I see how Maria uses these different sources of power, but she has authority. Isn't Mongkut teaching us how to lead people without having authority?"

"She has no authority except these sources of power," Faa said. "No one appointed her to run the kitchen. She invited herself into the kitchen and began working. After several months the head chef asked her to lead the lunch staff."

"I think there's a crossover," said Tao, "where power eventually turns into authority because the purpose you pursue eventually joins an institution."

"Yes, but someone can take away the power of authority, but no one can take away the power we are learning," Muu said. "A person with authority in the palace can tell Maria to not come back, but she can lead others someplace else with the power she has already acquired."

They finished their journey in silence, primarily because they were thinking about the diversity of leaders who could exhibit the power of purpose, even in a kitchen.

Answer the reflection questions in the Reflect and Apply section about *Leaders in Your Life*.

32

THE POWER OF
BUILDING THE WHEEL

Sunan noticed that Tao was polishing his emerald instead of eating his breakfast. The stone was almost completely green, but it had a strange shape and its surfaces were scratched. He looked sad.

"Is anything wrong, Tao?" Sunan asked.

"I miss my family," he said without looking up from the stone. "When do you think I can go and visit them?"

Sunan had spoken to Mongkut about this, but he said that completing the training was more important than Tao's homesickness. Sunan had asked about inviting his family to Ayutthaya and Mongkut said that it may be a possibility, but he hadn't mentioned it again.

"Have you read the letters from your village? They are all proud of you."

"Yes," said Tao. "But it's not the same as seeing my family."

Sunan put her hand on Tao's shoulder and said, "Remember what I said about you and this stone?"

"You said it will take effort and time to polish both."

"That's right. But once the stone is polished, then its value will be revealed. The same with you. It may feel like it is taking too long to find your true value, but trust that the work you're doing will reveal it."

Tao relaxed and smiled at Sunan. He knew that he was here for a purpose and that he needed to persevere.

He slid the stone into his shoulder bag and jogged to school through the busy streets and over canals. He was now used to seeing people from different countries. Some wore long hair in knots down their backs. Others wore leg stockings and hats. Many of the white foreigners were tall and loud. The Muslims wore small round hats and the Chinese wore beanies. The French Jesuits wore dark robes that almost touched the ground and a cross on a necklace around their necks. The Buddhist monks wore saffron robes wrapped around their bodies with one shoulder exposed. The Chinese had white skin and the Indians had dark skin. But somehow, all of these groups worked together. Father Tachard had told Tao that Ayutthaya was the most diverse city on earth and only King Narai could orchestrate such a mixture of cultures, religions, and competing interests.

The other students were already kneeling at their desks when Tao quietly removed his shoes and entered the classroom.

Mongkut was sitting at the front of the room talking to a Chinese man who Tao had met a few weeks before. His name was Shen Kuo.

"Now that we are all here," Mongkut said with a corrective glance at Tao, "I want to introduce Shen Kuo. He is a scholar on the teachings of Confucius, Lao Tzu, and the history of the Chinese dynasties. He is also a trader who has brought many of the beautiful bowls, vases, and urns you may have seen in the markets. The

Chinese techniques for making porcelain are highly respected and very secret. In addition to his many talents, Shen Kuo understands the power of authority and the power of purpose. I've asked him to talk to us about the latter."

With this short introduction, Mongkut bowed slightly to Shen Kuo and moved his chair to the side of the room.

Shen Kuo stood and put his hands together in a unique way. The right hand made a fist, the other a flat surface, and then he pressed them together and gave a slight bow. He wore a golden silk robe embroidered with images of red dragons surrounded by many small flowers. A red hat stood high on his head and a long, thin mustache hung down below his chin and matched his short grey beard.

"I am honored to meet such fine students," he said in a loud, staccato voice with a strong Chinese accent. He began pacing with his hands clasped behind him. He would only stop when he wanted to emphasize a point by stomping his right foot and slowly raising his right hand.

"Mongkut asked me to teach you about a power that is highly valued in my country. If you do not know about China, we are ruled by the Qing dynasty and I represent the Kangxi Emperor. He has reigned for many years and provided stability for our people. I also represent the Grand Dowager Empress Xiaozhuang who provides wise counsel to the Kangxi Emperor. By applying her advice, he has made peace with many warring clans."

"I will start my lesson by telling you a story of another Chinese Emperor: Emperor Gaozu who was also known as Liu Bang. He lived almost 2,000 years ago and was born to a poor family in Jiangsu province in the east of China. His family worked in the rice paddies in a small town surrounded by canals, much like the villages not far from Ayutthaya."

Tao, who had been daydreaming of home, felt a shiver of surprise when he heard about a poor boy whose family grew rice. He sat up and took out his paper and pen. He immediately connected with the story of Liu Bang.

"Liu Bang did well on his civil service exam which opened doors for him to work in the provincial government. Some of you may be following the same path!" Shen Kuo exclaimed with a loud laugh.

"He married above his family's position in society and was one of a thousand civil servants who helped Qin Shi Huangdi, the first emperor of China, reign. However, Huangdi's son oppressed the peasants and they revolted. Liu Bang joined with general Xiang Yu to defeat the emperor. Eventually, however, they turned on each other. Xiang Yu oppressed the citizens to get resources for his army and fewer and fewer people followed him. In despair of losing a battle with Liu Bang, the general took his own life and the path opened for Liu Bang to become emperor. He was a wise ruler who insisted that his officials keep everything simple. He lowered taxes on farmers and expanded the empire by putting down revolts around the country."

Chang had stopped his usual doodling when Shen Kuo mentioned war. He raised his hand and asked, "Was Liu Bang a great warrior and general? Is that how he came to power?"

"Ah Chang! You are the son of Phetracha the great General! I would like to tell you that Liu Bang was a great general like your father, but he actually did not like fighting. He wanted peace for the empire. He knew how war devastates the poorest people through taxes, conscription, and the destruction of what little they own."

"Was he highly educated?" Faa asked.

"Unlike you," Shen Kuo said, "he hated reading books and even disrespected his teachers! But he did know one thing: citizens do not want corrupt leaders. His first experience leading others was when he joined some prisoners against a corrupt emperor. This emperor commanded the prisoners to toil in the mud for months to build a useless army made of terracotta clay. The prisoners agreed to follow Liu Bang as their leader."

Shen Kuo stopped, stomped his right foot, and exclaimed, "The real power that Liu Bang had was not military expertise, legal knowledge, nor education from books and teachers. We need to ask the question, 'How did a simple civil servant who grew up harvesting rice become emperor of the Han dynasty which eventually reached into the Persian and Turkish empires?'"

Shen Kuo paused for effect, and then walked to the board and drew a large circle.

"Liu Bang used what I call the *power of building the wheel*."

Shen Kuo began pacing again with his hands firmly clasped behind him.

"After defeating Xiang Yu, many nobles insisted that Liu Bang become emperor. He told them that he was not worthy to be emperor, but they continued to entreat him. He finally agreed if the nobles believed that it was good for the country. He was named Supreme Emperor Gaozu in February 202 BCE. He then assigned kings and nobles to manage different regions, and the armies were disbanded and the soldiers sent home."

"Grand Emperor Gaozu held a banquet in the Southern Palace of Lo-yang, and he invited the most influential people in the empire: poets, philosophers, musicians, and leaders of the military and the provinces. During the banquet he told his nobles and generals to speak candidly and answer a question, 'Why did I win the position of Emperor and Xiang Yu lost?'"

The students were listening to every word and even Mongkut found himself transfixed by the story.

"Two attendees boldly said that Gaozu was arrogant and insulting and that Xiang Yu was kind and loving. But after a battle, Xiang Yu kept all of the rewards and spoils for himself. Gaozu shared the spoils with the victors and even spread them to many others."

"Gaozu agreed, but said that they had missed the most important reason. Do you know?"

Shen Kuo stopped walking and looked at the students, but before they could answer he continued.

"Gaozu pointed to his main advisor Chang Liang and said, 'When it comes to strategy, commanding others, and negotiating treaties, I cannot compare to Chang Liang.' He pointed to Hsiao Ho his logistics chief and said, 'When it comes to organizing the state, making sure people are fed, and managing our supply lines, I cannot compare to Hsiao Ho.' Finally, he gestured to the military leader Han Hsin and said, 'When it comes to leading a million men and winning every battle and attack, I cannot compare to Han Hsin.' He concluded by saying, 'These three are all men of extraordinary ability, and it is because I was able to make use of them that I gained possession of the world. Xiang Yu had his one Fan Tseng, but he did not know how to use him and thus he ended as my prisoner.'"[8] Shen Kuo walked to the board, drew a smaller circle in the center of the larger circle, and then drew five lines – some thick and some thin, some close together and some far apart—from the outside of the circle to the center. He had drawn a wheel.

He regarded his drawing for a moment and then turned to the students and asked, "What makes this wheel strong?"

"The strength of the spokes," said Mot. "Bigger wheels must have stronger spokes."

"Yes, but what if you place the spokes like I have on this drawing? Will this wheel be strong?"

Mot shook his head. "That wheel would collapse or wobble because the spokes are not spaced properly."

"Listen to what Mot said," Shen Kuo said excitedly and stomped his right foot. "A builder of strong wheels must harmonize the spokes with the space in between them. Who was the master craftsman of the Han Empire?"

Shen Kuo let the obvious answer sit in the air as he erased the misplaced spokes and drew spokes that were at an equal distance from each other.

"Using the power of building the wheel, you create a harmonious group in which each person can use their strengths and develop their potential. The power you release will surprise you."

Shen Kuo returned to the board and wrote a short list.

THE POWER OF BUILDING THE WHEEL
1. *Select people with talent and potential*
2. *Create a space for them to do what they do best*
3. *Give them the credit*

"To use the power of building the wheel, first *select* the people who have the talent or the potential to do what you need done. These are the spokes. Selecting your key people is critical for achieving your goal. If you just use whoever is available or those who must be commanded to serve, your wheel will be weak and unbalanced. Look for the natural potential and talent in each person. Do not ask a sailor to drive oxen, and do not ask a merchant to sow seed. Selecting the right spokes takes time and observation, but with practice you will see who has the talent and potential you need to achieve your purpose. Then you use the power of invitation and ask them to join you."

Shen Kuo gestured to the students. "I will tell you a secret." In a loud whisper he said, "You are the spokes that Mongkut selected."

Tao sat back and the students looked at each other. Muu's family was in business. Faa's family was involved in foreign affairs. Chang's father was a general and Mot's family managed the palace. Tao was a farmer who knew the land and rural people.

Mongkut laughed. "Now Shen Kuo, don't reveal all my secrets! I see potential in each of my students and I'm doing my best to develop them to reach that potential."

Shen Kuo continued. "Second, the power of building the wheel requires you to provide *space* for your key people to accomplish their work. Some leaders find this is the most difficult part because they want to control everyone and everything. The power of building the wheel, however, requires space between the spokes and between you and the spokes. Give people freedom to accomplish what they do best."

Faa raised her hand and asked, "Is the leader the middle of the wheel or the outside of the wheel or another spoke?"

"Who is building the wheel?" Shen Kuo asked.

Faa thought for a moment and said, "The wheel maker."

"Correct!" Shen Kuo said.

"Sometimes leading others requires you to be part of the 'wheel', but the leader's task is to harmonize a team for a specific purpose. The leader builds the wheel and supports each part while the wheel fulfills its purpose. This is why the power of building the wheel requires the 'wheel maker' to give others space to accomplish their work."

Shen Kuo checked the first two items on his list and then stroked his thin mustache.

"These two – talent and space – must work together. The great Chinese teacher Lao Tzu describes how the Tao or 'the way' infuses the universe and all that is in it. The Tao – not you Tao – is always flowing like water, filling empty places and pouring out of full places. Talent and potential are like water that naturally flows unless it is blocked. As a leader, you need to create the space and boundaries for someone's talent and potential to flow."

Mot looked up from his notes and said, "Does this mean you just leave people alone? That doesn't sound like leading."

"Lao Tzu would say that a leader is not forcing anyone. Instead, you set up a position where people can go with the grain of their talents. It is easier to cut a piece of wood along the grain rather than against the grain. Imagine if Mongkut required you to write with your non-dominant hand. You would struggle to take notes. But in this class, you 'go with the grain' of your dominant hand and you are successful."

Shen Kuo paused and asked Mongkut for a cup of water as sweat was dripping from his chin. He drank the entire cup quickly, wiped his mouth, and then continued.

"Finally," Shen Kuo said, "you must give each person *credit* for what they've accomplished. Consider that the sun is sharing its light with the trees and in response the trees stretch toward the sun. Emperor Gaozu was not interested in being honored or receiving all of the glory. He shared his vision with these talented people, he helped them accomplish their best work, and then he gave them the credit and honor. They naturally responded with devotion to him and his vision."

Chang spoke up, "Why shouldn't the Emperor keep credit for himself? If he is the leader, then he deserves credit for uniting the empire."

Shen Kuo became quiet, nodded slowly, and again stroked his wispy mustache with his thumb and forefinger.

"Chang, you point out the hardest part of the power of building the wheel. To lead others without authority is to be willing to give all the credit away. Too many leaders can't imagine doing that, so they seek the power of authority to ensure that they always receive the praise and honor. But what difference does receiving credit make if it only satisfies one person's desire for fame while discouraging those who actually did the work?"

He walked over to Mongkut and whispered something to him. Mongkut nodded and asked the students to follow him and Shen Kuo.

The group walked out of the Wat and toward the river.

"Ajarn, where are we going?" Faa asked Mongkut.

"You'll see."

Mongkut and Shen Kuo led the students to the bank of the Chao Phraya river which was flowing quickly toward the south. Its brown water lapped against the stony bank where they stopped.

"Everyone, grab a stone." Shen Kuo ordered

The students picked up rocks of varying sizes. Muu and Chang picked up the largest rocks they could find.

"Now throw them in the river and watch what happens."

The rocks flew varying distances, but all only made small splashes and were quickly buried in the current.

"Do it again!" Shen Kuo shouted.

The students threw rocks into the river for five minutes. Eventually they became tired and covered in sweat. Shen Kuo saw them slowing down and then asked that they stop and sit down under a nearby tree.

"Isn't it tiring trying to make a big splash in a river that doesn't care?" he said. "No matter how big the rock, how far the throw, or how large the splash – where is it now?"

"It's gone under the water," Mot said through labored breathing.

"Yes. It's gone forever and the water will continue to flow over these stones and time will flow over our accomplishments. Receiving credit makes a splash for a moment, and then it is gone. So why seek something so temporary? Didn't you learn this from the power of the open hand?"

He let the students consider the question as they watched the river flow as if nothing had touched its rolling surface.

Shen Kuo then said, "Credit is to be shared, not hoarded. Credit is for nurturing others, not for lifting yourself above others. Credit is not a foundation for leadership. It is a tool for accomplishing things."

He pointed across the river at a large Chinese ship making its way down the river. The boat had two sails that were stretched with wind slowly pushing the boat.

"The power of building the wheel requires you to be the wind in someone *else's* sails. Blowing on your own sail while sitting in the boat only exhausts you and leaves you sitting still. Give away the credit and watch as their motivation returns and fills your sails. They will respond with gratitude and devotion. That is the lesson from Grand Emperor Gaozu."

Tao reflected on this lesson as they walked back. He would

never look at wheels the same again. He was also wondering when they would start using more of these sources of power. Only one source remained, and he was becoming impatient.

———————————————

Answer the reflection questions in the Reflect and Apply section about how you can apply the *Power of Building the Wheel*.

33
MASSACRE IN MERGUI

The king was coughing violently when Phaulkon rushed into the Main Hall and kneeled at his position. It was after four in the morning when a messenger had awoken him and demanded he come to the Main Hall.

Phetracha looked at Phaulkon with disgust, which was not new. Mongkut was talking to Rangsiman, but they stopped and glanced up at the king's red face as he struggled to catch his breath. The king's two brothers, Prince Aphathot and Prince Noi, knelt behind the throne and appeared worried.

A military messenger knelt in the aisle leading up to the dais. The king finally took a deep breath and relaxed. The messenger was breathing heavily and sweat poured off of him and dripped from his bowed head and onto the floor.

The king gathered his strength and sat back on his throne. Phaulkon glanced up and saw that the king's handkerchief was spotted with blood. The chirping of crickets and frogs filled the air as he spoke with a rasping voice.

"I've called you here at this late hour because I have received disturbing news. A massacre of British soldiers and sailors took place in Mergui yesterday. Some of you know that I received a letter from the British East India Company demanding £65,000 three days ago to compensate them for privateering losses."

The king cleared his throat and continued in a weak voice. "We all know that the British East India Company is poorly run and corrupt. They have no claim to this payment. They thought that they could blockade Mergui by anchoring two ships in the harbor. Soon, rumors spread that the soldiers and sailors were going to invade." He took a deep breath and then said, "Messenger, tell your story."

The messenger wai'd the king and sat up so that he could be heard, but kept his eyes on the floor.

"When the heavily armed British frigates arrived, governor Richard Burnaby invited the commander of the company to a meal. He and Captain White tried to persuade the commander that attacking Mergui was only going to harm trade with Siam. The commander loudly disagreed and threatened to fire on Siamese ships. These threats could be heard throughout the house."

"The next morning, the Siamese town and our naval officials feared that the company would take over the town. Instead of consulting with Governor Burnaby or Rangsiman, the Siamese ships opened fire on the warships. In a frenzy of fear, Siamese soldiers and citizens massacred every Englishman they could find. About 60 Englishmen were killed, including Burnaby. White has fled."

Rangsiman was visibly angry that he had not been alerted to these threats. He was also upset that Phaulkon had given Burnaby a position. He was a known pirate who regularly boarded ships that traded with Siam.

Rangsiman looked at Phaulkon and said, "What were Burnaby and White doing?"

"Burnaby's job was to manage trade and protect Siamese interests," Phaulkon said with hesitancy. "The real fight is between the British East India Company and the king. This obviously got out of hand because the commander threatened to fire on the town."

"Your English friends were stealing from the company," said Phetracha with a voice of restrained rage. "You have invited this upon the Siamese people!"

The king now spoke as loudly as he could without triggering another coughing fit. "Phaulkon, what do you recommend we do?"

"Your Majesty, the mission from France is just two days away from Mergui. I understand that they have six ships and 500 troops to secure their investments in Bangkok and Songkla. I recommend that we ask the French to manage Mergui."

Phetracha could not control his anger. He yelled at Phaulkon, "Your English puppets have failed the Siamese, and now you want to give Bangkok to the French? How long must we endure your incompetence?"

"What is *your* recommendation?" the king asked Phetracha.

"I will go and take charge of the situation! I can march 500 troops to Mergui leaving in three hours!"

Rangsiman spoke up. It was not like him to disagree with Phetracha, but in this case he knew that Phetracha was reacting without considering the consequences.

"Great king, I believe Phetracha has good intentions, but we must guard Ayutthaya and Lopburi. If the British East India Company sails up the Chao Phraya, they could attack us. This city of a million people must not be left unprotected, and for that we need our warships to stay here."

Phetracha listened and ground his teeth. He started to argue, but then he relaxed. He now saw his path to power by staying close to the sick king.

Phetracha said, "I agree with Rangsiman. Our forces will protect the heart of our kingdom."

"I agree as well," said the king. "Mongkut, what do you say?"

Mongkut had been listening quietly with his eyes closed.

"Great king, I agree with Phaulkon that we need the strength of the French to deter the British East India Company and force them to negotiate with us. I also agree with Rangsiman that we must prepare a defense of the capital."

The king considered Mongkut's words carefully. With great effort, he leaned forward on his throne.

"I have decided that we will ask the French mission commander to become governor of Mergui. I am also declaring war on the British East India Company until they drop their unfounded demand for £65,000."

The king coughed violently, took a deep breath and continued.

"Phaulkon, you will communicate our invitation to the French commander. Also, contact the French garrison in Bangkok and make sure that they protect the harbor chain that blocks the Chao Phraya river. Also, inform the commander of the Company that we are at war with them until they renegotiate their trade agreement. We will destroy any of their ships that enter our harbors unless they comply. Phetracha, you will implement our defense plans for Ayutthaya and Lopburi. We have six miles of wall to protect. Make sure our cannon crews are on alert as well as the messenger stations leading from Bangkok to Ayutthaya. No firing on ships until all parties understand our position."

The king stopped talking and breathed heavily. He finally said, "I am taking my family to Lopburi. My brothers, sisters, wives and children will travel with me. Phaulkon, Rangsiman, and Phetracha, I want you to come to me in Lopburi next week as I have important matters to discuss with you."

With those words the king dismissed the cabinet who bowed, stood and walked out. Mongkut, however, stayed.

"Great King," he said, "do you need help in Lopburi with organizing your meetings?"

Both the king and Mongkut knew that right now the main concern was who would succeed King Narai in case his health deteriorated.

The king gave half a smile. His two brothers looked surprised.

"My friend, I already have a plan and Rangsiman will come with me. The kingdom is in good hands. I only wish your students were ready to lead us through these challenging times."

He rested for a moment and said, "I have the power of a king, but your students have the power of the people. I hope to see you soon."

Mongkut walked out of the hall and saw Rangsiman whispering with Phetracha in the hallway. Rangsiman was upset. He said, "Even if the king is sick, the succession is up to *him*. It is not up to *you*."

Mongkut joined them and said, "The king will establish his succession plan soon. I hope that *all of us* will honor his wishes." He looked at Phetracha and Rangsiman.

Rangsiman exclaimed, "On my honor and my life I will obey the king's command."

Phetracha sneered and said, "Oh *great* Mongkut. Who am I as a lowly general to question the king's plans? You go along and teach children how to lead. Leave the real leadership to me."

Mongkut stared into Phetracha's eyes and leaned forward into his face. His boldness surprised Phetracha. He had forgotten that Mongkut had also been a senior military leader as a young man.

"You may not realize it," Mongkut said in a strong voice, "but 99-percent of the real leaders in Siam are people without a government title. Merchants, sailors, monks, farmers, teachers, doctors, cooks, cleaners, water carriers, shepherds, and bankers. I appreciate your defense of our kingdom which is critical for our survival. But without these other people who make the kingdom run, you would starve within a week. You need to ask yourself, who is leading whom?"

"Don't lecture me on leadership!" Phetracha fired back with a tremble in his voice. "You are safely hidden if the Lan Na or the Khmer attack!"

Mongkut took a step back.

"I served in the army for eight years while you were still a boy playing with wooden swords in the palace. I have killed my share of Khmer soldiers. I've seen my friends crushed under the feet of elephants and torn apart by cannon balls." He pulled back his right sleeve. Mongkut's arm skin was shredded and scarred from his wrist to his shoulder. He winced as he pulled up his sleeve. Rangsiman drew in his breath and put his hand over his mouth.

"I've experienced the fire of battle while you sit safely on an elephant at the top of a hill. You only see the world through personal victory and honor. I see the world through different kinds of battles – ones with engines of war and ones with engines of peace. I prefer the latter."

Mongkut carefully pulled his sleeve down and turned to walk away, but then stopped and said over his shoulder, "I wonder if the real enemy of Siam is outside our palace walls or inside?"

The sky was orange in the east as Mongkut stepped outside.

Two giant pagodas stood like loyal sentinels silently guarding the palace.

Mongkut saw Maria walking towards the kitchen which reminded him that he had not eaten. He called her name and they walked together across the dew-soaked lawn.

34
THE POWER OF PATIENCE

Tao walked out of the hospital door with Suchart by his side. The soldier had fully recovered and was returning home to Nakhon Ratchasima province after visiting Mongkut.

"Thanks for visiting me," Suchart said. "You've been a healing medicine."

Tao looked down and said, "You've been an uncle to me."

Suchart dropped his sack of belongings to the ground and embraced Tao. Tao was surprised, but hugged Suchart.

"You go to school now," Suchart said. "Come and visit me. I have a big house and some land so you can bring your family."

Tao said that he would visit and started running through the crowded streets toward the Academy. He hadn't seen Mongkut when he woke up and he wanted to find out what had happened last night.

He bounded up the steps to the classroom and stopped when he saw Muu and Faa emptying their desks. Chang and Mot were talking in excited tones by the far wall. Both of them had shaved heads and wore their soldier uniforms.

Muu said, "You need to organize your notes and empty your desk. Today is our last class."

"What?" Tao didn't know how to react.

"Mongkut just told us that after this class we will be going into jobs where we can practice what we've learned."

Chang and Mot joined the others. The students put their notes in order from the first class to the last and stacked them on their desks. Faa and Tao had the most notes. Chang had none.

Chang leaned over to Tao and said, "My dad has scheduled an emergency military exercise and Mot and I are going to Lopburi with the king's family."

"What's going on?"

Chang told him about the Mergui attack on British sailors and how the French would now secure Mergui and Bangkok.

"The British and the French are the ones creating all of the problems," he said. "If I were in charge, I would kick them out of the kingdom, and especially that traitor Phaulkon."

"How do you know Phaulkon is a traitor?" Tao asked.

Chang became guarded as if he had a secret he couldn't reveal, "I just know that he is trying to take over, but my father and I will make sure that Siam will always be ruled by a Siamese king."

Mongkut and a royal messenger walked into the main room and Chang became silent. The messenger took two documents that Mongkut had finished reading and placed them in a brown leather bag hung on his shoulder. He closed the bag, wai'd Mongkut, and ran out of the classroom.

Mongkut called his pupils together. They knelt on their mats and he sat down on a chair facing them.

"We have come to our last class too quickly," he said with a sigh. "Today we will finish by learning about the eighth source of power. But first, let's review. What two types of power have we discussed?"

"The power from authority comes from institutions, and the power from purpose comes from different sources," Mot said.

"The power of purpose usually comes from creating more freedom for others," said Faa.

"Correct," Mongkut said with a satisfied smile.

"We need the power from authority to do many things like manage trade or defend our borders. But you do not need a high position or a title to lead others. You can give yourself the permission to change the world with the power of purpose which has eight sources."

Mongkut stood, walked to the chalkboard, and drew the tree from the first class.

"Let's finish this drawing of our tree with the eight branches which represent the eight sources of power. Remember that the tree represents freedom. It provides a place of rest, protection, and resources for yourself and others."

Mongkut asked the students to recall the seven sources of power. He assigned each source of power to its own branch.

1. The Power of Invitation
2. The Power of the Open Hand
3. The Power of Praxis
4. The Power of Framing
5. The Power of Substitution
6. The Power of Solidarity
7. The Power of Building the Wheel

Mongkut let the students copy down the list. Chang sat staring.

When they finished, Mongkut said, "Before we discuss the last source, go outside and walk around the walls of the Wat. Return and tell me what you see."

The students walked out and started looking around. As they walked by the outer walls, they noticed two short pagodas near the river wall. They noticed flowers growing in sunny spots and the huge pagoda behind the coronation hall. A few young monks had climbed up its northern steps and were talking in its shade.

When they returned, they told Mongkut what they had seen.

"I believe you all mentioned the two short pagodas by the river wall. Today, I will tell you about the creation of Wat Ratchaburana and those two pagodas. The story will explain the importance of the eighth source of power and how critically important acquiring power without authority is for you and Siam."

Mongkut sat down and faced the kneeling students.

"King Intharacha ruled Ayutthaya two hundred and sixty years ago, before Wat Ratchaburana was built. He had three sons who ruled different provinces. Prince Chao Ai Phraya ruled Suphan Buri, prince Chao Yi Phraya ruled San Buri, and the youngest prince Chao Sam Phraya ruled Chai Nat in the north. Chao Ai Phraya and Chao Yi Pryaya competed to replace their father as king. They trained armies and tried to win the favor of their father. Chao Sam Phraya was content ruling Chai Nat and didn't desire the throne. He loved his brothers as the youngest child often does."

"When King Intharacha died, Chao Ai Phraya and Chao Yi Phraya rushed to Ayutthaya with their armies. The prize was the throne of Siam. Their armies fought each other and the city was in turmoil. Eventually the two brothers met on this very spot. The princes charged each other on elephants next to the Pa Than bridge. Dust filled the air and the noise of elephants trumpeting and spears clashing could be heard across the river. Crowds gathered to see who would win this battle to the death. Who would claim all of the authority in Siam?"

Mongkut took a deep breath and continued the story.

"The two brothers lunged at each other with long spears. Brother trying to kill brother for power. Anger and greed drove them on. Suddenly the elephants faced each other and the princes lunged at the same time. Both spears met their mark and the princes fell from their elephants with their throats cut. They died gasping for breath as the power and authority that they wanted slipped through their bloody fingers."

Faa had stopped writing. The students stared at Mongkut whose voice had begun to quiver.

"The youngest prince didn't fight for power, but he was called to Ayutthaya and crowned King Borommaracha II. He mourned the death of his father and his two brothers – all dead within one week. To honor his brothers, he cremated their bodies here and ordered that this ground become a monastery. He ordered that the two pagodas be built to honor his brothers."

Mongkut slowly stood and looked at the students.

"The fight for the power of authority can be deadly, so don't be surprised about the destruction it causes. It is part of human history. But I have taught you a different type of power which you can gain by connecting with others instead of fighting others."

He grabbed the chalk off of the tray and on the eighth branch he wrote *The Power of Patience*.

"The power of patience," Mongkut said, "is knowing when to act and when not to act. When you consider Chao Sam Phraya's actions after the death of the king, what makes him different from his brothers'?"

Tao raised his hand and said, "The two older princes acted immediately to capture the throne, but Chao Sam Phraya didn't get involved. He observed what was happening so that he would know what to do next. He didn't choose sides."

Mongkut nodded and under the branch wrote, *1. Understand before acting.*

"The power of patience requires you to observe and understand the situation before acting. I believe Chao Sam Phraya understood the conflict between his brothers long before his father died. By patient observation and thought, he protected his province and was ready to become king if the opportunity opened itself. He was also in touch with leaders in Ayutthaya during the battle which is why they sent for him after his brothers died."

Mongkut looked at Faa and said, "What else did Chao Sam Phraya do differently?"

"If he was in contact with people in Ayutthaya, then he pre-pared them for whatever was going to happen."

"Yes!" Mongkut wrote *2. Prepare for any outcome* under the branch.

"The power of patience is not the 'power of laziness' or 'the power of inaction.' Chao Sam Phraya prepared for any outcome. He prepared by ruling his province, training his administrators, learning how to fight, and building defenses for Chai Nat. I'm sure he was ready in case one of his brothers tried to attack him. If you can't use the power of praxis in the moment, you can use the power of patience and prepare while you're waiting."

He looked at the students and asked, "Can you prepare for ten years before fulfilling your dream? How about twenty years?

Will you give up if time drags on? Will you lose your passion and your hope?"

The students considered these questions. Ten years was a long time to prepare for something that may never come.

"I've waited 12 years to teach in this academy," Mongkut said with a sigh, "and it has been worth every year preparing for you five students."

Mongkut then looked at Muu and asked, "Why is patience a power? How can the power of patience influence others and lead them to greater freedom? Think of Chao Sam Phraya's eventual position."

Muu thought about the story and how the Siamese made Chao Sam Phraya king after the death of his brothers. He thought of how he honored his brothers and created Wat Ratchaburana instead of honoring himself. He did not build a pagoda to his own greatness.

Muu said, "I think that the power of patience inspires others because the leader is not trying to control everything. Instead, the leader has a vision of what the future can be, but is not forcing others to complete that vision now. In this situation, Chao Sam Phraya honored others and worked with his people instead of honoring himself. Does that make sense?"

Mongkut smiled at Muu and said, "It makes perfect sense and it is a perfect example." He wrote on the board, *3. Encourage your followers.*

"The power of patience requires you to focus on *where* you are leading people. *How* you lead others is also important. Instead of honoring yourself and commanding people, gently encourage them. Especially if you must wait years to achieve your purpose, people may lose hope. Encourage them, work with them, and also find someone who will encourage you!"

"Note that Chao Sam Phraya was *asked* to become king," Mongkut continued. "The people of Siam knew that he did not demand the throne, but instead he peacefully accepted the throne. Also, consider that by honoring his brothers he encouraged their armies and followers to join him."

"Are you sure patience is a source of power?" Chang asked. "If my father were here he would say that it shows weakness to wait for others to die. Why not take over with soldiers?"

Mongkut hid his surprise at Chang's question. He wondered what Phetracha had told his son about the king's succession plan.

Mongkut rephrased Chang's question for the class. "Class, how would you respond to a person who believes that soldiers, guns, and battle elephants would be *the best way* to secure power, especially given the story of the two brothers who did not capture the throne?"

Tao looked directly at Chang and said, "Battles are unpredictable and you may win or lose. The power of patience may be slow but it is always moving. It's like the Chao Phraya river. It constantly flows – sometimes fast and sometimes slow – but it is always moving toward the south. The one who wins the battle may not be able to stop a leader with the power of patience."

Tao looked up at Mongkut who was obviously pleased at his answer.

"Thank you, Tao. The power of patience is not an excuse for inaction Chang, as we learned from the power of praxis and the power of solidarity. But this power is a way for someone without authority to understand the situation, prepare themselves, and encourage people who may start to lose hope."

He looked at the students and said, "You now understand the power of patience, but now we must move on to the conclusion of our lessons."

Mongkut asked the students to rise.

"This is our last class for the next two months. The king requested that I work with him in Lopburi."

Tao looked at Mongkut and didn't know how to respond. Faa clasped her hands and stared forward.

"But don't be sad," Mongkut said in an encouraging voice.

"You now know the eight sources of power, and it is time for you to put them into practice. I am sending Muu and Tao to Bangkok where they will work with city leaders and the French commanders to make sure that what happened in Mergui does not happen in Bangkok. Chang and Mot are going with me and Phetracha to Lopburi."

"What about Faa?" Tao asked.

"My father says that I can't travel without him or my mother," Faa said. "They are going to Lopburi, and I'll start preparing a school in the palace." Tao forced a smile, but deep down he felt sad. He, Muu and Faa were now good friends.

Mongkut gestured for the students to come together. From a light brown teak box, he produced five small red silk bags. The top of each bag was pulled tight with a leather thong. The students bowed their heads as Mongkut placed a bag into their out-stretched palms.

"Well, don't just stand there. Reach in the bag," he said.

Tao reached into the bag and pulled out nine round metal coins. Each coin had a different symbol punched into one side.

Mongkut said, "Each of these coins represents a source of power." He explained which symbol matched the source of power.

The Power of Invitation

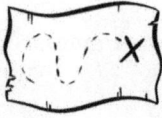

1. Ask someone to join you on a journey.
2. Together, determine:
   - where you are going
   - where you are
   - how to get there

The Power of the Open Hand

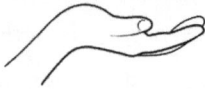

1. Compassion frees us from greed.
2. Generosity frees us from anger.
3. Curiosity frees us from ignorance.

The Power of Praxis

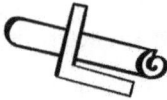

1. Match your knowledge and expertise with the need.
2. Practice in real situations.
3. Multiply the power of praxis through others.

The Power of Framing

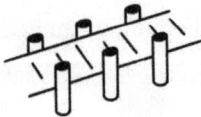

1. Address fears about the change.
2. Describe how the change will create more opportunities.
3. Reinforce the frame by asking others to describe their vision.

The Power of Substitution	1. Substitute ignorance with knowledge. 2. Substitute uncertainty with confidence. 3. Substitute fear with love.
The Power of Solidarity	1. Listen to the stories of others. 2. Invest in the dreams of others. 3. Bind your future to the future of others.
The Power of Building the Wheel	1. Select people with talent and potential. 2. Create a space for them to do what they do best. 3. Give them the credit.
The Power of Patience	1. Understand before acting. 2. Prepare for any outcome. 3. Encourage your followers.
The Purpose	Move toward freedom.

"If you find that you don't know what to do in a situation, reach into the bag and take out a coin. If you pull out the *praxis* coin, go learn something or practice what you know. If you take out the *open hand* coin, ask yourself if you are being curious or are you grasping something that you need to let go. If you take out the *substitution* coin, go substitute something bad in someone's life with something good."

Muu held the ninth coin with a tree symbol. "Ajarn, what does the coin with the tree represent?"

"That is the coin that reminds you of why you are acquiring power. The whole tree represents you as a source of freedom. It should also remind you that you have many sources of power. Avoid focusing on yourself as a lonely trunk. Stretch out your branches and interact with others."

The students thanked Mongkut. They slowly gathered their papers and bound them with leather covers and thongs that Mongkut had provided. Mongkut gathered his papers into a shoulder bag and erased the board. When he finished the faded outline of the tree with eight branches still glowed in the background.

The students said good-bye. Faa and Mot spoke quietly to each other and Muu talked to Mongkut. Tao walked up to Chang and reached into his bag.

"I've done everything I can with this rock," he said and offered the scratched emerald to Chang. "Why don't you take it and see what you can do with it."

Chang shook his shaved head.

"Why are you trying to be a friend to me?"

"I'm...I thought I was your friend."

Chang reluctantly took the emerald from Tao's open hand.

He rotated in his hand and as he examined its green surface his body relaxed.

"I guess I'm your friend too," Chang said quietly. "I don't know why, because I'm not like the rest of you. I'm a soldier who can't get too close to anyone. I have to do things that you'll never have to do."

He held the emerald up to the light. "I hope Mongkut is right about this power thing, because the world I live in thinks it is a waste of time. But when I see how we've turned this river rock into a jewel, it makes me believe that patience and practice could make a difference."

"I believe that too," Tao said.

"I'll take care of your rock until you get back from Bangkok," Chang said and turned to go. He turned at the door and said, "Be careful."

Mot joined Chang at the door and they left. Tao then said good-bye to Faa as she slowly walked down the steps. "I'll see you sometime," she called back.

Tao walked up to Mongkut and Muu and asked, "When do we leave for Bangkok?"

"In two days," Mongkut said. "I think it is best if you and Muu stay out of Ayutthaya for a while."

"Why?" Muu asked.

Mongkut didn't answer. Instead, he put his hands on their shoulders, leaned close to them and in a quiet voice said, "Whatever happens in the next few weeks I want you to remember a universal truth. Someone can have all authority – even over who lives and dies – and still people will not follow them. At the same time, someone else can have no authority and thousands will follow. Let's go."

Tao and Muu didn't know how to respond to Mongkut's mysterious words, but they followed him out of the classroom.

The sky over Ayutthaya was dark and thunder rumbled over the city from the east. Muu walked to his home. Tao put his bound papers in Mongkut's shoulder bag and walked next to him. Rain began to pour down like when Tao was in the rice field so long ago.

Tao and Mongkut rushed home in the rain, laughing and jumping. Tao clutched the red silk bag to his chest as if it were a new heart.

35
TROUBLE IN LOPBURI

The late afternoon heat and humidity was impossible to avoid on the boat to Lopburi. Mongkut sat under a canvas tarp stretched across a wooden frame in the middle of the boat. Each little breeze felt like a cool caress on his face. He hoped that cool weather would greet Tao and Muu in Bangkok.

Mongkut puzzled over the two letters he had received that morning. One letter from Rangsiman was sent a day earlier. He wrote that the king's health was failing, and that King Narai had appointed his daughter Kromluang Yothathep to be his successor to the throne. Phetracha, Phaulkon, and the king's adopted son Mom Pi were to act as regents until she chose a mate from one of the king's closest counsellors.

The second letter was from Phaulkon and arrived shortly after Rangsiman's letter. He said that Phetracha had filled Lopburi with troops and monks who are hostile to foreigners. Phaulkon insisted that Mongkut come and stabilize the succession of Kromluang Yothathep to the throne. He also said that he would personally guide the princess through this difficult transition.

Mongkut evaluated his alliances. While the royal family

trusted him, he knew that Phaulkon would use the family to gain more power for himself. Phaulkon may have a plan to become king by manipulating Mom Pi and Kromluang. Maria had shared this power-seeking aspect of Phaulkon's character with Mongkut, which is why she stayed in Ayutthaya with their son Jorge.

Mongkut also knew that Rangsiman would act in the best interest of the king and the kingdom. Also, Faa's mother Arinya oversaw the royal servants in Lopburi and if a coup occurred, she planned to remove all the servants until peace was restored.

Phetracha would be the aggressor if the king died. He would take the throne for himself. He had personally selected the Lopburi garrison soldiers and could make a powerful move to secure the throne.

Folding the letters and placing them in his bag, Mongkut looked at the approaching dock. He decided to stay close to Rangsiman.

He glanced at Suchart who was polishing a long knife. Mongkut had asked him to be his "private secretary" during the royal transition. Having a respected former military official at his side may keep the parties in line, and also save his life.

"Thanks for accompanying me on this visit. I hope it is uneventful." Suchart slid his knife into a hidden sheath in the small of his back and said, "I hope so too."

As the boat gently slid up to the dock, three sailors jumped out and tied it to the wooden pilings. Mongkut and Suchart climbed out of the boat and walked to the palace. The sun setting in the west cast a yellow glow over the far riverbank.

Rangsiman met them at the palace gate. He gave a strained greeting and then rushed them to his office. He told two of his personal guards to stand outside of the door.

"What's happening?" Mongkut asked. Suchart stood close to the door with his arms crossed.

Rangsiman's face was red with anger. "Phetracha held mock trials this afternoon. He had some of his most loyal generals and a few anti-foreign monks hear the cases against the royal family and Phaulkon. None of the councilors or cabinet were allowed into the hall."

Rangsiman walked away from the door and collapsed on a couch next to Mongkut.

"What is Phetracha's next move?" Mongkut asked calmly.

Rangsiman reached into a pocket and handed Mongkut a piece of paper. Mongkut uncrumpled the paper and saw a list of people found guilty of treason. Mongkut noticed several names he knew from the royal family. His and Rangsiman's names were not on the list.

"We need to talk to the king about this," Mongkut said and stood up.

Rangsiman buried his face in his hands and said, "The king is waiting for you. I wanted to tell you what's happening before you see him. My guards will take you to his bedroom."

Rangsiman stood and embraced Mongkut. "My friend, we need to live to fight another day. I'm leaving for Ayutthaya as soon as I can."

With two knocks, the guards opened the door. Mongkut and Suchart walked down the torch-lit hallways to a door with four royal guards standing in front of it with large spears pointing toward the ceiling. They bowed their heads to Mongkut and one opened the large wooden door.

Suchart walked down the hallway and stood by another door as Mongkut stepped into a dark room. He made out the shape of a large bed with oil lamps at each side. He saw the young prince Mom Pi kneeling on the left side of an elevated bed. His face appeared tired and nervous in the flickering lamp light. Mom Pi was only 15 and had served his adopted father well.

In a whisper, the king said, "You can go son."

Mom Pi looked at Mongkut as if pleading for help, stood, and then disappeared through a side door. Probably a room that was well protected.

The king spoke with a raspy voice.

"Mongkut, I am dying and Phetracha is ignoring my orders. He has his own soldiers ready to take over. What can I do?"

Mongkut knelt down by the bed and his eyes filled with tears.

"Great king, you have led us for many years. You have done all that a human can do. I will do my best to save your son, daughter, and brothers."

The king reached out his shaking hand and Mongkut took it in his.

"My friend," the king said, "you know I took power with a coup myself. I was young and foolish. I thought ruling was about being admired and acquiring whatever I wanted. But you taught me that using power to please myself is hollow and lonely."

He tightened his grip on Mongkut's hand.

"But then I used my power to build a strong and healthy people," he said. "A strong kingdom admired around the world. I'm not empty and lonely at the end ... but I am upset at Phetracha for taking the kingdom for himself."

Mongkut brushed away his tears as the king released his hand. He whispered, "I need to sleep. Take care of Siam while I am gone."

The king stopped talking. Mongkut could hear his breathing

become deeper as if he were asleep. With his head down, he walked backwards to Mom Pi's door.

He knocked gently but there was no response.

Mongkut quickly moved to the door from which he had entered and knocked. The door opened and Suchart pulled him out. "We've got to go!" he whispered and rushed Mongkut back to Rangsiman's office. The door was open but Rangsiman was gone.

Suchart and Mongkut walked quickly through the palace courtyard. They heard men cheering loudly from around a corner. A soldier ran out and said, "The traitors are dead!"

Mongkut pulled away from Suchart and asked the soldier. "Which traitors are dead?"

The soldier thought Mongkut looked important so he said, "Sir! Prince Aphathot and Prince Noi have been executed as well as Mom Pi. We knew they were part of the Makassarese rebellion. Phetracha is now regent."

Suchart grabbed Mongkut by the arm, but Mongkut turned and asked the soldier one more question. "Where is Phaulkon?" The soldier smiled and said, "The Greek traitor was also executed."

Mongkut felt Suchart at his side and allowed himself to be led toward the dock. Outside the palace gate Mongkut could see Rangsiman, Faa, and Arinya in the boat under watch by two of Rangsiman's personal guards.

Turning one last time toward the palace, Mongkut saw Chang watching from a tower in his military uniform. Gesturing to Mongkut with his head, he lifted his sword above his head and yelled, "This is real power!"

Mongkut shook his head and walked on to the boat. The passengers sat in shock as more palace staff rushed to find a seat.

The group rode back to Ayutthaya in silence to await instructions from the new king.

36
WAITING IN BANGKOK

Tao and Muu were tired of waiting. They had waited in the Siamese fort in Bangkok for Mongkut's instructions for a month. No news came from him. They worried for his safety, but kept themselves busy by exploring Bangkok and helping Muu's relatives in the teak business. They also practiced French and English with any trader, sailor, soldier, or merchant they could find.

Johannas Keijts, commander in the Dutch East India Company, ate dinner with Tao and Muu a few nights a week. He told them of the elaborate funeral for King Narai. A royal procession of boats and barges carried the king's body from Lopburi to Ayutthaya. He said the boats were gilded with gold and saffron colored silk tapestries and more flowers than he had ever seen. King Phetracha and Prince Luang Sorasak (Chang) sailed on their own barges to the palace.

Keijts had just returned from Ayutthaya after spending a week working with the new government. When he arrived for dinner on Saturday night, Tao and Muu begged him to share what he learned.

Keijts was tall and had to lean down to eat at their table. As he ate he described how the French were being expelled from all positions of power– except for the doctors and surgeons who were valued by the new royal family and the nobles. He was happy to say that the Dutch had gained favor with King Phetracha. They had sent a few ships up the Chao Phraya to welcome Phetracha to Ayutthaya.

"What's going to happen to the Lopburi palace?" Muu asked.

"Phetracha gave it all away as a sign of his commitment to the common people of Siam. He turned the main buildings over to those who supported his coup. The seminary and school that Phaulkon founded were given to the Chinese officials. Any buildings used by the English and French are now owned by Siamese officials. The king also gave away all property owned by Phaulkon in Ayutthaya. Of course, the French camp in Ayutthaya has been plundered and several French administrators are in prison."

Keijts took another bite, but Tao and Muu didn't feel like eating.

"What of Maria, Phaulkon's wife?" Tao asked.

Keijts looked up from his meal and said, "She was in prison for a while. But I heard that Phetracha likes her cooking, so she is now a slave in the royal kitchen. Given that her husband had conspired with Mom Pi to kill the king, I think she got off easy."

"Phaulkon led a conspiracy?" Tao asked.

Keijts took a drink of whiskey to cool his tongue.

"My sources in Lopburi say that a court official was arrested under suspicion of treason. He had a document outlining a plot by Phaulkon and Mom Pi to kill Prince Noi, Phetracha, and several other officials when King Narai died. Supposedly King Narai saw the document and knew that he couldn't stop Phaulkon's execution. At least that's what I heard."

"So, what's next?" Muu asked. "We know that General Desfarge is waiting for the king to return his sons in exchange for handing over the fortress in Bangkok to the Siamese. Also, Bishop Laneau was released."

Keijts became more guarded with his words. He pushed back from the table, filled his pipe, and struck a match.

After a few puffs he said, "First, remember that I am neutral on the new king and his son. He's being kind to the Dutch because we are neutral. We are not like the French and British who received special favors from Phaulkon."

He looked through the rising pipe smoke and said, "That being said, King Phetracha has banned Europeans from bearing arms. He continues to punish non-Siamese people. Two weeks ago, he took children who have European fathers and Chinese or Siamese mothers and distributed them as slaves in the palace . . ."

Keijts was visibly upset. He pulled harder on his pipe, stood and walked to the window.

He turned and said, "I spent last Thursday convincing the king that these Eurasian kids should be returned to their grieving mothers. The prince and Mongkut agreed with me and eventually the king rescinded his order. But now they are trying to find the kids because they were distributed all around the court. A Dutch surgeon Daniel Brochebourde and Kru Sunan are getting the kids back to their mothers."

Telling about the resolution of the separations seemed to calm Keijts. He came back to the table and sat down.

"Anyway, Phetracha's the king now and is busy establishing his royal credentials. He married Kromluang Yothathep and also one of King Narai's sisters so that he can have some royal legitimacy. He's also cutting the taxes that Phaulkon raised which he hopes will make the people happy. Just another day in Siam."

Keijts finished smoking, tapped out his ashes, and placed the pipe in his side coat pocket. He thanked Tao and Muu for a delicious dinner. As he opened the door he turned, winked at them, and said, "I'm *sure* you'll get your orders soon."

With a slight bow he grabbed his hat off of a chair and walked out. Tao and Muu looked at each other.

"What are we going to do?" Tao asked. "Mongkut didn't teach us anything about what to do when the king dies, the French are expelled, and we are close to civil war. Now Chang is in line to be king and he helped execute Phaulkon and Mom Pi."

Muu shook his head. "Mongkut is probably busy transferring property and responsibilities from Phaulkon's office to the new Chinese Phrakhlang."

In French Tao said, "I didn't know the power of patience would require so much waiting."

A loud knock on the door made them jump.

"Come in," Tao said.

Faa opened the door and said, "Why are you guys hiding in the fort?"

They were speechless. Tao and Muu hadn't seen Faa in a month. Tao finally said, "We're not hiding! We're waiting for instructions from Mongkut."

Faa held out an envelope to Tao and said, "These are our instructions. He said that you are to read them to us when we're all together."

Tao broke the wax seal on the envelope and unfolded the letter. The page was almost completely blank, but in the middle Tao recognized Mongkut's tight handwriting. He had written six words.

"Find people who need more freedom."

37
SEARCHING FOR THOSE WHO NEED MORE FREEDOM

Faa and her family had sailed from Ayutthaya with Keijts and were staying at a house they owned near the main government buildings. Most days her father Rangsiman was busy with his duties as foreign minister. Her mother still communicated with the palace staff.

Faa, Muu and Tao met several times during the next week to determine what Mongkut meant and where they should start. One day Rangsiman sat down with them. He told them of the many military and trade negotiations he had with foreign governments and companies. Everything had changed now that France was no longer in control of the Bangkok fortress.

"Papa," Faa said, "Mongkut said that our assignment is to find people who need support and freedom. Who do you think these people are?"

"Ah, he wants you to start becoming a tree," Rangsiman chuckled. He stopped and thought for a minute. His brow furrowed and he said, "Come with me tomorrow to the main docks. You won't find anyone sitting in this house talking. Also, consider that you may need to split up to match your expertise with the needs of others. What did Mongkut call it? The power of praxis?"

As the sun rose over Bangkok the next day, Rangsiman and his three guests found themselves rocking back and forth in an ox-drawn carriage riding to the docks. He let them out by a saloon and said, "Take a good look around. I'm sure you can find your way home by dinner."

Businesses, restaurants, and trading stalls stretched for miles along the mouth of the Chao Phraya river. Ships flying the flags of different nations rocked next to docks while more ships and barges were anchored further out in the flowing water.

A man's piercing shouts caught their attention. He was speaking English and dragging a young Siamese woman out of the saloon by her hair. He threw her on the ground and she covered her face.

"You agreed to three coins, not five! You weren't even trying!"

He threw three coins on the ground next to the cowering woman and stumbled past Muu.

Faa ran to the woman who was on her knees searching for the coins. Faa helped her stand and asked where she lived. The woman was too scared to answer. She looked at Faa, clutched her and began to weep.

Faa said to Tao and Muu, "I think I'll stay with this woman and find out where she lives. Solidarity, right?"

Two other women ran out of the saloon and started talking to Faa.

Faa waved Tao and Muu away, so they started walking south along the docks. "My father sells teak to a company down here," Muu said. "I remember working there about three years ago. Let's see if we can find their office."

The rising sun's yellow light slowly crept up the front of the buildings. After about thirty minutes Muu said, "This is the place. *Songsaman's Warehouse.*"

The warehouse had two ramps leading from the dock to a large door. A Portuguese ship was tied close to the dock and a bald sailor with a beard watched Tao and Muu as they walked up one of the ramps.

Muu knocked on a small wooden door next to the large door. After a minute, they heard the sound of a wooden cross bar being removed from the door. The door opened and a short Siamese man said, "We are not ready to load yet! Come back in an hour."

As his eyes adjusted to the sunlight he recognized Muu.

"Songsaman! It is me, Muu. How are you doing? Can my friend Tao and I come in?"

The man smiled with teeth colored black from years of chewing tobacco. He grabbed Muu by the hand and said, "Come in! My, you are big and strong! Have you come to work for me?"

Soon hot green tea and stale Chinese pastries were sitting on a beautiful teak table. Muu and Songsaman caught up on each other's lives and Tao talked about growing up on in village that grew rice.

"What is a problem you think people around here need solved?" Muu asked. "Who needs help?"

Songsaman did not hesitate in answering. "Two things. First, all of us merchants must pay someone from each of these foreign companies to negotiate our deals. There is always a middleman who charges us for doing nothing. All he does is say, 'I've got three French ships that want teak. Pay me 10% and I'll arrange the times.' We don't speak their language, so we let them negotiate our prices and schedule our sales. That money could be going to the people who grow and deliver the teak."

Muu said, "My dad complained about these middlemen too. They don't add much value to the transaction and they're always adding extra fees."

Tao could tell that Muu was interested with this problem. After ten minutes of talking about the monopoly these resellers had on the docks, Tao interrupted.

"Sir, what is the second problem? You said that there are two?"

"Yes, but I don't see how you can fix the second one. Never mind."

Tao sat forward and said, "I would like to hear it anyway."

Songsaman glanced at the sun coming in the window and must have realized that he had to start work. He cleared the table and carried the chipped cups and dishes into his small office.

Tao shrugged his shoulders at Muu. Then Songsaman walked back to the table and put a piece of paper in front of Tao. He said, "Solve this!"

Tao read the document which was written in French. It was a loan application for 5,000 Francs at an interest rate of 30%. It was from the Merchants Bank of Siam which Tao had never heard of before.

He looked at Songsaman who was staring at him. "The only loans Siamese in Bangkok can get are from this bank which is run by foreigners. Persians, French, Dutch, British and Portuguese combine their money and then offer to loan us money at a high interest rate. I'm not educated like you two, but I know that this is what the Jesuits call usury. Between the middlemen taking their cut, the government taking its tax, and the high interest rates, how can we ever get ahead? What if we could buy our own boats to take rice to China and bring back pottery? Solve that and you'll free all of us to do more for ourselves."

The men turned as the large door opened with a creak and two Siamese and one Makassarese worker entered and started stacking long teak boards on wooden trollies.

Muu and Tao thanked Songsaman for the tea and said they would be in touch.

They decided to walk back to the saloon and check on Faa. They talked of how Muu could work with businesses to create their own distribution network. They also talked of how Tao could contact Aqu and set up a Siamese bank.

When they arrived at the saloon, it was empty except for two Chinese workers sweeping the floor. They asked where the women were and one of the workers pointed to a back door.

Muu and Tao walked through the door which led to a narrow alley with a wooden walkway. On both sides were curtains, some open and some closed. It was a brothel.

"Faa? Are you here?" Muu said.

Tao turned as three children rushed out of a curtain laughing. He looked past the curtain and saw several young women talking with Faa. Some laughed and others covered their mouths and looked away.

Faa introduced Tao and Muu to the young women. She had already learned their names and where they were from.

"These women want more freedom," she said. "I'm going to help them."

38
MUU DISRUPTS THE TEAK TRADE

The next day, Muu looked at his class notes. They weren't very clear because he often got distracted. He talked to Tao and they selected two powers that he would use to help the local merchants: the power of invitation and the power of praxis.

He would start with the power of invitation. He remembered reviewing Siriporn's plans for the Wat Mahathat school and how the architect met with many people before designing the building. Muu needed to listen to the sellers about where they are and where they want to go. He wrote a draft business plan so that the sellers could react to it.

Muu created a five-point plan to replace the middle-man resellers:

1. Invite the local sellers to a meeting and listen to their problems and goals

2. Set up a company with trained negotiators who would look out for the interests of the farmers and sellers.

3. Create an agreement with the sellers to use his new company for negotiating prices

4. Create an agreement with the farmers to let him negotiate with the sellers.

5. Reach agreements with the foreign shipping companies to use his company.

Looking through his notes, he was reminded that not everyone would accept his invitation. In fact, some may have special deals with the middlemen that they won't break. That was OK with Muu. He would work with those who wanted his help.

Songsaman agreed to use his warehouse as a meeting place. Muu then invited the teak and coconut sellers up and down the docks to a meeting. He told them that the meeting was to discuss negotiating directly with the foreign companies like the British East India Company, the Dutch East India Company, and leave out the resellers."

Some of the sellers looked at Muu suspiciously and asked, "Who are you?"

Muu explained that he and his family were teak farmers and sellers. They had been growing and selling teak for over 30 years. He said that he was working with Songsaman to explore ways to increase the amount of money that stayed with the farmers and the local sellers. Some said they would come to the meeting and others said that they liked their current arrangements.

As Muu left each business he reached into his pocket. He felt the "Praxis" coin and repeated to himself, "Praxis requires knowledge, practice, and it multiplies." He knew the teak business and how to negotiate good deals. Now he needed to invite others who also knew about the value of their products.

At the meeting, only four sellers showed up. Three were teak sellers and one sold coconuts.

Muu welcomed them and then explained the complaints against the resellers. He asked the attendees if these were real problems for them.

The teak sellers agreed that the additional fees were a problem. One young seller – probably the son of a business owner – said that the Bangkok Retail Company was the worst. Everyone nodded.

"Why are they the worst?" Muu asked.

"Because they charge fees for things they don't do. They charge an inspection fee, a negotiation fee, a scheduling fee, and a finder's fee. I'm surprised they don't charge a fee for scratching their butts!"

The men howled with laughter, and all agreed that the fees didn't produce any value.

"Another problem I have," said the young man, "is when they lower the price for so-called damaged wood. We inspect all of our stock and we don't sell damaged wood."

"Yeah! That's always happening," said Songsaman. "It cost me a quarter of my sales last week. And then they don't return the wood because they say they 'destroyed it.'"

The coconut seller was a quiet man whose clothes were worn and whose face was darkened from a life working in the sun. He listened intently and crossed his arms tightly around his chest.

"Do you have any comments, sir?" Muu asked.

"My name is Watana and I sell coconuts for twelve farms. I cannot join this organization at this time because my reseller has agreements with the largest companies. I cannot put my farmers at risk."

He took a deep breath and continued, "However, if you negotiate agreements for selling teak to the European companies, then I will talk to my farmers about letting you negotiate for coconuts."

The meeting adjourned with all agreeing that Muu and Songsaman begin contacting the large teak buying companies.

Muu and Songsaman started the Siamese Trading Company with support from Rangsiman. Over the next three months, Muu scheduled meetings with the companies in the teak supply chain. He believed that focusing on one commodity was the best way to start. The competing resellers didn't take him seriously, but they did tell lies about his background and promised bigger kickbacks to the company buyers. Muu used the power of substitution to replace ignorance with knowledge about how the system actually worked against the farmers and sellers. Also, his confidence in the plan and relationships with the farmers and sellers removed their uncertainty.

Muu decided that he was ready after 30% of the teak sellers agreed to allow him to negotiate with the companies. Also, Muu's older brother came to Bangkok with ten carts of teak and agreed to let Muu negotiate the terms directly with the Dutch East India Company.

The largest reseller sent their best negotiator to Muu's meeting with the Dutch – Samuel White. After the disastrous privateering collapse in Mergui, White had called in favors from his friends in the shipping industry.

White arrived at the meeting and acted like Muu was wasting the time of the adults. He was well dressed, smelled of liquor, and his eyes were ringed with red. While Muu had organized ship manifests, pricing tables, and a list of all available teak (by quality and size) from his members, White had a snuff box and a walking stick. He smirked at Muu and stared out the window for most of the negotiation.

The Dutch buyer was Hans De Vries. He had heard good things about Muu from Keijts. Because of the government dislike of foreigners with a bad reputation like White, he needed to get a good price, make a profit, and work closely with the Siamese.

The negotiations went quickly. White, who had negotiated with De Vries before, said that he represented over 50% of the teak sellers and was ready to sell three ship loads for 5-pence a square foot. Muu shifted in his chair and leaned forward. He knew that White had agreed to 1.5-pence a square foot with the farmers and sellers. His cut would be huge.

De Vries made some notes on a small piece of paper and then turned to Muu.

"What is your sales price?" he asked.

Muu had practiced negotiating with Tao and his brother for three days, but this was different.

"We are offering to sell at different prices based on your demands," he said confidently. "If I may, please let me show you a table of how much teak we have. Note that I have graded the teak by quality. The best teak for floors and furniture, we will sell for 5-pence a square foot, and then 4-pence for teak for other building projects and crafts. We don't deliver poor quality teak."

White and De Vries glanced at each other. White cleared his throat and readjusted his chair to face the table.

"Based on your orders last year and discussions I've had with other buyers," Muu continued, "I estimate that an overall price of 4-pence a square foot would meet your needs and the needs of my suppliers."

De Vries studied the price list carefully. He then looked up at White who appeared to be trying to wake up from a deep sleep. He moved his mouth and only mumbling came out. He finally said, "Four and a half pence per square foot, and like our last order, you will receive appropriate compensation."

Now Muu felt afraid. He didn't want to pay a bribe. If he went along with the practices of the big resellers, they could always pay a larger bribe than he could.

"Consider the cost savings you realize by buying at 4-pence," Muu interjected. "Also, because our quality is clearly identified we are saving you time and waste. Finally, you can charge more for the best teak in the Netherlands. The compensation I offer is an additional .5-pence per square foot when you arrive in Amsterdam."

This was his best offer thanks to inside information from Keijts. De Vries wrote a few more notes on his small piece of paper and excused himself. He walked out and took Muu's list with him.

White's face was red. He was either angry, needing another drink, or both.

"Listen 'Sir Siam,'" he growled, "I negotiate teak and the big companies buy from me. Stay out of my way."

"Sir, I know that you worked for Phaulkon and your incompetence and piracy indirectly led to the Mergui massacre and the death of your friend Burnaby. Given that King Phetracha is a sworn enemy of Phaulkon's friends, I think making threats against the Siamese is an unwise negotiating tactic."

White's face went slack, and he seemed unable to breath. He finally looked away and leaned his forehead on his walking stick.

De Vries opened the door and White sat up and tried to smile. Muu's heart was pounding so hard he wasn't sure what to do with his hands, so he left them in his lap.

De Vries sat down and pushed a pile of papers to Muu.

"We are going to buy the amounts indicated from the Siamese Trading Company at an average of 3.8 pence a square foot."

Muu looked at the numbers and agreed with the price. He asked to be able to review and complete the forms by sunset and De Vries agreed.

De Vries looked into the face of a shocked White.

"Thank you, Mr. White. Perhaps in three months you will offer a better price and quality than your Siamese competitor."

Over the next ten years, the Siamese Trading Company continued to win contracts. The organization reduced costs and increased profits for farmers and dock sellers. Muu eventually negotiated almost all agricultural sales with European companies in Bangkok and Ayutthaya. He hired and trained five additional negotiators and buyers including Rangsiman when he retired from the government.

39
FAA RESCUES SEX WORKERS

"Get out! You're driving away my customers!"

The woman who operated the brothel Faa visited two weeks ago yelled at Faa. She flailed her arms as if shooing away a stray dog. She was in her mid-50's, her hair had already turned grey and she had it tied up on top of her head. She wore thick make-up.

Faa stood her ground at the entrance of the alley brothel. "I would like to talk to you, ma'am," said Faa and she took three steps toward the woman. "I just want to talk to you about helping your business."

The woman stepped in front of Faa, placed her hands on her hips, and examined her body from toe to head.

"Why would a skinny rich girl like you want to service sailors all night long? Why don't you go find a husband?"

"I don't want to become a prostitute," Faa said sternly. "I want to teach your girls other professions. I want to teach them how to read and make things."

The woman now became angry. She stepped forward and shoved Faa onto the ground.

"My husband and I own these girls! You want to take them from us and leave us to starve? Get out!"

Faa stood up, brushed off her clothes and then relaxed. Behind the woman Faa saw the faces of young women peering out from behind curtains along the alley.

"I live in an apartment across the street," Faa said loudly for all to hear. "If anyone wants to come and see me during the day they can. I will have lunch everyday which will save you money!"

The mention of money caught the woman's attention. Faa could see her thinking about the financial savings of not having to provide lunch for 15 women.

"My girls can go to your place for lunch, but they must be back here by 4:00."

"I knew we could come to an agreement. Feel free to come to lunch yourself."

The woman smirked and spat on the ground. She walked back to her room at the end of the alley.

Faa stood alone in the alley. She heard quiet whispering and continued to stand in silence.

Eventually their uncertainty was substituted with Faa's steadfast confidence and courage. A woman who was a little older than Faa walked forward with three younger women hiding behind her.

She bowed to Faa and said, "Thank you for inviting us to lunch. My name is Watchara and I have lived here for three years."

Watchara then leaned in and whispered, "Watch out for the owner's husband. I've seen him beat people unconscious. I'll bring the girls for lunch, but not all of them at once."

Faa nodded and told Watchara where the apartment was located. "It's on the second floor above the laundry. I'll hang a blue scarf out of the window when I'm ready."

Faa returned to the apartment that she had rented a week earlier. On the back porch she started boiling rice and grilling fish over a fire.

Faa was thankful that Sunan had come to Bangkok the week before when she heard what "tree" Faa was going to grow. Sunan bought the food so that Faa could focus on what she would teach the girls.

When discussing Faa's plans, Sunan shared that her older brother had refused to let Sunan be placed in a brothel. Her brother took her to Ayutthaya where she worked for a wealthy Portuguese trader whose wife was Siamese. Sunan learned to read, write, cook and sew. Mongkut saw her at a trade dinner and sought her family's permission to marry. Sunan held Faa's hand tightly and in a resolute voice said, "Go get those girls."

Faa set a covered bowl of rice and a plate of fish on a table that Muu and Tao had built. She then hung a blue scarf out of the front window.

She sat and waited. Would anyone come? Was this a good idea?

She reached into her apron pocket and pulled out three of the coins that Mongkut had provided. She placed them on the table and then recited to herself what each one required.

"*Solidarity* is listening, investing in the dreams of these girls and binding my future to theirs. *Framing* their future requires addressing their fears and describing a new future that is safe. I am *substituting* the ignorant lies they've been told about their worth with the knowledge of their value. I am substituting their fear with love."

A gentle knock at the door brought a smile to Faa's face. She gathered the coins, dropped them in her apron pocket, and opened the door.

Watchara brought four girls that afternoon and four different ones each day. The girls were all 14 to 18 years old. They laughed and talked. Faa listened and asked questions. The girls didn't hesitate to tell stories of growing up on farms or in the slums of Bangkok. They didn't talk much about the brothel.

Faa wrote the name of each girl on a piece of paper along with a goal they had for the future. She tacked them to the back of a closet door and kept the door closed in case the brothel owners showed up, which they did twice. However, they eventually stopped checking on the apartment.

After a month, all 15 girls came to Faa's apartment for lunch. Sometimes children of the older girls sat on Faa's lap and leaned against her. When Sunan was in Bangkok, she taught them how to repair clothes and gave each of them a sewing kit.

In the second month, one of the girls, Achara, was killed by a drunken sailor. The owner beat the man and demanded that he pay for the woman. Faa realized that the girls needed to move if they ever wanted to be free.

Faa worked with Watchara and two of the older girls to develop an escape plan. Faa addressed their fears of the violent owners by focusing them on how they could escape to the Nakhon Ratchasima province in the north. She framed a future of going to school and learning a trade that would serve the nobles in the province. They agreed, but were still unsure and cautious.

The next lunch when all the girls were present, Faa opened the closet door and explained how they must start now to achieve their dreams. She pointed to each name and each goal. Finally, she pulled off Achara's piece of paper and said, "She wanted to return to her home near Lopburi."

The room became silent. A few girls wiped tears from their eyes.

After they left, Faa heard a hard knock on the door. She was not thinking and unlocked the door.

In stepped a soldier with a sword and armor. Faa jumped back shocked. But after a few seconds she recognized the smiling face of Mot.

"Mongkut asked me to help you," he said. They embraced each other.

That night Mot, Muu, Tao and Faa ate at her parent's house. Mot explained that Chang had become more and more unstable because of drinking. King Phetracha had enemies from the different provinces who were trying to overthrow him. Ayutthaya was always on a war footing.

"I'm sure you've heard that a friend of King Narai's brother Thammathian almost overthrew Phetracha. Also, the governors of Nakhon Ratchasima province and Nakhon Si Thammarat province don't recognize Phetracha as king. They refuse to follow his edicts."

"Why did you come now?" Tao asked.

"I thought working with Phetracha and Chang would be a great way to serve Siam. But now I see that Phetracha just wants to stay in power. The army is afraid of their unpredictable plans. If a general loses a battle, he is executed. Several soldiers have returned to their provinces and refused to return to Ayutthaya. If it weren't for paying soldiers more money, many more would leave. But the money comes from higher taxes, which upsets the people in Ayutthaya. I'm reconsidering how I can serve Siam."

"The power of building the wheel!" Muu said. "I knew you would come if we created a space for you!"

The four laughed.

After dinner they outlined their plan for taking the girls to a safe place. Faa explained that the girls were fully committed to a new future in Nakhon Ratchasima.

Two weeks later the girls arrived in Faa's apartment. Mot was dressed as a sailor and stood on the sidewalk.

They ate quickly and then went out the back door. Faa led them through dark alleys until they emerged on a street next to a large boat. Muu was stationed across the street. He saw Faa and walked into the street and looked both ways. He didn't see the brothel owners, so he took off his hat as a sign that it was safe.

Faa sent pairs of girls across the street so as not to create a scene.

Tao lifted a large piece of canvas that covered the front of the boat. He had them sit in the bottom of the boat under the canvas. They didn't say anything. He could see the excitement in their eyes as they huddled closely together.

"This is what freedom looks like," he thought.

Watchara was the last one to cross the street with Faa. Watchara was trembling and stopped in the middle of the street. Faa turned and said, "Come on. We're almost there."

"I can't! They'll find us and kill us!"

Faa rushed to her side and gently pulled her to the boat and helped her climb under the canvas. Watchara's hands were shaking and she was weeping.

She finally looked up from tear-soaked eyes and said, "No one has ever cared about me. Why are you doing this?"

"Because you need to know the truth. You are a leader. Look!"

Faa pointed to the 13 young women and three children huddled together under the canvas. "You led them here. You need to lead them to the end. You can come back if you want."

"We've got to go!" Muu shouted as he jumped into the boat. "The owner's husband is waiting in front of the apartment and yelling! Someone started a fire in the brothel!"

Watchara wiped her eyes and stared at the girls. A slender girl holding her son looked around at the shocked faces and said, "We're never coming back!"

Two sailors who worked for Muu's trading company untied the boat from the pier and began rowing the boat out toward the mouth of the Chao Phraya river. Mot sat next to Faa while Muu and Tao helped guide the boat into the harbor.

When the boat was a few miles from the pier, Faa lifted the canvas. The girls sat up and looked toward Bangkok. They saw giant ships and barges resting in the harbor. They also saw a thin stream of black smoke rising to the sky and gently blowing out to sea.

Faa rescued 233 girls during Phetracha's reign. Almost all of them learned a skill and were quickly employed by wealthy families or local businesses. Some returned home and some older girls missed the income and excitement of Bangkok and went back. Watchara became the leader of Faa's rescue operation while Faa and Mot developed a school.

40
TAO RETURNS HOME

Tao struggled to find a group of people who needed the "tree" that he could become. During his first year in Bangkok, he helped Muu set up his business. While Muu negotiated with merchants, Tao traveled to farms and lumber operations. He explained how using Muu's organization would benefit the people in the country. Most of them seemed amused by the idea of working with a Siamese dealer until Tao explained the financial benefit of receiving more of the selling price.

Muu and Tao created a simple contract for village leaders to sign which gave Muu's company priority in negotiating the sale of their wood. The contract also established quality criteria and required the farmers to replant trees.

But Tao was not passionate about negotiating lumber contracts. After a year, Tao visited Faa's school and talked to her about his future. They sat under a tree while girls practiced sewing in a pavilion that Mot had built.

"I don't know what I should do," he said. "It seemed so easy for you and Muu to find people who needed your help. You've empowered a lot of people. I'm sort of lost."

"You've helped both of us get started," she said. "You are a strong spoke in our wheels."

They laughed because the reference was silly, but they knew it was true.

"I think you need to go home for a while," Faa said. "Visit your parents and your sister. Take some time to observe the world and to hear your own voice. You're smart and quick to serve others. But if you are always rushing to serve others, you won't have the space to see a need that requires your specific talents."

Faa reached into Tao's shoulder bag and pulled out his red bag of coins. She searched through the bag until she found what she was looking for. She handed Tao the power of patience coin.

Tao sat and looked at the picture on the coin.

"Understand, prepare, and encourage. I'll go back home tomorrow," he said.

In the morning Tao started the five-day journey. Mot, who was now the all-purpose school handyman and security guard, gave him some food and water for his trip.

As Tao walked through villages and open fields, he tried to understand his surroundings. He watched kids swimming in creeks. He saw water buffalo pulling plows for farmers. He ate at small huts with workers, soldiers, and craftsmen. Loud people, quiet people, stray dogs, and shaven monks crossed his path each day. He saw everyone exchanging something for something else. Eggs for rice. A plowed field for two goats. Gold pieces for fine silk. A story for a drink of water.

He began to relax. He didn't need to solve everyone's problems. He needed to be who he was at this time and in this place. But who was that?

Tao walked into his village at dusk. The rice plants waved

gently in a breeze and the quiet of the village surprised him. He went to his house and no one was there except a couple chickens and the water buffalo.

He walked toward the temple and saw everyone kneeling on mats around the main building. Tao walked up to the group. Several people turned their heads, nodded, and then turned back to the front where five monks were chanting and holding incense sticks.

Tao felt a pull on his hand and saw his sister smiling at him. He picked her up and noticed that she was heavier than he remembered.

"What's happening?" he whispered.

"Your teacher Phra Somdej died three days ago. Today we are saying good-bye."

Tao felt a hand on his neck and turned to see his mother with tears in her eyes. She embraced him and his father joined them in a silent celebration.

After the ceremony, six men carried Phra Somdej's body wrapped in white linen to a funeral pyre next to the river. The villagers stood back as the flames took their beloved teacher away.

"That man was my tree for support and comfort," Tao thought as he watched the sparks fly into the night sky. "He was in solidarity with me and invested in my future. He invited me to become more than a rice farmer."

During the next two weeks Tao enjoyed playing with his sister, talking into the night with his parents, and helping around the village. It was harvest time and he joined the villagers in the rice paddies. Ayutthaya seemed like a strange dream. He wrote Mongkut and asked if he and Sunan were well. He explained that he was still searching for those who needed more freedom. He wrote in French to show him that he had not forgotten his lessons.

No ideas for a project came to Tao. The people in his village were as free as birds. Poor, but happy and free.

One-night Tao was staring up at the stars while his father smoked and his mother repaired one of Nu's shirts.

"You should go back to Ayutthaya or Bangkok," his mother said. "Your teacher Mongkut invested so much in you, and we are doing fine here. But we hear of big changes outside of our village. We hear stories about the new king attacking other provinces. We hear of large foreign ships with guns sailing up and down the Chao Phraya river."

"If a power struggle happens, we will all be pulled into it," his father said. "We need to sell our rice for a certain price, or we can't survive." The end of his pipe glowed orange and he blew a blue cloud of smoke into the darkness.

"If you have a role to play on the bigger stage, you need to play it."

Tao nodded and thanked them for their advice.

After the rice was dried, threshed, and placed into large cloth sacks, Tao offered to deliver the sacks to the barges on the Chao Phraya with five others. He said good-bye to his parents and Nu. Just as he did almost two years earlier, he watched with mixed emotions as those he loved disappeared around the corner in the road.

For two days the five men walked their carts full of rice toward the trader's market on the Chao Phraya. Two of them carried spears and they all had knives for protection. When they arrived, Tao helped unload the rice sacks onto a large scale and then onto a barge destined for the markets in Ayutthaya. Two government officials weighed the bags and handed the men a piece of paper for them to present at the government office for payment.

Tao walked with the village leader to the office to receive payment. While waiting in line, he heard a familiar voice say, "Tao. Would you like to work for me?" He turned and saw Aqu standing in the corner.

41
TAO AND AQU
START A BUSINESS

Tao said good-bye to the villagers and went with Aqu to a cafe for steamed rice and stew.

"Mongkut said you were coming back to Ayutthaya after delivering rice," Aqu said, "so I waited here to intercept you. Ayutthaya isn't a safe place for my family right now. King Phetracha and Prince Sorasak are unpredictable. Phetracha says that he wants Siamese in positions of power, but he actually means Chinese officials. In fact, a Chinese official is now Phrakhlang since Phaulkon . . . well you know what happened."

Tao shook his head in disbelief. He couldn't believe that Chang had turned so quickly to violence, but then he recalled their last conversation and Chang's insistence that he had to do things that Tao could not do.

"What are you working on?" Tao asked.

"I am expanding my power of solidarity to support small business owners with financing. I still have connections with senior Siamese leaders as well as French and Persian investors who have lived here for decades. They don't want King Phetracha and the Chinese to monopolize all business and trade. They want to empower people at the ground level. These are people that Ayutthaya ignores."

"You mean like the support you gave to Ahmed Muhammed with his cows?" Tao asked.

"Exactly like that!" Aqu was excited that Tao had remembered.

"I like your idea, but I don't see how I can help. What would I do?" Tao asked.

"I need you to do what Mongkut trained you to do – to jump on an invitation and start something new that many people need. You read and speak French. You know math and trading. You make friends easily, work hard, and you have all the skills we need to change the lives of some very poor and talented people. I will teach you how to finance small businesses."

Tao didn't know if this was the right path. His doubts began to rise up, but then he glanced down at the silk coin bag attached to his belt. He reached in and pulled out a coin and set it on the table.

Aqu glanced at the coin with the picture of an open hand and continued eating.

But Tao stared at it and asked himself, "What am I grasping? What won't I let go?" A voice inside him said that he was grasping his limitations and his fears. He needed to practice compassion and generosity, and Aqu was opening a door. Like Buddha, he had to leave the safety of the bodhi tree.

Tao opened both of his hands under the table and shook them as if he were shaking invisible shackles from his wrists. No more fear. No more holding on to his doubts.

He placed the coin back in the bag and began eating.

"While walking back to my village," he said, "I noticed people exchanging goods, money, skills, animals, land – everything! The

Siamese are born to exchange and that is why Ayutthaya is one of the greatest trade centers in the world. I want to help these people."

Aqu stared at Tao in amazement. Then he leaned across the table and said, "Come to my office in Bangkok and we'll create our plan."

Aqu and Tao secured passage on a Portuguese ship traveling to Bangkok via Ayutthaya. They sat on two stools late into the night and leaned on a barrel that sat between them like a table. An oil lamp cast an orange flickering light on their faces. Aqu explained the business model that he was proposing.

"In the government, power is measured by how many people you can call on to work for you. This power comes from the top and is based on owning land, storing wealth, trading with ships, and having a big supply of rifles and cannons. If the Khmer attack, the provincial leaders call in their men to fight, not only for Siam, but for their own land."

"But you and I are going to spread out power at the bottom – the people who don't own much. We will lend money to common people who want to grow their businesses, but are ignored by banks and other lenders."

"Why are these people ignored?"

Because they can't pay high interest payments. For example, a person in Bangkok – let's call him Abdula – may own one oxcart to deliver vegetables to market, but he could use two to grow his business. If he wants a loan to buy the second oxcart, most Bangkok lenders won't even have a meeting with him. Those who do see him will charge him so much interest that he won't be able to pay back the loan. Abdula is stuck even though he is making money."

Aqu moved the lamp over and pulled five silver coins from his pocket and placed them in front of Tao.

"These five coins represent Abdula's monthly profit. Imagine that Abdula takes out a loan of 100 coins for his oxcart. With the cart he earns another five coins."

Aqu placed another five coins in the pile and continued as Tao watched.

"If a bank will even talk to Abdula about a loan, it will charge him three coins – 30% interest – for a loan every month and three coins to pay off the loan."

Aqu moved six of the coins away from the pile. "This means that the bank is taking his profits just because he needed to buy an oxcart. I don't believe taking interest from Abdula is fair because the lender isn't doing anything to grow his business."

"Our business will be based on the principle that we do not charge interest. Many Muslims and Christians subscribe to this way of lending because it protects the borrowers from becoming poorer while the wealthy get richer from interest."

Aqu moved the six coins back into the pile in front of Tao.

"Now imagine Abdula comes to us and wants to buy the second oxcart. Instead of *loaning* him 100 coins and charging interest, we *buy* the oxcart for him for 100 coins. Now we are business partners and Abdula is earning ten coins each month with the new oxcart. He agrees to pay us two coins a month to buy the oxcart from us, and we receive three coins in profit from our oxcart. What does this mean for us?"

As Aqu spoke he removed two coins from the pile for buying the ox-cart and then three more for the shared profit.

Tao looked at the five coins Aqu moved and thought about the problem. "Abdula will pay us back, but without interest?"

"Yes," Aqu said and pointed to the two coins.

"And we are going to share in the profits of his business since we are partners?"

"Yes," Aqu said and pointed to the three coins.

"So . . . he will repay us on a schedule, and we will take some of his profits since we are his partners. If he makes no profits, then we don't get anything. After, we are paid back we can continue or dissolve the partnership."

"Exactly!" Aqu exclaimed. "Abdula gets his oxcart, we are paid as a partner, and the risk in his business is shared by him *and* us. This means that we will help him succeed instead of sitting back and demanding interest. We will be in solidarity with him – his dreams become our dreams! His risks become our risks!"

Tao now saw the business plan clearly.

Aqu gathered the silver coins and placed them back in his pocket. "We have three rules for lending money. First, we will only invest in businesses that don't harm others or take advantage of the poor. Second, we will avoid big risks by interviewing potential borrowers and determining that they would be good partners for us. Finally, we will not charge interest. Instead, we are taking a stake in the business. The new oxcart is partly ours – for better or worse – until the debt is paid. We are partners, not lenders."

The next day they arrived in Ayutthaya and stayed two weeks with Mongkut and Sunan. Even though Aqu's wife Duangka-mol was Siamese, she had moved to Bangkok with one of her daughters to avoid King Phetracha's unpredictable behavior. Aqu's oldest daughter Yasmin was living with Mongkut and Sunan and attending the re-opened Siam Leadership Academy.

One night over dinner Mongkut explained that King Phetra-cha had given permission to reopen the Academy with a new group of students. Shen Kuo and Phra Vimutti had lobbied the king strongly. Using the power of framing, they explained that just as the Chinese, British, and Buddhists have schools to prepare future leaders, Siam needed the leadership academy to prepare Siam's next generation of leaders. The story they presented reduced the king's fears.

Mongkut said, "Because King Phetracha and Chang are always on alert for rebellions and battles with the provinces, they leave me alone. We have nine students who have just learned the power of building the wheel. Right Yasmin?"

Yasmin nodded to Mongkut and said, "Yes Ajarn. And I hope to learn how Tao is using his lessons." She looked at Tao. He felt a jolt of excitement as she stared into his eyes and then he turned away.

The next morning, Yasmin and Tao walked around Ayutthaya and ate breakfast at a neighborhood food stand. She told Tao that Mongkut encouraged the students to look for people who desire more freedom and talk to them.

"Who are you attracted to?" Tao asked. Yasmin looked down and then up at Tao with a shy smile. Tao suddenly realized what he had asked could be taken two ways.

"I mean, uh, whose lack of freedom attracts you? What cause is calling to you?"

Yasmin laughed and said, "I am attracted to children who need good teachers. I receive an education because my family is respected and wealthy. I think any child who wants to learn should have the opportunity." She paused. "And I am attracted to your adventurous spirit."

Tao took a deep breath and said, "I have to be adventurous

because I don't know who I want to serve. But your dad has a vision that I can follow, so I'll follow that vision for now."

He dipped his pineapple into some salt and Yasmin did as well.

"I am attracted to talking with you," Tao said earnestly. "Would you like to go to breakfast tomorrow?"

Yasmin said yes. With Aqu's permission, they went out for breakfast and long morning walks every day over the next two weeks.

In the afternoons, Aqu and Tao met with Persian and Siamese investors who signed documents agreeing to Aqu's business plan. Tao took notes, edited the contracts, and memorized the financial terms used by Aqu. Yasmin went back to the Academy in the afternoons and also continued her Chinese language lessons.

The days flew by and Tao wished they would not end, but eventually Aqu said they were booked on a ship to Bangkok.

On the last day in Ayutthaya, Mongkut pulled Tao aside and said, "I'm proud that you are working with Aqu. He'll teach you how finance works, and you can empower people to improve their lives."

"I'm sorry that I didn't create some organization like Muu or Faa," Tao said apologetically.

Mongkut put his arm around Tao's shoulders and walked him into the backyard.

"Do you see that orange tree and that lemon tree? Do you think the orange tree feels inferior because it isn't a lemon tree? Or that the lemon tree envies the orange tree?"

Tao chuckled as the lesson hit him. "No."

Mongkut laughed as well. "Neither do I. I'm glad I have

oranges *and* lemons. It makes life more vibrant when we have variety."

He then became serious and looked Tao in the eyes with a kind but corrective stare. "And self-pity doesn't fit you. It will take your strength. Remember the power of substitution and replace fear with love. Love the people you serve, and you won't feel inadequate." Tao stood a little taller and said, "Yes Ajarn."

Yasmin, Sunan and Mongkut took Aqu and Tao to the ship the next day. Tao kept looking back at Yasmin who stood on the dock waving until the ship passed from sight.

Upon arriving in Bangkok, Aqu rented an office near the main fish market and Tao turned the upstairs into a small apartment. Later in the week, workers arrived and installed a black, steel safe in the upstairs closet. After they left, Aqu and Tao installed a thick wooden door to the closet and attached a padlock and reinforced hinges. After locking the padlock Aqu turned to Tao and said, "*Never* risk your life for this money. If it is meant to go, then let it go."

The first investments they made were with some of Muu's tree farmers. One needed a water buffalo and another needed three new saws. While the farmers were suspicious of a Persian who spoke Siamese, they felt comfortable with Tao. The partnership loans were small and had to be paid back within six months.

Eventually, Tao and Aqu set up a table in the market on Tuesdays and Thursdays. They turned down about half of the requests because they were for risky businesses, gambling, liquor, or ideas that had not been tested. Many of the approved partnership loans went to small business owners who needed to buy more inventory or expand their existing operations.

Tao also offered financing to women business owners. Several women used the money to buy materials for tailoring, sail repair, fishing net repair, and other businesses which could be done at home. Aqu was not sure about this market, but when the women paid back the loans faster than the men, he knew that Tao had found a new way to spread wealth.

Tao was responsible for updating a large book with each transaction and the payment schedules. Aqu made a trip to Ayut-thaya every three months on a private boat with two trusted guards. He returned profits to his investors and reported on the businesses. When Aqu was gone, Tao closed the office and spent time traveling with Muu or visiting Faa and Mot, who had gotten married.

After the first year of steady profits and 98.9% repayment of their partnership loans, Aqu received a letter saying that his three biggest investors were coming to Bangkok. He and Tao reserved a suite in a French hotel. On the first night, the investors sat at a large table with Tao and Aqu in the hotel. A crystal chandelier lit the room as they enjoyed drinks before dinner.

One of the investors was a Persian merchant who previously traded in rugs and spices, but now enjoyed reading and studying astronomy. The second was a Siamese businessman whose family specialized in selling Chinese pottery in Siam and the Khmer kingdoms. He and his wife had been unofficial message carriers between King Narai and the Khmer royal family. The third investor was a Frenchman who built houses in the different foreign camps using Siamese labor. Tao watched as Aqu praised them for their wise investing, their efforts to uplift small business owners, and their skill in sharing what they had learned with others.

Tao thought of the power of building the wheel. Aqu had selected people who were experts in trade, politics, and building. They each had achieved some wealth, and now Aqu was giving them the space to achieve something that was even greater – uplifting others. Aqu then gave them the credit for the success even though he and Tao did all the work. Aqu, like a master craftsman, had balanced the wheel and rolled it into the lives of people who needed a small investment. The result was more freedom as Mongkut predicted.

Tao felt like he was watching Liu Bang surrounded by his team.

The investors enjoyed talking with Tao and quizzing him about the different businesses he had approved. The next day they toured the little office and met with five people who had received and paid back their partnership loans.

One older woman with fat cheeks, few teeth, and gleaming eyes excitedly explained that she used her loan to employ five women who repaired fishing nets at her house. "My husband is away on the Portuguese barges," she said, "and I don't like to sit around. Thanks to your support, I now earn about as much as him." She then laughed loudly and said, "He may become *my* employee next year." The investors laughed loudly until tears came to their eyes. Tao marveled that these wealthy men had never distanced themselves from regular people. They had practiced the power of solidarity and it had served them well.

Tao and Aqu continued to operate their business and never strayed from their core principles. The profit they made was not huge, but Aqu explained that the purpose of the business was not to take as much as they could. They would always balance giving as much as they could while making enough to grow their investments. Aqu's way of doing business reminded Tao of a lesson on justice that his French tutor gave between lessons and eating fresh bread. He said that the Greeks believed that a just person gives people what they are owed, and an unjust person takes more than what is rightfully theirs. Tao liked this definition of justice and saw Aqu living this kind of just life each day.

One morning Tao came down from his apartment and was surprised to see Yasmin sitting at her father's desk.

"What are you doing here?" he asked in surprise. He tried not to appear as excited as he felt.

"I graduated from the Academy. Didn't my father tell you?"

"He must have been too busy. Are you going to work here ... with me?"

"No, but I am going to work as a tutor for children of my mother's friends. I am looking for ways to create more freedom, like you did. Want some breakfast?"

Tao nodded and they walked to Tao's favorite breakfast vendor.

Now that Yasmin was in town, Tao ate dinner at Aqu's house four times a week. Tao and Yasmin also went to breakfast almost every morning. They talked of a future together and possibly starting a school. Yasmin recommended that they start pooling their savings to start a school, and Tao agreed to put their money in the safe.

Over the next year, Tao slowly lost enthusiasm for his work. He enjoyed working with people, but deep in his soul he longed to teach. He wanted to set up an academy like Mongkut did. Yasmin expanded her tutoring by teaching Siamese and French writing to the children of government officials and aristocrats in Bangkok.

In the spring of his second year in Aqu's business, Tao decided it was time to share his and Yasmin's plans with Aqu. During lunch, Tao pulled a coin from his pocket.

"I carry this coin in my pocket all the time," he said and showed Aqu the coin for the power of patience. "Mongkut taught us that while we are waiting to act, we can do three things."

"What are those?" Aqu asked.

"First, I *understand* that more Siamese and foreigners have moved to Bangkok because of King Phetracha's edicts, taxes, and the constant battles with the provinces. They are bringing their children here and they need a place to go to school. Second, I've been *preparing* to open a school. Yasmin and I found a central location and have saved our money for furniture, books, and paper. Finally, I have been *encouraging* our customers to seek education for their children. If I were to open a school next year, I would have at least 40 students whose parents would pay a small amount."

"Who will teach these students?" Aqu asked, even though he knew the answer.

"I'll teach French, science, and business, and . . ." Tao paused, "Yasmin will teach math, Chinese, reading, and writing. She's already agreed if you give her permission."

"I like your plan, and I'll help you if I can." Aqu paused to let Tao say something else if he desired. Tao took a deep breath and stood up.

"And I would like to marry Yasmin if you give me permission."

"It took you long enough!" Aqu exclaimed and reached out and patted Tao strongly on the shoulder. "Yes! Yasmin's mother and I discussed this already and I also received approval from your parents just in case you asked. We would be proud to join our families together."

Tao let out a visible sigh of relief, thanked Aqu, and then said he wanted to tell Yasmin. Aqu was about to dispense some advice, but Tao had already rushed out of the door.

42
MEETING THE TIGER KING

Messengers visited Muu, Tao, Mot, and Faa in the spring of 1703 and ordered them to come to the palace in Ayutthaya. King Phetracha had died and Chang – now King Suriyentharanthibodi or King Surasuk – ruled Siam.

They all met at Mongkut's house before the meeting. Sunan greeted them with big hugs and joyous laughter. Each of the former students had visited individually or with their families over the last 15 years, but this was the first time they had visited together.

Faa and Mot now had three girls. They had expanded their rescue work to include escaped enslaved people from the Portuguese and Spanish compounds. Faa funded their school with small businesses that taught the students a trade. They also bought a coconut plantation with help from Aqu's investors. The plantation had become one of the largest coconut sellers to Japanese traders.

Muu had not married and was happy being an uncle to his brother's kids. Tao and Yasmin had two boys who were staying with Aqu and Duangkamol. They had poured themselves into developing the primary school in Bangkok. Father Tachard had sent two Jesuits to teach science at their school and they had just finalized plans to create a college for graduates.

Mongkut sat in a comfortable chair and asked questions of his former students. His voice was more quiet than usual, and he often asked the students to repeat what they said.

"I hope I prepared you well," he said. "I wish the lessons weren't cut short by the death of King Narai."

Each of the students explained how the eight sources of power had changed their lives and created more freedom for others. Muu laughed as he pulled a worn red bag of coins from his pocket. Everyone watched as he reached his hand in and pulled out a coin.

He placed the power of solidarity coin on the table so that Mongkut could see it. The room became silent. Tao stepped forward and said, "Thank you for investing in our dreams. You and Sunan have made us freer people."

Sunan touched Mongkut's shoulder and said, "Thank you Tao. I try to tell Mongkut that his life's work has been important, and he has graduated over 100 students from the Academy, but . . ."

"Unfortunately," Mongkut interrupted, "I don't think it changed the life of King Sorasak. Before his father died, Chang killed his half-brother Phra Khwan to make sure everyone knew who would be the next king. You must be cautious when you go to the palace tomorrow. Some nobles call him the Tiger King because he is cruel to his servants and drinks heavily."

Mongkut sighed and sat back in his chair.

"You will be safe," he said reassuringly. "King Sorasak asked me to visit the palace a few times to hear my advice on winning over the provinces. He listened and asked good questions, but his mind wanders."

The next day the four former students rode in a horse drawn

carriage to the palace. They stopped at Wat Mahathat first and found the wall they had built many years ago. They then rode up to the large wooden palace gates. The guards checked their papers carefully and made sure that they didn't have any weapons.

Muu observed that hundreds of soldiers were camped on the palace grounds as if an attack would come at any time. Their guns leaned against the wall of a new barracks. Faa whispered, "Chang always liked the military, but it looks like he is a prisoner in his own palace."

They rode up to the main palace and climbed out of the carriage. Two palace staff members met them, bowed, and walked them up the stairs and into the palace.

"The king requests that you tour the palace before going to the meeting hall," one staff member said.

The four walked through rooms full of servants who seemed to be waiting for them, though they just stood and nodded as they passed. The staff members then took them to a room full of open wooden chests filled with pearls, golden chalices, rubies, and emeralds. Two tough-looking guards stood at each doorway and closely observed the visitors with their right hands resting on their swords.

Though the four didn't say a thing, they knew that Chang was letting them see his wealth and authority before meeting them.

The two staff members finally ushered them into the main audience hall. They knelt down on small, thick Persian rugs. The elevated throne sat in front of them. It was much taller and larger than King Narai's throne. On each side of the throne were huge stone lions with their paws raised as if in attack; a male on the right and a female on the left. A longsword and a musket hung on the wall behind the throne. All was silent, until a court messenger entered and banged a long wooden staff on the floor.

"All bow before King Suriyentharanthibodi," he yelled.

Tao put his face to the carpet and heard the footsteps of someone entering the room. He then heard breathing and the creak of wood as someone sat on the throne.

"You may look up."

Slowly they looked up to see the face of their old classmate. He looked older than his age. He had a large scar on his right cheek, his face was thin, his eyes darted around the room, and he continually grasped and released the arms of the throne.

"I wish you good health and wealth, great king," Muu said.

"Thank you, Muu. And to all of you as well."

He adjusted his posture so that he leaned to his left while still nervously grasping and releasing the arms of the throne.

"I hope you enjoyed the palace tour," he said with a disinterested look. "I have so much," he continued "and I thought . . . how can I share something with my old friends. I've called you here to hear your requests."

He leaned back and without releasing the arms of the throne. In a loud voice he said, "I've heard about your schools, businesses, and other small adventures. But now that I have all the *real* power in the kingdom, what would you ask of me? Money, servants, introductions to powerful people? Name it and you'll have it!"

The four were quiet, not knowing what to say.

"Ask! Don't you know that I can give you anything! Isn't that what those ridiculous classes were about? Gaining power? Well now I have it, so ask!"

Tao looked at his old classmate and felt pity and not fear.

"Great king," Tao said in a friendly voice, "thank you for your generous offer. I need more desks and paper for our Bangkok school if you are willing to share your wealth with us."

Chang was visibly frustrated with such a modest request. He stood up.

"All you want is paper and desks?" he exclaimed. "I can offer you anything – servants, ships, guns, elephants . . ." he trailed off as if losing his train of thought.

"All I need is paper and desks at this time," Tao said. "In the future I may need something else."

Chang looked at Faa, Mot, and Muu as if they should be jumping up with requests for gold and property. They said nothing, more from shock than a lack of ideas.

"You know," Chang said in a thoughtful tone, "I've spent my entire life waiting to sit in this chair, and here I am." He tapped the armrest of the throne and frowned.

"I have the power of life and death, but I feel no desire to live or die. I have Egyptian sheets on huge beds, but I cannot sleep. I can eat anything I want, but all I want is liquor to dull my senses. I can go anywhere I want, but I am afraid to leave the palace because of plots against me. I've asked Mongkut to come and advise me, but he is afraid to tell me the truth."

Chang looked exhausted, but he continued. He pointed at Tao and said, "We studied together. We built a wall together. We *are* friends."

He pointed at Mot and said, "We fought together and protected the palace during the uprising."

He shook his head and looked directly at Faa. "Faa, you are smarter than the rest of us. Tell me the truth. What do I need to be free?"

Faa looked at Chang and said, "You've spent your life believing that authority gives you freedom. But the authority you have makes others fear you. Use the power you have to lighten the burdens of your people and you may find that your burden is lightened as well. That is the truth."

Chang was staring at the ceiling to his right while Faa spoke. Tao wondered if he had heard what she said. They waited.

Finally, Chang laughed loudly and rubbed his eyes with the palms of his hands.

"It's too late," he exclaimed. "The people who surround me sense weakness. I am the king of an empire built on fear, and if people do not fear me then they will kill me and take over."

Faa was about to say something, but Chang started walking toward the exit. The students pushed their heads down to the ground.

They heard him mumble, "You can't understand," and then the sound of a closing door.

At Mongkut's and Sunan's house, the friends recounted the strange meeting with Chang. Mot seemed upset at his old friend's behavior. Mongkut, however, addressed them from his chair.

"Chang still plays a part in Siam for better or worse. You must *also* play your part . . . to create more freedom in Siam. You are not alone. Over 100 Academy graduates are out there creating more freedom. Some have positions of authority and use the power that comes from authority. Others, like you, practice the power of purpose. As each of you uses the eight sources of power, freedom is multiplied in the largest palaces and smallest rice paddies in Siam. Why, I know of five graduates who are often in the court of the Chinese Emperor, and two who regularly advise French aristocrats."

Mongkut then sat up a little straighter and spoke a little stronger. "Keep your heads up. You are tapped into a universal power that runs through all life. If you are willing to serve, you will always find power."

After two more days in Ayutthaya, the students reluctantly said good-bye to each other and traveled back to their homes and families.

Tao never saw King Suriyentharanthibodi again. But two months after the visit to Ayutthaya, three carts of beautiful wooden desks and Persian rugs arrived at Tao's and Yasmin's school along with reams of writing paper and ink.

Before returning to Ayutthaya, the palace messenger who delivered the desks handed Tao a small wooden box. "This is from the king to you," he said.

Tao opened the lid and removed a red silk cloth. Under the silk he found his emerald, beautifully polished and cut. A note was tucked under the emerald. Tao unfolded the small piece of paper and read the note.

"To my friend who is freer than the King of Siam."

EPILOGUE

King Suriyentharanthibodi became known as King *Sua* – King Tiger – because of his abuse of his servants. The Siamese grudgingly accepted him as king, and all feared him. He died in 1709 after six years on the throne.

His son Prince Phet was crowned and referred to as King Thai Sa ("end of the lake") referring to the pond that surrounded the palace. He had a relatively long and peaceful reign. During that time, he built strong ties to China. He died in 1733.

Maria Guyomar de Pinha was forced to work in the palace kitchen until King Phetracha's death in 1703. She became the head chef of the kitchen and was reunited with her son Jorge. She lived on a pension from the French East India Company until her death in 1728.

Father Guy Tachard returned to France in 1687. Other French Jesuits were imprisoned after Phetracha became king. They were eventually released.

REFLECT AND APPLY
WHAT YOU'VE LEARNED

Ready to change your world using the power of purpose? You begin by knowing yourself, your situation, and your opportunities. Use the reflection and application questions in the sections below to explore how you can use the power of purpose and practice the eight sources of power. I recommend you write your answers in a journal that you can take with you each day. Then you can revisit your responses and add new insights about your personal leadership path. You can also write each source of power on a small piece of paper and select one or two each day as a way to reflect on how you are pursuing a purpose.

You will gain the most from these reflections by being honest about yourself and your circumstances while maintaining optimism about what is possible. Many leaders have followed the path you are starting and I include several stories of ordinary people who successfully led others with the power of purpose.

REFLECTION ON OPPOSITION AND RESILIENCE

Have you ever tried something new and immediately faced opposition? Did you want to give up? These are common experiences on the path of leading without authority because you don't have the institutional legitimacy or position backing you up.

Remember that in the long run we admire those who face opposition and keep trekking on toward their goals. Answer the following questions about being resilient, even when you feel like quitting.

1. Recall an instance in which you faced opposition to your ideas or even your presence. How did you feel and what did you do?

2. Now that you are away from that situation, what would you have done differently in that situation, if anything? Can you do the same thing now?

3. Developing resilience is important so that you can manage opposition and not let it stop you. Consider these resilience strategies:

    1. Reduce stress in your life and get enough sleep. These have been found to increase your resilience reserves.
    2. Accept that some people will never accept you, and that is their problem. Avoid taking their words or actions personally. In most cases, their opposition is about their insecurity or fear of losing power.
    3. Seek emotional support. Note how Sunan and Mongkut provide the stability that Tao needs to keep going.
    4. Don't give up because of what others think. Only choose another path because the current path no longer meets your needs, the timing is not right, or you are not prepared.

REFLECTION ON TWO TYPES OF POWER

I define power in terms of leadership. To have power is to *take an action that motivates others to follow you*. I present a view of motivation that assumes that people naturally move away from certain situations and toward certain situations. All moves seek to increase freedom and a leader can tap into this natural movement.

1. List some of the people, organizations, habits, and/or situations you moved *away from* to improve your life. Describe the freedom that each move gave you?

2. List some of the people, organizations, habits and/ or situations you *moved towards* to improve your life. Describe the freedom that each move gave you?

Mongkut describes two types of power.

THE POWER OF AUTHORITY	THE POWER OF PURPOSE
1. The power of authority requires institutions	1. The leader identifies a purpose that increases freedom
2. The institution justifies rewarding and punishing	2. Followers share their power in pursuit of the purpose
3. Authority can be delegated to others	3. The leader uses the eight sources of power

The questions below and in several of the *Reflect and Apply* sections will guide you to make a specific change in your world. If you have not identified a specific change you want to lead, answer the questions for your own personal leadership development.

1. What aspect of your world would you like to change as a leader?

2. Ideally the change should be a real need and not just a personal desire. Avoid pursuing a change that no one wants, like building a park in a place where no children live or creating a product no one needs. Observe what people need to increase their freedom. Consider how the need fits with your natural motivations and abilities.

3. Write a one-sentence purpose statement that describes the change you want to see. If you are working with a group, ask them for input in creating a shared purpose statement. The statement could follow this format: "We are going to (*Action*) for (*Target Population*) with the result of (*Result*)."

    For example:

    a. "We are going to redesign our product packaging for our consumers with the result that landfill waste and plastic will be greatly reduced."

    b. "We are going to provide tutoring for at-risk children in our school with the result of higher grades."

    c. "We are going to start a baseball league for underserved youth with the result that children exercise and learn teamwork."

    d. "We are going to redesign the compensation system for our organization with the result that we reward employees fairly and eliminate historical bias."

5. If you are in a position of authority to make the change, what is stopping you from making the change? (e.g. resources, motivation, people, circumstances, time, etc.)

6. List the people – even if it is only you– who also see the importance of this purpose and may join you.

EXAMPLE OF THE POWER OF PURPOSE

Jaime Escalante was a son of a math teacher and a physics teacher in Bolivia before emigrating to the United States. He worked different jobs, learned English, earned an additional math degree, and then began teaching math at Garfield High School in Los Angeles, California. The high school was plagued by gangs and drugs. Escalante was told by an administrator to just give students passing grades to protect the school's accreditation, but Escalante refused. He convinced students that they could have a future working in technology and computers if they learned math. He is quoted as saying, "The day someone quits school he is condemning himself to a future of poverty."

One school administrator resisted Escalante's efforts to implement new math programs and even threatened him with dismissal. Henry Gradillas was hired as a new principal and supported Escalante's *purpose of uplifting his students* through achieving in algebra and calculus. In 1978 he and fellow teacher Ben Jiménez taught five students calculus and two of them passed the Advanced Placement (AP) Calculus exam. By the end of his and Jiménez's career at Garfield High School, 570 students had taken advanced placement exams and many former students attended college.

Escalante's power of purpose was depicted in the movie *Stand and Deliver.*

REFLECTION ON TEARING DOWN AND BUILDING UP

When our purposes are challenged or criticized, we may react by dominating or punishing the person (fight), running away (avoiding conflict), or becoming silent (shutting down). If you are going to lead others to make a change, these options will not serve you well. The authors of *Crucial Conversations: Tools for Talking When Stakes Are High* explain that choosing among only three options is a "fool's choice." Their extensive research shows that effective leaders react to criticism by creating a *safe place* where others are respected and the team can continue to pursue their purpose. You can create a safe space by restating the purpose in a way that acknowledges the criticism and how these issues can be addressed now or later.

Using this method protects you from taking criticism *personally* which can sap your energy or produce unproductive anger. You can uplift others in the face of criticism by restating a broader purpose that addresses the criticism and the fears that may be behind it (see the chapter on the *Power of Framing*). Answer these questions about how you can manage criticism and praise.

1. How do you typically react to people who criticize you or your ideas? Describe one such episode and how you felt. Next, write down what you could have said to open a safe space so that the criticism and your purpose could co-exist in a respectful dynamic.

2. Consider the change you identified in the earlier

reflection. What could be some criticisms people will make about you or the change? Write down what you can say to open a safe space for their criticism and your purpose to co-exist in a respectful dynamic.

3. What questions could you ask a person who criticizes the change so that you can avoid reacting emotionally and taking their words personally?

4. What is your most natural and effective way of building people up? Conversation, emails, texts, new assignments, lunch, compensation?

5. How do you typically react to people who seek to build you up? How would you prefer to react to those who are building you up? Three possible reactions are:

    a. Self-deprecating: "I didn't do anything. I got lucky."

    b. Self-aggrandizing: "It's about time you recognized my awesomeness."

    c. Appreciation and relationship building: "Thank you for your comments. I hope that together we can achieve even more."

EXAMPLE OF TEARING DOWN AND BUILDING UP
THE WRECKERS

I watched them tearing a building down,
A gang of men in a busy town.
With a ho-heave-ho and a lusty yell,

They swung a beam, and the side wall fell.
I asked the foreman: "Are these skilled--
And the men you'd hire if you had to build?"
He gave me a laugh and said: "No, indeed!
Just common labor is all I need.
I can wreck in a day or two
What builders have taken a year to do."
And I thought to myself as I went my way,
"Which of these roles have I tried to play?
Am I a builder who works with care
Measuring life by a rule and square?
Am I shaping my deeds to a well-made Plan,
Patiently doing the best I can?
Or am I a wrecker, who walks the town
Content with the labor of tearing down?"
—H.S. Harp[9]

REFLECTION ON THE POWER OF INVITATION

One of the main differences between the *power from authority* and the *power from purpose* is making invitations instead of delivering commands. When leaders have authority, they can tell followers to do something, and they must do it to receive a reward or avoid a punishment. A person in authority doesn't need to ask you if you *want* to do something.

Leaders who use the power from purpose, however, need to invite others to join them. An invitation respects a person's freedom to say "yes" or "no". It also establishes the equal status between the leader and the follower because both need each other to achieve the purpose. Finally, receiving an invitation to start planning a change is exciting and motivating. As the one who invites others, this is your opportunity to create a team and facilitate a vision and a plan. Answer these questions to determine how you can use the power of invitation.

1. Review the list of people from your Two Types of Power reflection. Who will you invite to join you in planning the change?

2. At this early stage, invite those who understand the change, whose support and resources you need, and/ or those who have expressed their desire to make the change. You may want to avoid inviting those who consistently tear down ideas or who are committed to maintaining the status quo. You can invite others later as the plan starts to become a reality.

3. As the leader and/or as a group, answer the following questions about the change you want to make. Use a sheet of paper, a flipchart, or a whiteboard.

   • *Where are we going?* On the far-right side, describe in detail the new state of affairs you want to see.

   • *Where are we now?* On the far-left side, describe the current state of affairs that you and your stakeholders are experiencing.

   • *How will we get there?* Starting on the right side (future), work backwards to the left side (current state) and list the steps needed to get to where you are going. You do this by asking "What do I need to do to achieve the next goal?" This is called *backward planning*.

4. Your plan is alive! Revise your plan as information is gathered, goals are achieved, and priorities are changed.

EXAMPLE OF BACKWARD PLANNING

Where are we now?	3. How to achieve the next goal?	2. How to achieve the next goal?	1. How to achieve the next goal?	Where are we going? (start here)
Ninety-five percent of our employees drive to work.	Move budget from parking to IT support and software.	Invest in laptops and cameras for people to work at home.	Have employees work remotely on Wednesdays and Fridays.	Reduce the carbon footprint of our workforce using remote work.

With practice, you will find that backward planning is a powerful method for a team to plan a change.

EXAMPLE OF THE POWER OF INVITATION

In the American South before the mid-1960s, discriminatory state and city ordinances, known as the Jim Crow system, required Black Americans to use different water fountains, bathrooms, hotels and restaurants. During this time, Martin Luther King, Jr. earned a bachelor's degree from Morehouse College in Atlanta and his doctorate from Boston University's School of Theology. Before graduating with his doctorate in 1955, he and his wife Coretta decided to take a pastorate at the Dexter Avenue Baptist Church in Montgomery, Alabama – a city whose Black residents cried out for freedom from the segregated bus system. In this system, Blacks were told to sit in the back of the bus and give up their seats to White riders even though Blacks made up 75 percent of bus riders.

Jo Ann Robinson, the head of Montgomery's Women's Political Council, had already written to the mayor of Montgomery about the mistreatment of Black bus riders. In March 1955, fifteen-year-old student Claudette Colvin was arrested for violating the segregation ordinance. Robinson, King, Rosa Parks and other Black leaders met with city and bus company officials about making changes. When Parks was arrested for not giving her seat to a White person on December 1, Robinson immediately sent out fliers asking Black bus riders to stay off the buses the following Monday.

The young Martin Luther King, Jr. was *invited* to become the leader of the Montgomery Improvement Association (MIA). He worked alongside Robinson, E.D. Nixon, Rufus A. Lewis, and Parks to organize the Montgomery bus boycott. The MIA's modest demand was that a dividing line be put in the buses to separate the races, but if the White section filled then they would have to stand instead of requiring a Black person to give up their seats. The boycott lasted 381 days and required organizing carpools, filing court cases, and standing up to threats and violent intimidation including the bombing of King's house. Many grassroots groups provided funding to support the women and men who would rather walk or ride in carpools than support an oppressive system.

Because King was new to the city, he relied heavily on local leaders to plan the boycott and maintain support for those who needed transportation. In the preface to King's book *Stride Toward Freedom*, Clayton Carson writes, "There can be little doubt of King's sincerity in downplaying his role [in the Montgomery movement] since MIA records reveal that his leadership was tenuous, particularly during the early months of the boycott ... He found it necessary to consult regularly with other MIA leaders, bridge internal differences, and rely on the assistance of many dedicated coworkers." King states, "I neither started the protest nor suggested it. I simply responded to the call of the people for a spokesman."

On November 13, 1956, the US Supreme Court upheld an earlier ruling that segregation on public buses was unconstitutional. The city passed an ordinance allowing Blacks to sit anywhere they chose.[10]

REFLECTION ON MANAGING POWER RELATIONSHIPS

Power is often in the eye of the beholder. If you are following a leader, then you are committing part of your life to that person and the purpose they are pursuing. But if you disagree with the leader and go in a different direction, a conflict may occur. The leader may try to win you back, ignore you, punish you, or even agree with you and change their own direction. Managing complementary and conflicting power relationships requires you to identify conflicts and decide how to manage them. Answer these questions to determine how you can manage power conflicts, especially if you are having conflicts in your change project.

1. *Identify Assumptions* - What assumptions are you making about the leader's direction and plan? What assumptions is the leader making about *your* direction and plan? Test each assumption to see if it is based in reality and directly supports achieving your

shared objective. If the group is acting on conflicting assumptions, discuss this with the leader.

2. *Map Power Dynamics* - Who speaks in your meetings and who does not speak? Who completes tasks and who does not? Who makes the final decisions? Identify these people so that you can determine who is *actually* making change happen and who is watching from the sidelines. Talk to those who are actively involved (individually or as a group) about how they would resolve the conflicts about the direction of the project or conflicts with other groups.

3. *Decide to Stay or to Go* - Is the change you are pursuing more important and urgent than the leader's purpose? If "yes", then break free and start your own team to make the necessary change. If "no", then resolve the conflicts and remove obstacles for your current team.

EXAMPLE OF MANAGING POWER RELATIONSHIPS

Re-read the story of Jaime Escalante and Ben Jiménez above. Reflect on how they patiently continued their plans until a new principal arrived to support them. Also, note how Dr. King was invited to work alongside Jo Ann Robinson, Rosa Parks, E.D. Nixon and other Montgomery leaders to complement their leadership with his ability to inspire others, preach, and create a moral vision for desegregation. These are actual examples of leaders who identified and actively managed conflicts so that their purpose was achieved.

REFLECTION ON THE POWER OF THE OPEN HAND

Leading others to change the status quo is hard work because most of us do not like change. Just take a minute and write your name with your non-dominant hand, or spend the night sleeping on the floor, or skip dinner. Even if we know a change is needed, we may cling to what is comfortable. The power of the open hand provides you with the tools to free yourself and others from clinging to ideas, values, and practices that may be obstacles to much needed change. Answer these questions and reflect on how you can apply this power.

QUESTIONS ABOUT HOW YOU USE AN OPEN HAND

1. In what areas are you harsh and not gentle towards yourself?

2. What would it look like to show yourself compassion (e.g. caring for yourself and not feeling sorry for yourself)?

3. What can you share with others that will give you more freedom?

4. Be curious about yourself. What are you grasping (ideas, things, relationships, locations, habits, entertainment) that may be blocking you from gaining more emotional, spiritual, and physical freedom?

QUESTIONS ABOUT HOW YOUR TEAM USES AN OPEN HAND

1. In what areas are you harsh and not gentle toward others?

2. What would it look like to show them compassion?

3. What can you share with others that will give them more freedom?

4. Be curious about your team. What is the team grasping (ideas, things, relationships, habits) that may be blocking them from gaining more emotional, spiritual, and physical freedom?

5. Be curious about the change you want to create. Why hasn't anyone made the change already? What power structures are resisting the change? Who has successfully made this change in another time or location, and can you imitate them?

EXAMPLE OF THE POWER OF THE OPEN HAND

Poonsapaya Navawongs na Ayudhya was born in 1910 in what is now Bangkok's Phra Nakhon district. Her father was a German jeweler and her mother was a lady-in-waiting in the palace. Queen Saovabha Phongsri gave her the name Poonsapaya. As an adult Poonsapaya graduated from Chulalongkorn University and later earned a master's degree in education from the University of Michigan. Realizing the importance of the growing field of education, she started earning a graduate degree in education at Columbia University. Instead of returning to Thailand during World War II, she joined the Free Thai resistance movement as a radio broadcaster.

In the 1950s she returned to Chulalongkorn University as a faculty member. Observing emerging developments in teacher training, she expanded the teacher training program and helped found the Faculty (or College) of Education in 1957. She was the first woman to serve as Faculty dean in Thailand. She introduced new teaching and learning theories, concepts, and practices such as seminar classes and course credit systems. Through her leadership, she established the Chulalongkorn University Demonstration School, which continues to provide teacher training and educational research opportunities. I was invited to teach at this school in 1988-1989 as part of an innovative program to have native English speakers teach English.

Poonsapaya worked to advance opportunities and training for women. She founded the Thai chapter of Zonta International and the Thai Association of University Women. After the death of her husband, she donated her residence as a learning center and library. She died in 2015 at the age of 105.[11]

REFLECTION ON THE POWER OF PRAXIS

In my research on those who lead others without authority, I found that almost all of them acquired or were actively acquiring knowledge and expertise in some area. Knowledge, expertise, experience, a credential, or even actively pursuing more education signals to followers that you are competent and can be trusted. Applying the power of praxis requires you to gain the knowledge and expertise to initiate the change you want and then lead others to move from knowledge to action. Answer these questions about how to apply the power of praxis. The next section will ask you about the specific knowledge and expertise you want to acquire.

1. Using your responses to the power of invitation questions, review the purpose statement you wrote. What disciplines, authors, leaders, and researchers have analyzed the change and how to make it a reality? What are the solutions or methods that they proposed and which ones seem to best meet the change that you've identified?

2. Using your responses to the power of invitation questions, research how to best implement each of the sub-goals toward your main goal. What additional knowledge or expertise do you need to achieve these goals? Use an online survey, an email, or a phone call to gather more information from those who will be involved in the change.

3. Who is responsible for achieving the sub-goals? What data, information, or expertise do they need in order to succeed? (See the power of building the wheel about how to delegate responsibilities.)

EXAMPLE OF THE POWER OF PRAXIS

Leymah Roberta Gbowee was born in the East African country of Liberia in 1972. She was a teenager when the first Liberian civil war began in 1989. In 1996, warlord Charles Taylor overthrew president Samuel Doe and was then elected president in 1997. Opposition to Taylor grew and the second Liberian civil war began in 1999. Meanwhile, Gbowee trained as a social worker and volunteered at St. Peter's Lutheran Church in Monrovia where her mother was a women's leader. In the Trauma Healing and Reconciliation Program (THRP), Gbowee tried to bring healing to former child soldiers of Taylor. She continued her training in reconciliation and peacebuilding by attending conferences and reading works by Martin Luther King Jr. and Gandhi. Gbowee connected with the Women in Peacebuilding Network (WIPNET) and found mentors among women from other African nations. She became the unpaid leader of WIPNET in Liberia while her sister took care of her five children (one adopted) in Ghana. In 2002, Gbowee had a dream that God told her to, "Gather the women and pray for peace!" With support from her friends, she reached out to Muslim and Christian women to pray for the peace of Liberia and she organized a women's peace movement. To reduce religious divisions, she held workshops and asked women questions like, "Does a bullet care if you are a Christian or a Muslim? Does a rapist ask if you are a Christian or a Muslim?"

The violence in Liberia continued as factions began moving to take over the capital Monrovia. Eventually president Taylor could not ignore the women's peace movement which included protests and prayers in the markets and beside the road he travelled each day. The women wore white t-shirts signifying their desire and demand for peace. On April 23, 2003, Taylor invited more than 2,000 women to the executive mansion. Gbowee delivered a speech and said, "We are tired of war. We are tired of running. We are tired of begging for bulgur wheat. We are tired of our children being raped. We are now taking this stand, to secure the future of our children. Because we believe, as custodians of society, tomorrow our children will ask us, 'Mama, what was your role during the crisis?'"

Peace, however, would not be secured until the warlords and government officials agreed to a peace accord. Gbowee travelled to peace talks in Ghana with other Liberian women who prayed and waited for over a month while negotiating parties wasted time and enjoyed the comforts of their hotels. Fed up with the lack of urgency and the continuing violence and rape occurring in Liberia, Gbowee led over 100 women into the hotel where they blocked the delegates from leaving the conference room until they completed a peace agreement. With this pressure and the insistence of General Abubakar who was a former president of Nigeria, the delegates finally completed the agreement during the next few days. The Accra Comprehensive Peace Agreement was signed on August 18, 2003.

The Women of Liberia Mass Action for Peace movement set the stage for Ellen Johnson Sirleaf to become the first elected female president of an African nation in 2005. Gbowee completed her Masters of Arts in Conflict Transformation in 2007. She and Sirleaf were awarded the Nobel Peace Prize in 2011 along with Tawakkol Karman.[12]

REFLECTION ON IDENTIFYING AND GROWING YOUR EXPERTISE

Few people can or should become an expert in every topic needed to make a significant change, and that is why we need the expertise of others to achieve our purpose. The power of praxis requires you to gain the knowledge and experience to lead others AND/OR to find the people who have the knowledge and experience you need. Note that having "knowledge" does not require you to have a college degree, and having a degree may not take the place of extensive experience. To better align your knowledge, experience and contacts with your purpose, reflect on and answer these questions.

1. Consider the change project you are leading. In what area(s) do you consider yourself knowledgeable enough

to lead others? In what area(s) do you have extensive experience and/or contacts so that you could lead others?

2. Consider the change project you are leading. What area do you want to dive deeper into and start becoming an expert? How will you acquire this knowledge and experience?

3. Who can mentor you so that you can knowledgeably and actively lead others to fulfill the purpose you are pursing?

EXAMPLE OF GROWING YOUR EXPERTISE

Reread the story of Leymah Roberta Gbowee and identify the organizations she joined to learn how to lead, how to reconcile people, and how to build peace. Note also her leadership positions and how she had a close group of people to complement her own expertise and experience.

REFLECTION ON THE POWER OF FRAMING

We all make decisions based on how we frame or narrate our lives and the world. You may be following a narrative that needs to be changed. Reframing a narrative involves identifying, questioning, and testing the stories we are telling ourselves and others. Do these stories and our assumptions track with reality? For example, if a company frames the natural environment as an unlimited resource for water, air, trees, animals, and soil, then they will implement strategies that use as many resources as they want with no regard for conservation or reducing waste. But if a leader *reframes* the natural environment as containing limited resources that must be conserved to secure the future of the company and society, then the company's strategies will change and focus on sustainability. Nothing changed in the world except for the leader's frame. Reflect on the items below in regard to your change project and write your responses.

1. Start by committing to *embrace reality* as presented in data and experience. Embracing reality requires you to:

   a. avoid being overly optimistic and confident, *and*

   b. avoid being overly pessimistic and overly cautious.

   c. Note Supawadee's *positive objectivity* in the story.

2. Describe what will actually change if your project is successful. By yourself or with your team, list the fears you and others have about the change (for example, who will have to give up something, what will change about daily work, who wins and who loses).

3. Address each of these fears by researching if they are based in reality or only in worry. How will you address any real consequences if they arise?

4. List and describe ways that the proposed changes will create more opportunities, benefits and freedom. Be specific.

5. Reinforce the frame by asking others to describe their positive and realistic vision of the change in one year. What does each person see in your new future?

EXAMPLE OF THE POWER OF FRAMING

Dr. Muhammad Yunus was born in 1940 in what is today Bangladesh. In the 1950s and 1960s, Yunus earned undergraduate and graduate degrees in economics which included a PhD from Vanderbilt University in the United States in 1971. During the Bangladesh Liberation War of 1971, he founded the Bangladeshi Information Center with other Bangladeshis in the US to support people seeking liberation from West Pakistan.

After the war, Yunus returned to Bangladesh and eventually became head of the Economics department at Chittagong University. In 1974 he was working with the poorest households in a village near the university. He observed how small loans could make a huge difference in the lives of the poor, but the available loans had high interest that took most of a small businesses' profits. In particular, he saw poor women who made bamboo furniture paying most of their profits to lenders. Yunus created a new frame of what loans are and who is eligible. Instead of loans being high-interest financial disbursements by large banks to the wealthy, he framed loans as small financial disbursements with low interest to fund small projects. Those without collateral would now have a bank.

He tested his "microcredit" idea by loaning 42 women a total of $27. The women made a profit of $.02 on their loans ($.84) and paid back the principal. In December 1976, Janata Bank supported Yunus' frame of microcredit for projects that poor villagers wanted to pursue. By 1982, the lending group had 28,000 members and in 1983 Yunus' project became Grameen Bank ("village bank"). The bank uses a system of "solidarity groups" which are small groups that apply for loans. The group members support each other by co-guaranteeing loans and helping members advance economically in their projects.

Yunus' concept also created a new frame about how to address some forms of poverty using loans and solidarity groups instead of only relying on charities and non-government organizations. The microcredit frame assumes that many people want some financial support to pursue initiatives that create value for themselves, their families, and their communities. Unfortunately, credit is often reserved for the wealthy in many countries because of existing frames about what loans are for and who should receive them. Another challenge is that some larger banks claim to be in the microcredit and microfinance space but are charging exorbitant interest.

In 2006, Yunus and Grameen Bank both received the Nobel Peace Prize. In 2019, Grameen Bank boasted 9.6 million members and 97-percent of them were women.

Yunus' latest book attempts to reframe some of the world's largest problems. The book's title presents three new frames: *A World of Three Zeros: The New Economics of Zero Poverty, Zero Unemployment, and Zero Net Carbon Emissions* (2018).[13]

REFLECTION ON THE POWER OF SUBSTITUTION

Using the power of substitution requires research, commitment, and empathy. You need to research where there is ignorance and then find the knowledge that can remove it. Imagine people are sick in your town. It takes research to find out what is causing it and the knowledge to prove it. Then, you need commitment to a solution to substitute uncertainty with confidence, while always leaving space for admitting what you don't know. Finally, you must empathize with others enough to understand their fears and then love them enough to help them find safety. Your love in action can remove fears.

While ignorance, uncertainty and fear distract and repel followers, knowledge, confidence and love attract followers. They also increase trust in you and your shared purpose. Explore how you can acquire the power of substitution by answering these questions and reflecting on your responses.

1. When you consider the change that you want to make, what is not known (i.e. ignorance) by you and how will you find the knowledge to replace this ignorance?

2. What do your followers not know, and how will you effectively communicate the knowledge to them? For example, select the right time, the right method (email, face-to-face, one-on-one, phone, group meeting), and the right amount of sharing. This could take some time.

3. What are you uncertain about regarding the change you want to make (e.g. consequences to yourself and others, funding and resources, timing)? List these items and then decide how to substitute uncertainty with confidence. Commit to using the knowledge you find, ask questions, and seek advice to build your confidence and the confidence of your team.

4. What are the top three fears that you have about making the change? Describe how your love (that is, desire to further the interests of others) can overcome these fears. For example, Rosa Parks lovingly and courageously sacrificed her freedom and was arrested to increase the freedom of others.

EXAMPLE OF THE POWER OF SUBSTITUTION

Triveni Acharya is an Indian journalist in Mumbai. In 1993 she was covering a famous actor who was going to visit a red-light district in the city. She walked into the brothel and saw small rooms and met three young girls. She thought they were the daughters of the sex workers, but then discovered that they were victims of sex-trafficking. The girls told Triveni that they were abducted from Nepal and wanted to leave. An older woman came out and shouted at them and they hid.

This incident impacted Triveni greatly and she told her husband Balkrishna Acharya of her shock. She continued working as a journalist, but the event stayed with both her and her husband. Years later, her husband met a salesman who wanted to marry a sex worker if he could free her. Triveni and Balkrishna decided to rescue the girl. At the brothel, 15 more girls pleaded with them to rescue them as well. With help from the police, they freed the girls. Some girls returned to their families, but many families rejected their daughters. These girls were placed in a rehabilitation home for Nepalese girls.

Triveni said, "It was then that my husband felt the need to work towards rescuing and rehabilitating young girls who are abducted and trafficked and we decided to pledge our lives to them." They were no longer uncertain about their purpose and moved forward with confidence and love.

Balkrishna started going to brothels undercover and he found more young girls who were sex slaves and who wanted to escape. In the early days, the couple housed the girls in their own home. Balkrishna gave up his business while Triveni worked as a journalist during the day and a rescuer at night. They created the Rescue Foundation which was the organization they used to rescue and rehabilitate these girls. The website states, "Rescue Foundation, given the heinous nature of the crime it works against, was a result of the twin pillars of love and compassion that drove our founding members."

In 2001, they won the Reebok Human Rights award which gave them recognition and attracted support. In 2003, they received a seven-story building to shelter the girls. However, the more girls they rescued the more threats came from those who profited from sex trafficking and also from corrupt government officials. In 2005, Balkrishna died in a car accident, though Triveni felt it may have been intentionally caused because of his work.

Triveni mourned for her husband and then became president of the Rescue Foundation where she continues to rescue and provide for girls. The foundation has 100 full-time staff, over 100 informers, and four shelter homes in the largest Indian cities. The rescued girls have access to vocational training, schooling, mental health counsellors, HIV and medical treatment, and also legal help in returning home. Since beginning in their home, the Rescue Foundation has rescued over 6,000 girls and has rehabilitated and repatriated over 15,000 girls. [14]

REFLECTION ON THE POWER OF SOLIDARITY

It is powerful knowing that someone stands with us, no matter what. Our load is lightened, and we often feel more confident. It is the experience of the power of solidarity.

In the story, Aqu outlined three ways to acquire the power of solidarity listed in order of the commitment they take. Sometimes all you can do is *listen to the stories of others* and ask questions. Other times you will *invest your time and resources* in someone's dreams as you pursue a shared purpose. The ultimate step is when you *bind your future* with those you are serving. Given the many roles we have in life, a person can only bind their future with others by letting go of some commitments and roles. Carefully consider how much solidarity you have to give, because committing to everyone in need can lead to ineffectiveness and burnout. Respond to the items below and reflect on your answers to better understand and apply the power of solidarity.

1. List the commitments that you have in your life (family, work, volunteering, school, exercise, recreation). If you are going to use the power of solidarity, which commitments are you going to prioritize as your highest? Do you have to let go of some commitments in order to pursue your purpose? Which one or ones?

2. For the purpose or change you are pursuing, how can you better listen to the stories of your followers? For example:
   a. rephrase what was said to make sure you have understood
   b. no interrupting
   c. ask questions
   d. sit down with the person and look at them
   e. schedule another time when you can be alone or focus on what is said

3. For the purpose or change you are pursuing, how will you invest in the dreams of your followers? For example:
   a. daily or weekly time to devote to the purpose
   b. make donations
   c. share your network of connections

   d. provide educational support (books, pay for
       tuition)
   e. give someone a job
   f. share your story
   g. give guest lectures at schools and colleges
3. For the purpose or change you are pursuing, how will
   you bind your future with your followers' future? For
   example:
   a. move to where the change needs to happen
   b. change jobs
   c. make a significant financial investment
   d. start a new organization

EXAMPLE OF THE POWER OF SOLIDARITY

Greg Boyle was born in Los Angeles in 1954 as one of eight children. He attended Loyola High School in Los Angeles and was inducted into the Society of Jesus (the Jesuits) after graduation. He earned several college degrees and was ordained a priest in 1984. He spent a year serving as a priest in Bolivia to learn Spanish before returning to the US. Father Boyle was appointed the parish priest for the Delores Mission Church in East Los Angeles. The area was surrounded by public housing projects and the neighborhood was known for having more gang activity than any city in the United States. Father Boyle told one interviewer, "I just said, I want to cast my lot with the poorest folks I can find."

In 1988, Father Boyle and his parish started positive projects to help gang members escape the violence and poverty surrounding them. This included starting a daycare and assisting gang members in finding employment. In 1992, the parish started Homeboy Bakery as a social enterprise to provide training and jobs for former gang members. The bakery also helped fund other social enterprises under the new umbrella organization, Homeboy Industries.

Since the early 1990s, Homeboy Industries has grown into the largest gang intervention, rehabilitation and reentry program in the United States. It also operates the largest tattoo removal service in the nation. Homeboy Industries now operates Homeboy Electronics Recycling, Homegirl Catering, Homeboyfoods.com, and other social enterprises with a staff of 176. Because the parish and Father Boyle bound their future to gang members and their families, a new way of preventing violence and crime has evolved.

The young people Father Boyle helps have jarring stories to tell of their broken lives. They tell of mothers who died from overdoses, fathers who beat them or are incarcerated, and friends being killed in front of them. Father Boyle has performed over 150 funerals for his "homies."

He often talks about *kinship* which he explains requires us to stand with the most vulnerable. In a 2019 talk at Loyola Marymount University in Los Angeles, he stated, "For Jesus, it wasn't about taking the right stand on issues. It was about standing in the right place. You go to the margins, and you brace yourself because people will accuse you of wasting your time. You don't go to the margins to make a difference. You go to the margins because you want those voices to be heard."[15]

REFLECTION ON LEADERS IN YOUR LIFE

The power of purpose is not new. People have used it to make important changes. It works regardless of location, culture, income, or language. Look around you and think about your life journey thus far. Who have you seen use the power of purpose or any of the sources you've learned in this book? Interview someone– even if they are famous – and ask them the following questions:

1. What motivated you to make this particular change in the world?
2. How did you invite those who you needed on your team?
3. How did you acquire the knowledge and experience you needed to lead this change?
4. How did you describe your purpose to others?
5. How did you address your fears and the fears of others?
6. What and who gives you confidence when you lead others?
7. How do you build bonds with others on your team?

REFLECTION ON THE POWER OF BUILD-ING THE WHEEL

When you have a plan and followers who are prepared to execute the plan, it is time to put them in a configuration that releases their potential. The power of building the wheel starts with the power of invitation – invite people with talent and potential to take on specific jobs. Next, give them the space, resources, and credit that they need. If you have the right people with the right knowledge and the right motivation, you will not need to micromanage them. Your job is to give them the space, resources, and recognition they need to succeed. If you are at the point of organizing your team, reflect on these questions and your responses to use the power of building the wheel.

1. What are the two or three critical goals that must be achieved to reach your purpose and make your change?

Describe them in detail (See your power of invitation responses).

2. Who on your team has the talent and potential to achieve these goals? If you do not yet have these people, where can you find them?

3. What training and education can you give your existing team members to develop their talent and potential?

4. When your key people are working on the critical goals, what can you do to create a space for them to do what they do best? For example:

    a. Remove bureaucratic obstacles

    b. Provide additional funding and resources

    c. Answer questions and requests for help quickly

    d. Connect them with supportive mentors

    e. Provide personal support when they are tired or experience a set-back

    f. Hold meetings with your team to share progress

    g. Communicate often and praise progress

    h. Remove or reassign team members who are not completing their tasks or are disrupting your key people

5. How will you recognize your key people and give them the credit in a way that they wish to accept it? For example:

    a. Send a team email or text praising a person's specific accomplishment

    b. Spend time with the person discussing their work

    c. Forward progress reports to senior managers and include the person

d. Give a day off for achieving a milestone

e. Ask questions about the goal

f. Open additional positions or responsibilities

g. Ask each person to present their work to the entire team

h. Send the person in your place to a conference or meeting

i. Recognize each person's contribution in public instead of taking credit yourself. Make it genuine and sincere.

EXAMPLE OF THE POWER OF BUILDING THE WHEEL

Ursula M. Burns was born in New York City to Panamanian immigrants. She was raised by a single mother in a New York City housing project along with her two siblings. In high school she was advised to be a nurse, a nun, or a teacher. Instead, she capitalized on her math abilities, reviewed different careers like engineering that offered the most money, and found the best colleges for entering these careers. She earned a bachelor's degree in mechanical engineering from Brooklyn Polytechnic Institute and then a master's degree in mechanical engineering from Columbia University in 1980. After an internship with Xerox, she joined the company full-time and worked in product development for ten years.

In 1990, senior executive Wayland Hicks asked Burns to become an executive assistant and learn about the entire company. She later became the executive assistant to Xerox CEO Paul Allaire. Through this mentoring process, Burns learned about different company functions and senior management positioned her to lead various businesses. She continued to achieve her objectives and became vice president for global manufacturing in 1999 and senior vice president for corporate strategic services in 2000. Her boss Anne Mulcahy became CEO in 2001 when Xerox was going through a time of intense competition, restructuring, and accounting irregularities. Burns became president of business group operations and continued to work closely with Mulcahy to right-size Xerox.

Burns became president of Xerox in 2007 and was asked to be CEO in 2009, becoming the first Black female CEO of a Fortune 500 company. During her tenure she moved Xerox into different markets, acquired Affiliated Computer Services and split Xerox into two companies: Xerox and Conduent Incorporated. She stepped down as CEO in 2016.

According to Burns, Xerox's culture was built on valuing difference, talent, and potential. They did this by placing people in different positions so that they could grow and develop. In an interview for the book *Triple Crown Leadership: Building Excellent, Ethical, and Enduring Organizations* by Bob Venourek and Gregg Venourek, Burns made the following points about what leading requires:

- What are the most important things leaders can do to create the conditions for high-performance and integrity?
  - First, they define the possibilities. They set the agenda, the tone of the organization.
  - Second, they select. They select the key leaders in the next echelon of the company, help select the leaders after that, and so on. So, they have a big, big people component.

- Third, they empower. After selecting correctly, they have to empower these people to actually do the job.
- Next, they set the correct expectation for what excellence looks like, what greatness looks like.
- Then let them go.

- If you had to define great leadership in a sentence or two, how would you do it?

  - Persons who can define a purpose, select a great team, empower that team appropriately, enable them to understand what greatness is about, and then let them go.

Burns continues to give credit to others, especially her mother.[16]

REFLECTION ON THE POWER OF PATIENCE

How long are you willing to work (not wait) to make your purpose a reality? When you get tired, when key followers leave, when your enemies seem to be winning, you need the power of patience. Some changes may take a month, others a year, and some will take two or three lifetimes. But the power of patience is not about sitting and waiting. It is about learning about the situation, preparing yourself and others for the next move, and encouraging others to stay in the game. If you are faced with immovable obstacles and find yourself losing focus, reflect on these questions and your responses.

1. What is the situation you are confronting? Describe the situation from your perspective and also from the perspective of those who are hindering your progress? Is there any way to have them join you or step back so that they can achieve something as well?

2. What obstacles are you facing and what help do you need to overcome them? Consider help from new sources without compromising the core purpose. For example, can you exchange your knowledge and expertise for the knowledge and expertise of someone else?

3. What are three scenarios that may play out in the future? With your team, describe in detail best-case, worst-case, and realistic-case scenarios.

4. How will you prepare for each scenario? Implement your best plan.

5. How can you encourage your followers for the long journey? Note that simply being with your followers and communicating with them about any progress can keep them engaged.

EXAMPLE OF THE POWER OF PATIENCE

Václav Havel was born to a wealthy family in Prague, Czechoslovakia in 1936. His grandfather and father were real estate developers, his uncle built a large film studio, and his mother also came from an influential family. During his first 12 years, his family endured World War II and the 1948 coup d'état by the Communist Party which was supported by the Soviet Union. The Party removed all privileges from the former upper-class, which meant that Havel had limited academic opportunities. He studied as a chemist and took evening courses, but he could not study humanities for political reasons.

Havel pushed himself to live out the humanitarian values that his family espoused even though he had limited opportunities. He worked as a stagehand at Prague theaters and studied dramatic arts through a correspondence course. Havel wrote his first full-length play *The Garden Party* and it was performed in 1963. The play received international praise. He continued writing plays, the most famous being *The Memorandum* which satirized the ridiculous efforts of bureaucracies to make people conform, even in how they speak. The result is struggles for power. Havel had found a way to write and criticize a government that controlled the country.

In 1968, protests and liberal reforms were taking hold in Czechoslovakia to decentralize the economy. The Prague Spring upset hardline communists in the Soviet Union and surrounding nations. After the Prague Spring was suppressed, he was banned from participating in the theater and he decided to become more politically active. Havel continued to write plays and essays which were distributed via an underground network of "self-publishers" who hand-wrote and passed on censored materials. He and other dissidents wrote a document called Charter 77 that criticized the government for not supporting the human rights provisions of treaties and other documents it had signed. Those who signed Charter 77 were prosecuted. Havel was a political prisoner from 1979 to 1983.

Upon release, he continued to seek the removal of the controls imposed by the communist government. In 1985 the Soviet leader Mikhail Gorbachev was speaking of Glasnost (openness) and Perestroika (restructuring). The Czech communist leadership did not make many changes, but in 1988 and 1989 citizens began demonstrating over poor living conditions and a weak economy. The Berlin Wall fell on November 9, 1989 and Czechoslovakia and its neighbors began to remove their totalitarian rulers.

In what was called the Velvet Revolution of November 1989, theater members and students went on strike and carried on protests around the country. Havel and other leaders established the Civic Forum as a movement to dismiss government leaders who were responsible for violence and to release political prisoners.

Demonstrations of over 100,000 people continued and Prime Minister Ladislav Adamec met with the Civic Forum leaders several times as the protests continued and some freedom of the press was allowed. On November 29, the Federal Assembly officially ended communist rule by deleting the constitutional provision that the Communist Party would have a "leading role" or "ruling position" in the government.

On December 29, 1989, the Federal Assembly unanimously voted Václav Havel president of Czechoslovakia. In 1990, the Civic Forum party and its Slovak counterpart won strong majorities in the legislature and Havel remained president. On February 22, 1990, Havel spoke to a joint session of the US Congress. In his speech he talked of the responsibility humans have to create a moral world. He said, "In other words, we still don't know how to put morality ahead of politics, science, and economics. We are still incapable of understanding that the only genuine core of all our actions – if they are to be moral – is responsibility. Responsibility to something higher than my family, my country, my firm, my success. Responsibility to the order of Being, where all our actions are indelibly recorded and where, and only where, they will be properly judged." In 1993, the country split into the Czech Republic and Slovakia and Havel became president of the Czech Republic from 1993 to 2003. After the presidency he continued to write plays and speak out for creative freedom. He died in 2011.

In 2012, the Václav Havel Prize for Creative Dissent was established by the Human Rights Foundation with support from Havel's widow Dagmar Havlova, Google co-founder Sergei Brin, and PayPal co-founder Peter Thiel. The prize is given to individuals who challenge injustice through creative dissent. The award is given through the Oslo Freedom Forum.[17]

RESOURCES FOR
YOUR JOURNEY

THE POWER OF INVITATION

- *The Abundant Community* by Peter Block and John McKnight (Berrett-Koehler Publishers, 2010)

- *Community: The Structure of Belonging* by Peter Block (Berrett-Koehler Publishers, 2018)

THE POWER OF THE OPEN HAND

- *Unlearn: Let Go of Past Success to Achieve Extraordinary Results* by Barry O'Reilly (McGraw-Hill Education, 2018)

- *The Universe in a Single Atom: The Convergence of Science and Spirituality* by Dalai Lama (Harmony, 2006)

THE POWER OF PRAXIS

- *Great by Choice* by Jim Collins and Morten T. Hansen (Harper Business, 2011)
- *Episteme* and *Techne* by Richard Parry, Stanford Encyclopedia of Philosophy (March 7, 2020) https://plato.stanford.edu/entries/episteme-techne/

THE POWER OF FRAMING

- *The Power of Framing: Creating the Language of Leadership* by Gail T. Fairhurst (Jossey-Bass, 2010)
- *Crucial Conversations: Tools for Talking When Stakes Are High* by Kerry Patters, Joseph Grenny, Ron McMillan, Al Switlzer (McGraw Hill, 2012)

THE POWER OF SUBSTITUTION

- *Braving the Wilderness: The Quest for True Belonging and the Courage to Stand Alone* by Brené Brown (Random House, 2019)
- *Creative Confidence: Unleashing the Creative Potential within Us All* by Tom Kelley and David Kelley (Currency, 2013)

THE POWER OF SOLIDARITY

- *Tattoos on the Heart: The Power of Boundless Compassion* by Greg Boyle (Free Press, 2011)

- *Barking at the Choir: The Power of Radical Kinship* by Greg Boyle (Simon and Schuster, 2018)

- *The Masnavi, Book Three* by Jalal al-Din Rumi (Oxford World's Classics, 2014)

THE POWER OF BUILDING THE WHEEL

- *Good to Great: Why Some Companies Make the Leap and Others Don't* by Jim Collins (Harper Business, 2001)

- *Creativity, Inc.: Overcoming the Unseen Forces that Stand in the Way of Future Inspiration* by Ed Catmull with Amy Wallace. (Random House, 2014)

THE POWER OF PATIENCE

- *Man's Search for Meaning* by Viktor Frankl (various publishers)

- *Long Walk to Freedom: The Autobiography of Nelson Mandela* by Nelson Mandela (Little Brown and Company, 2008)

- *This Child Will Be Great: Memoir of a Remarkable Life by Africa's First Woman President* by Ellen Johnson Sirleaf (Harper Perennial, 2010)

NOTES ON THE HISTORY OF SIAM

The story you've read is fictional, but many of the people and events presented are real. The following is a short list:

- King Narai the Great ruled Siam from 1656 until 1688. He negotiated many treaties with many countries.

- Constantine Phaulkon did become the finance minister and was killed after King Narai died.

- Aqu Muhammad Astarabadi and his family were finance ministers for Siam for three generations.

- Maria Guyomar de Pinha was Phaulkon's wife and worked in the palace kitchen voluntarily and then as a slave under Phetracha's reign. She was released as indicated in the epilogue above. She is also credited with bringing the "foi tong" or golden thread dessert to Siam from her Portuguese upbringing.

- Phetracha and his son Sorasak did take over after King Narai died of an illness.

- The Makassarese rebellion did occur and also the Mergui massacre, but on a different timeline than presented in the story.

- The British and French military officers did the actions presented in the story, including acting as privateers for Phaulkon and protecting Bangkok.

- The French Jesuits built and operated hospitals and schools in Ayutthaya until Phetracha expelled them.

ABOUT THE AUTHOR

DAVID C. BAUMAN, PHD is an accomplished academic and industry expert who is passionate about empowering leaders to make ethical decisions and inspire their teams. As a Professor of Business and Chair in the Anderson College of Business & Computing, Regis University, he shapes future business leaders through his teaching and research. Leveraging his deep-rooted experience in Fortune 250 companies and academia, David offers practical strategies, tools and resources for individuals and organizations. A sought-after speaker and author, he delivers thought-provoking professional seminars that inspire managers and employees to embrace ethical leadership. David taught English in Bangkok, Thailand during college where he developed a deep respect for the Thai people, their culture, and their history. He lives in Colorado. Learn more at www.davidcbauman.com.

ENDNOTES

1   Elie Wiesel, "One Must Not Forget," interview by Alvin P. Sanoff, *US News & World Report,* October, 27 1986.

2   The Lord Acton Letter to Bishop Mandell Creighton, April 5, 1887. Transcript published in *Historical Essays and Studies.* Edited by J. N. Figgis and R. V. Laurence. London: Macmillan, 1907.

3   "We must never forget that we may also find meaning in life even when confronted with a hopeless situation, when facing a fate that cannot be changed. For what then matters is to bear witness to the uniquely human potential at its best, which is to transform a personal tragedy into a triumph, to turn one's predicament into a human achievement. When we are no longer able to change a situation—just think of an incurable disease such as inoperable cancer—we are challenged to change ourselves." Victor E. Frankl, *Man's Search for Meaning.* New York, Washington Square Press, 1985, 135.

4   "French Depiction of King Narai," 1750. *Les Missions Etrangeres.* Public domain. Downloaded December 2, 2023.

5   "La Ville de Judia." 1684. In Monsieur Glanius, *Les Voyages de Jean Struys en Moscovie.* Free Image Archives: http://www. ancestryimages.com/proddetail.php?prod=g0942 . Permission granted by Steve Bartrick on December 1, 2023.

6   Rumi, Jalal al-Din, *The Masnavi, Book Three.* Trans. Jawid Mojaddedi, (Oxford: Oxford University Press, 2008), p. 32.

7 Rumi, Jalal al-Din, *The Essential Rumi.* Trans. Coleman Barks with John Moyne, A.J. Arberry, and Reynold Nicholson, (New York: HarperCollins Publishers, 1995), Pg. 246.

8 Su-ma Ch'ien, *Records of the Grand Historian of China, Translated from the Shih chi - Volume I.* Trans. Burton Watson. New York: Columbia University Press, 1961. 107-108.

9 The poem has been attributed to three authors online: Edgar Guest, Charles D.F. Benvegar (aka Carmello Benvenga), and H.S. Harp. An extensive review of over 980 Edgar Guest poems reveals that "The Wreckers" is not listed and therefore was probably not written by him. The poem was published in a poetry collection *Songs of the Free State Birds* in a poetry anthology edited by Vincent Godfrey Burns, Poet Laureate of Maryland, (New World Books of Washington D.C. 1967) and attributed to Charles Benvegar or Carmelo Benvenga (1913-1989). I have permission from his son to publish the poem, but we have reason to believe that his father may not have written the original poem. My research shows that the poem appears in the mid-1930s and 1940s under the name H.S. Harp in two sources: "This Do and Thou Shalt Live" (1943) which attributes the poem to H.S .Harp and says permission was received from *Family Circle* magazine and a Pacific Electric newsletter from May 1937 which attributes the poem to H.S. Harp. The earliest instance of the poem I found is in a National Broadcasting Company receptionist staff newsletter from February 1935 which states that J.L. Kraft of Kraft Phenix Cheese Corporation read the poem "Builder vs. Wrecker" at an NBC Eastern Salesman's banquet. These are in addition to multiple newspapers and other publications using the poem without attribution in the 1930s and 1940s. There is a possibility the Herbert S. Harp, the president of Ready-Jell Manufacturing of Troy, NY (a pudding and Jell-O competitor) may have written the poem given his company's focus on food and his advertising copy. This could also connect him to *Family Circle* magazine in the early 1930s and J.L. Kraft. Given that the poem was published pre-1935, the copyright for pre-1936 issues of *Family Circle* magazine was not renewed, and the poem copyright was not renewed in 1961, the poem appears to be in the public domain.

10 King Jr., Martin Luther. *Stride Toward Freedom.* Boston: Beacon Press, 2010.

11 "Education Pioneer Thanpuying Poonsapaya Dies," *Bangkok Post*, October 24, 2015. https://www.bangkokpost.com/thailand/

general/741464/education-pioneer-thanpuying-poonsapaya-dies. See also, Srisa-an, Wichit. "Professor Thanphuying Poonsapaya Navawongs na Ayudhaya: The Intellectual Jewel of Thai Teacher Education," October 3, 2018. http://www.thaistudies.chula. ac.th/2018/10/03/professor-thanphuying-poonsapaya-navawongs-na-ayudhaya-the-intellectual-jewel-of-thai-teacher-education/ .

12 Gbowee, Leymah and Caro Mithers. *Mighty Be Our Powers: How Sisterhood, Prayer and Sex Changed a Nation at War.* New York: Beast Books, 2011. Also, Reticker, Gini, director. *Pray the Devil Back to Hell.* New York: Fork Films 2008.

13 Yunus, Muhammad with Alan Jolis, *Banker to the Poor: Micro-Lending and the Battle Against World Poverty.* New York: PublicAffairs, 2007. See also, *Grameen Bank*, Last modified December 2019. http://www.grameen.com/introduction/ .

14 Mahajan, Queeny. "This Journalist's Mission Has Saved 5,000 Girls from Sex Trafficking," *YourStory* January 30, 2018. https://yourstory. com/2018/01/rescue-foundation . See also *The Rescue Foundation.* Last modified 2022. https://www.rescuefoundation.net/ .

15 Long-García, J.D. "Father Greg Boyle's solution to an unjust criminal justice system: radical kinship." *America: The Jesuit Review.* April 04, 2019, https://www.americamagazine.org/faith/2019/04/04/father-greg-boyles-solution-unjust-criminal-justice-system-radical-kinship . See also *Homeboy Industries.* Last modified 2022. https://homeboyindustries.org/ .

16 "A Vision of Great Leadership" *Triple Crown Leadership,* December 3, 2012, http://triplecrownleadership.com/a-vision-of-great-leadership/ . See also, Burns, Ursula M. *Where You Are Is Not Who You Are: A Memoir.* New York: HarperCollins, 2021. See also, Nolen, Jeannette L. "Ursula Burns." *Encyclopedia Britannica*, September 16, 2023. https://www.britannica.com/biography/Ursula-Burns .

17 Editors of Encyclopaedia Britannica. "Václav Havel." *Encyclopedia Britannica*, December 14, 2023. https://www.britannica.com/biography/Vaclav-Havel . See also, *Vaclav Havel Center,* Last modified 2023. https://www.havelcenter.org/ . See also, "Vaclav Havel Distinguished Leadership Award 2009 ILA Conference," ILA Official, YouTube video, June 17, 2009. 5:22. https://www.youtube.com/watch?v=vl-oTKw21xQ .